VALUATION

ISBN 0-13-034804-X

9 790130 348042

90000

Financial Times Prentice Hall Books

For more information, please go to www.ft-ph.com

Deirdre Breakenridge
Cyberbranding: Brand Building in the Digital Economy

William C. Byham, Audrey B. Smith, and Matthew J. Paese
*Grow Your Own Leaders: How to Identify, Develop, and Retain
Leadership Talent*

Jonathan Cagan and Craig M. Vogel
*Creating Breakthrough Products: Innovation from Product Planning
to Program Approval*

Subir Chowdhury
The Talent Era: Achieving a High Return on Talent

Sherry Cooper
Ride the Wave: Taking Control in a Turbulent Financial Age

James W. Cortada
*21st Century Business: Managing and Working
in the New Digital Economy*

James W. Cortada
*Making the Information Society: Experience, Consequences,
and Possibilities*

Aswath Damodaran
*The Dark Side of Valuation: Valuing Old Tech, New Tech,
and New Economy Companies*

Sarvanan Devaraj and Rajiv Kohli
*The IT Payoff: Measuring the Business Value
of Information Technology Investments*

Jaime Ellertson and Charles W. Ogilvie
*Frontiers of Financial Services: Turning Customer Interactions
Into Profits*

Nicholas D. Evans
*Business Agility: Strategies for Gaining Competitive Advantage
through Mobile Business Solutions*

FINANCIAL TIMES
Prentice Hall

In an increasingly competitive world, it is quality
of thinking that gives an edge—an idea that opens new
doors, a technique that solves a problem, or an insight
that simply helps make sense of it all.

We work with leading authors in the various arenas
of business and finance to bring cutting-edge thinking
and best learning practice to a global market.

It is our goal to create world-class print publications
and electronic products that give readers
knowledge and understanding which can then be
applied, whether studying or at work.

To find out more about our business
products, you can visit us at www.ft-ph.com

Pearson
Education

VALUATION

AVOIDING THE WINNER'S CURSE

Kenneth R. Ferris

Barbara S. Pécherot Petitt

FINANCIAL TIMES
Prentice Hall

An Imprint of Pearson Education
London • New York • San Francisco • Toronto • Sydney
Tokyo • Singapore • Hong Kong • Cape Town • Madrid
Paris • Milan • Munich • Amsterdam

Library of Congress Cataloging-in-Publication Data
Ferris, Kenneth R.
    Valuation : avoiding the winner's curse / by Kenneth R. Ferris and Barbara S. Pécherot Petitt.
      p. cm.
    Includes bibliographical references and index.
    ISBN 0-13-034804-X
    1. Corporations — Valuation — Handbooks, manuals, etc. 2. Consolidation and merger of
corporations — Handbooks, manuals, etc. I. Petitt, Barbara S. Pécherot. II. Title.
HG4028.V3 F477 2002
658.15 — dc21

                                                2001055424

Editorial Production/Composition: *G & S Typesetters, Inc.*
Acquisitions Editor: *Jim Boyd*
Marketing Manager: *Bryan Gambrel*
Buyer: *Maura Zaldivar*
Cover Design Director: *Jerry Votta*
Cover Design: *Anthony Gemmellaro*
Art Director: *Gail Cocker-Bogusz*
Interior Design: *Tech Graphics*
Project Coordinator: *Anne R. Garcia*

© 2002 by Prentice Hall PTR
Prentice-Hall, Inc.
Upper Saddle River, New Jersey 07458

Prentice Hall books are widely used by corporations and government agencies for training, marketing, and resale.

The publisher offers discounts on this book when ordered in bulk quantities.
For more information, contact: Corporate Sales Department, Phone: 800-382-3419;
FAX: 201-236-7141; E-mail (Internet): corpsales@prenhall.com; or write Prentice Hall PTR, Corp.
Sales Dept., One Lake Street, Upper Saddle River, NJ 07458

Printed in the United States of America

10 9 8 7 6 5 4 3 2 1

ISBN 0-13-034804-X

Pearson Education LTD.
Pearson Education Australia PTY, Ltd.
Pearson Education Singapore, Pte. Ltd.
Pearson Education North Asia Ltd.
Pearson Education Canada, Ltd.
Pearson Educación de Mexico, S.A. de C.V.
Pearson Education — Japan
Pearson Education Malaysia, Pte. Ltd.

Contents

Preface

Valuation is the essence of finance. It asks the question, "What is the 'fair' price to pay for an asset that has a set of uncertain future cash flows?" In the past, the answer to this question was provided by time-tested methods. In recent years, however, new approaches have emerged as practitioners have sought improved ways to assess value. New approaches have also evolved in response to the development of the "new economy" and the many e-commerce companies that were privatized without a history of either earnings or cash flows.

With the backdrop of a rapidly changing valuation environment, this book presents a practitioner-oriented view of the fundamentals of firm valuation. The focus is on valuation for acquisition purposes. In large measure, an acquisition is viewed herein as equivalent to the purchase of any productive asset, namely, as a capital budgeting exercise. Furthermore, valuation is considered to be an art, not a science. Consequently, the reader will find that there are many "rules of thumb" but few inviolable principles to guide them.

The metrics used for valuing companies are not well defined, varying often according to the objectives of the valuation and often with the companies themselves. Consequently, executives and equity analysts face many choices and dilemmas as they try to assess value. Throughout this book, practical solutions are suggested for dealing with these dilemmas and for helping the reader make informed choices. The methods discussed are principally for use in nonfinancial companies; the topic of valuing financial companies is beyond the scope of this book.

To use this book effectively, the reader will need an understanding of the fundamentals of accounting and finance. Furthermore, a background in spreadsheet software, such as EXCEL™, is also beneficial.

This book is the result of numerous years of teaching, research, and industry experience. It is also the result of considerable advice from respected friends and colleagues, to include Barry Graham, Michael Moffett, and Anant Sundaram but especially Francis Nzeuton, Graeme Rankine, and Tom Selling. Our thanks go to Torrey Mann, who processed the manuscript throughout its many stages of development.

Kenneth R. Ferris and Barbara S. Pécherot Petitt
June 2001

1   Valuation: An Overview

MARKET VIEW
Eli Lilly and Company—
A Question of Assumptions

On 24 June 1997, the major financial newspapers carried a significant press release from Eli Lilly and Company, one of the world's leading pharmaceutical companies.* The company indicated that it would take a $2.4 billion charge against its second-quarter 1997 results to write down the value of its investment in PCS Health Systems. Three years earlier, Lilly had purchased PCS in an acquisition transaction valued at $4.1 billion.

The company indicated that two unanticipated factors had caused its investment in PCS to decline by more than half of its original value. First, Lilly had expected two other drug companies to buy stakes in PCS and, in so doing, reduce Lilly's exposure in the investment. Those investments failed to materialize after the U.S. Federal Trade Commission began scrutinizing the acquisition because of antitrust concerns. Second, the outlook in the health-care industry had shifted dramatically since 1994. A U.S. health-care program overhaul proposed by the Clinton administration in 1993 that would have substantially expanded the market for PCS's services did not obtain the necessary congressional support for passage.

*See T. M. Burton, "Lilly Will Swallow $2.4 Billion Charge," *The Wall Street Journal,* 24 June 1997, A4; M. Freudenheim, "Lilly Cuts Distribution Unit's Book Value by $2.4 Billion," *The New York Times,* 24 June 1997, D7.

Most Wall Street analysts agreed that the PCS situation provided an excellent illustration of the dangers of making assumptions about future events in merger and acquisition transactions. Lilly's PCS Health Systems debacle eventually came to an end in 1998 when PCS was sold to Rite Aid Corporation for $1.5 billion, bringing Lilly's total acquisition error to $2.6 billion.

● ● ●

Probably no question in the financial community is asked more often than "What is this investment worth?" Whether the investment is a bond, a share of stock, or an entire company, assessing the economic value of an investment is often the ultimate objective of the corporate executive or equity analyst.

The fundamental tenet of investment valuation is well established in corporate finance: *The value of an asset today is the present value of the future cash flows that the asset is expected to provide its owners.*[1] Valuation thus becomes an exercise in modeling the future cash flows of an investment and deciding how to value those cash flows. Because financial modeling can be quite time-consuming, and often imprecise, valuation analysts have frequently turned to short-cut techniques that (they hope) yield equivalent results with a reduced time expenditure. Alternative valuation metrics have also emerged because not all investments have sufficiently predictable cash flows to permit effective modeling. This was particularly true for many of the "dot.com" companies that characterized the Internet industry in 1999 and 2000. In the chapters that follow, a variety of valuation frameworks are considered: discounted cash flow analysis, earnings multiples analysis, adjusted present value analysis, equity method analysis, revenue multiples analysis, and economic value analysis. We consider each of these frameworks in the context of corporate valuation for merger or acquisition purposes, although the methods discussed can be used for a variety of valuation objectives.

This chapter addresses the following key questions:

- What are the principal reasons that companies merge or acquire one another?

- Why do acquirers pay a premium over the preannouncement share price in takeover transactions?

- What are the typical steps followed when a company is being valued?

- What are the most frequently used methods for assessing firm value?

Why Firms Merge or Acquire:
A Historical Perspective

Companies merge with or acquire one another for a variety of reasons. The 1890s, for example, witnessed what is considered to be the earliest "wave" of mergers and acquisitions as companies in the United States tried to gain monopoly power in their respective industries through the formation of trusts — in essence, an extreme form of **horizontal integration.** Examples of this include The Standard Oil Company of New Jersey in 1899, the United States Steel Corporation in 1901, and the International Harvester Corporation in 1902. After the Sherman Antitrust Act successfully outlawed this practice, acquisition-oriented companies turned their attention to the use of vertical integration mergers as a means of growth. **Vertical integration** is perhaps no better illustrated than by the U.S. oil and gas industry; companies that began as pure oil exploration businesses eventually moved into refining, transportation, and ultimately retailing of oil and gas products.

The 1970s witnessed a second major wave of mergers as companies tried to diversify their revenue streams and, in so doing, reduce their perceived riskiness. This trend led to the creation of conglomerates and holding companies composed of many diverse businesses. General Electric Company is one of the most successful examples of this trend. Today's capital markets, however, no longer place a premium on the value of these highly diversified entities. In fact, the share prices of most holding companies today are subject to a **conglomerate discount** as the equity markets struggle to place a fair value on these complex enterprises.[2] In essence, the equity markets now prefer a "pure play" — that is, a single-industry business — to a highly diversified entity, in large part because of the transparency of operations provided by these more easily understood, and consequently more easily valued, businesses.

In the 1980s, a third wave of mergers and acquisitions occurred, but for very different reasons. This period was characterized by relatively high inflation rates and consequently high borrowing costs. Thus, many firms merged in an effort to lower their financing costs, which reached as high as 25 to 30 percent in some instances. Still other firms merged during this period to gain size and thereby take advantage of the economies of scale associated with larger volume producers. These size-driven mergers and acquisitions were also motivated by the inflationary environment of the 1980s as companies tried to become low-cost producers and ultimately survive the industry "shake-outs" that inevitably characterize such economic periods.

The 1990s saw the emergence of still new justifications for merging or acquiring. Some firms used acquisition transactions as a means to acquire knowledge-based assets. This was particularly true in the late 1990s when the "first mover" advantage became highly prized. With the evolution of the global economy, many companies saw merger and acquisition as the quickest and least expensive means for acquiring a presence in a foreign marketplace and thus preserving their place in the global economy. This latter trend was largely driven by the formation of multination trade pacts such as the European Union (EU), Mercosur, and the North Atlantic Free Trade Agreement (NAFTA). Owning a business within the EU or NAFTA member countries meant that a foreign parent company could avoid the high cost of trade tariffs or other barriers to cross-border trade. Finally, some entities saw merger and acquisition as a means to "roll up" or consolidate those industries characterized by excess market participants, and hence marginal profitability. These "consolidators" recognized that not every participant could survive such economic conditions and consequently fostered a mentality of "acquire or be acquired." Examples of this global trend included the energy industry (e.g., BP Amoco Plc and ExxonMobil Corporation), the pharmaceutical industry (e.g., Pharmacia Corporation, a merger of Pharmacia and Upjohn with Monsanto Company; and GlaxoSmithKline, a merger of SmithKline Beecham and Glaxo Wellcome), and the automobile industry (e.g., the mergers of Daimler and Chrysler and Ford, Volvo, and Jaguar).

Not all of these mergers and acquisitions, however, created shareholder value. In fact, most destroyed value. Although evidence clearly indicates that the shareholders of a target company profit from a takeover, that cannot also be said for the shareholders of the acquirer company. An abundance of evidence shows that although the share price of almost all target companies rises after the disclosure of an intended merger or acquisition, the share price of most acquirer companies declines (for a review of the literature, see Jensen and Ruback 1983). This evidence suggests, among other things, that the securities market has become increasingly skeptical about the value-enhancing effects of merger and acquisition transactions. Whether offer prices are seen as excessive, the proposed synergies are thought unlikely to materialize, or current management is perceived as incapable of successfully merging two different cultures, today's capital markets appear to doubt the value of most merger and acquisition transactions.

Exhibit 1.1   Stock Market Performance of Acquirers
            After a Merger or Acquisition

Source	Market	Period	Performance
Agrawal, Jaffe, and Mandelker (1992)	U.S.	60 months	−10.26%
Gregory (1997)	U.K.	24 months	−11.89%
Loughran and Vijh (1997)	U.S.	60 months	−15.90%
Rau and Vermaelen (1998)	U.S.	36 months	−4.04%
Pécherot (2000)	France	36 months	−25.41%

Sadly, the markets are correct: *Few merger and acquisition transactions achieve their anticipated gains.* In 1995, for instance, *Business Week* magazine reported that for a sample of 150 mergers and acquisitions from 1990 to 1995, only half produced positive returns to the acquirer shareholders. Similarly, in a 1997 book, *The Synergy Trap,* author Mark Sirower reported that of the 168 mergers and acquisitions analyzed from 1979 to 1990, more than two-thirds destroyed shareholder value. Finally, in a study of 700 mergers and acquisitions from 1996 to 1998, KPMG International found that more than 80 percent of the transactions failed to increase shareholder value and that more than 50 percent actually destroyed shareholder value.

In short, the latest research on the long-run performance of mergers and acquisitions shows that, on average, acquirers experience a destruction of wealth. For instance, as shown in Exhibit 1.1, Agrawal, Jaffe, and Mandelker (1992), Loughran and Vijh (1997), and Rau and Vermaelen (1998) indicate that U.S. firms involved in a merger or acquisition underperform the market by 10 to 15 percent.[3] Gregory (1997) and Pécherot (2000) likewise confirm this result for the English and French capital markets. To help understand why so few mergers and acquisitions actually enhance shareholder value, it is instructive to consider recent data on the premiums paid in these transactions, to which we now turn.

Merger and Acquisition Premiums

A substantial body of evidence indicates that merger and acquisition premiums average 20 to 30 percent above a target firm's preacquisition share price. For example, in a study of 855 takeover offers between 1987 and 1996, Hand and Lynch (1999) found that the mean target price increase averaged 20.3 percent. In general, merger and acquisition premiums, which are sometimes referred to as "control premiums," are thought to be demanded by the capital markets as compensation for transferring controlling interest in a target firm to an acquirer. Majority control in a firm conveys many valuable rights and benefits, including control over all operating policies and decisions, the selection of management and the board of directors, and the distribution of funds to shareholders.

Merger and acquisition premiums can also represent compensation for other economic benefits, for example:

- **Synergy benefits** from the installation of a more efficient target management team, improved production techniques, the redeployment of assets to more profitable uses, the exploitation of increased market power, and/or cost efficiencies from economies of scale

- Target firm **operating tax loss carrybacks and carryforwards** that may be used to shield acquirer-firm operating profits from taxation

- **Capital market pricing inefficiencies,** wherein target companies may be undervalued because of the market's preoccupation with short-term earnings or a poor industry outlook

If merger and acquisition transactions yield these valuable economic rights and benefits, why then do most destroy shareholder value? The reasons are many, but the five principal explanations for value destruction appear to be the following:

1. Overestimation of target firm growth and/or market potential (i.e., a forecasting error problem)

2. Overestimation of expected cost and/or revenue synergies (i.e., another forecasting error problem)

3. Overbidding (or what is sometimes called "executive hubris")

4. Failure to undertake a thorough due diligence of the target firm's operating and financial risks

5. Failure to successfully integrate an acquiree after a successful merger or acquisition

In essence, in about one of every two mergers or acquisitions, the acquirer management commits some type of critical error — in the assessment of target-firm value, in the bidding process, or in the postacquisition integration of the acquiree. How to avoid each of these pitfalls is beyond the scope of this book; instead, we focus on the *process* of assessing firm value, namely, the specific accounting, finance, and taxation issues that the analyst must successfully deal with in order to assess economic value, to which we now turn.

The Process of Valuation

Analysts refer to five types of "firm value": book value, break-up value, economic value, liquidation value, and market value.

Book value refers to the accounting value of a company — that is, its total assets minus its total liabilities. It is the residual value remaining assuming that a company's assets can be sold for their reported book values and the proceeds used to satisfy all liabilities at their recorded values. **Break-up value,** on the other hand, refers to the amount that could be realized if a company were split into saleable units and disposed of in a negotiated transaction; this concept is principally relevant for those companies composed of a variety of individual business units or segments. **Economic value** refers to the after-tax cash flows that a company is expected to provide to its owners over its expected economic life; it is a forward-looking concept, measured by assessing a firm's potential future cash flows. **Liquidation value** refers to the amount that could be realized if a company were liquidated in a distress sale. Finally, **market value** refers to the consensus value of a company based on values established in an organized and orderly marketplace such as a securities market.

Although all five values may be used for valuing a company, this book deals primarily with the determination of *economic value* because it represents the "ongoing" value of a company. Thus, the value of a company is defined herein with reference to the future cash flows expected to be provided by a company to its owners over the entity's expected economic life.

The process of valuing a company is usually undertaken in five steps:

1. Identify and screen potential merger and acquisition target candidates thoroughly to ensure that the proposed transaction is an appropriate one from a *strategic* standpoint.

2. Analyze the historical performance of the potential acquiree to ensure that the target company is an appropriate partner in a

financial sense, as well as to gain a thorough understanding of the target's operations and business model.

3. Model the future performance of the target company through the preparation of pro forma financial statements. Although much is made about selecting the appropriate valuation multiple or discount rate, *nothing* is more important in assessing firm value than a complete and accurate modeling of a target firm's operations. This critical step requires a thorough understanding of the target's business model — its revenue and cost drivers — as well as the development of realistic assumptions about the target's future operations.

4. Estimate the operating value of the target company after its free cash flows and its continuing value are calculated.

5. Estimate the equity value of a target firm and assess the sensitivity of the key pro forma assumptions on the target's equity value.

As we will see, steps 4 and 5 can be avoided when short-cut valuation techniques, such as earnings or revenues multiples analysis, are used.

Alternative Valuation Frameworks

Several valuation approaches are available depending on whether a target firm is a start-up or a mature entity and also on the target's industry. We focus on the mainstream methods, and the most popular of these can be segmented into two categories: (1) relative valuation methods, and (2) direct valuation methods. Relative valuation methods, by definition, do *not* provide a *specific* assessment of firm value; that is, relative valuation methods do not reveal whether a security is fairly priced but only whether it is fairly priced *relative to* some peer group. Thus, these methods are most useful when an acquirer is making an intraindustry acquisition; but when an acquirer is considering a number of alternative acquisition targets from a variety of industry settings, these methods provide little comparative insight. This group of methods includes earnings multiples valuation, revenues multiples valuation, and book value multiples valuation.

Direct valuation methods, on the other hand, use various conceptual viewpoints to yield specific assessments of the present value of the future cash flows that an acquisition transaction can be expected to provide to its owners. These methods include the discounted cash flow approach, the adjusted present value approach, the equity method approach, and the economic value approach. Each of these methods has as a central tenet the notion that value is a function of the cash flows provided by an investment.

That there are multiple direct valuation frameworks, all essentially grounded in the same economic tenet, suggests two important observations:

- The financial community is in relative agreement as to what drives value — future cash flows; but

- the financial community is not in agreement as to what drives share price.

In today's global economic setting, it would be naïve to suggest that security prices are driven by any *single* factor. Indeed, the proliferation of alternative valuation frameworks reflects in part the financial community's inability to agree on exactly which factors are the primary drivers of share prices — revenues, accounting earnings, book value, economic income, or discounted cash flows. The dominant viewpoint, however, and hence the framework endorsed in this book, is that (ceteris paribus) discounted cash flows are most closely related to share price *value* movements.

We now turn to a closer examination of the relative and direct valuation frameworks.

Relative Valuation Methods

The notion that "time is money," or stated alternatively, that "time is an expensive and limited commodity," is one of the principal reasons for the presence and use of relative valuation methods. Other reasons are that they are simple to apply and easy to understand. In essence, relative valuation techniques provide executives and equity analysts with a "quick and dirty" way to analyze the value of a company that the potential acquirer can readily understand.

The three most commonly used relative valuation metrics are

- Market price per share–to–earnings per share
- Market price per share–to–revenues per share
- Market price per share–to–book value per share

The market price per share–to–earnings per share metric, more commonly known as the P/E ratio or P/E multiple, provides an indication of how much investors are willing to pay for a company's earnings as a surrogate for the company's future cash flows. For instance, a company whose P/E ratio is 10 is said to be selling for ten times earnings and suggests that investors are willing to pay $10 for each $1 of current or future earnings. Companies with high earnings growth prospects usually carry higher P/E multiples because these firms will presumably be able to reward investors with a quicker and larger return on their investment in the form of dividends, increases in share price, or both.

Because the earnings of a company are influenced to varying degrees by how a business is financed — with debt or with equity — some analysts have turned to a variant of the P/E ratio that removes the effect on earnings caused by alternative capital structures, namely, the market price per share–to–earnings before interest and taxes per share metric (P/EBIT).[4] Still other analysts, worried about the distortive effects on earnings sometimes associated with the alternative accounting policies with respect to the amortization of intangible assets and the depreciation of fixed assets, prefer to use the market price per share–to–earnings before interest, taxes, depreciation, and amortization per share metric (P/EBITDA). The P/EBITDA metric is also popular because of the close proximity of EBITDA to a company's cash flow from operations.

The P/E, P/EBIT, and P/EBITDA metrics all presume the presence of positive accounting earnings. But not all companies, particularly new ones, may have attained positive operating earnings. For these firms, analysts must look elsewhere for relative valuation metrics; the most popular of these is the market price per share–to–sales per share ratio (P/Sales). The P/Sales (or P/Revenue) metric may be used in the early stages of an entity's life cycle when growth in market share and marketplace acceptance are considered to be the two best indicators of the company's likely future operating performance. For instance, as the Internet emerged as a viable economic medium of commerce, technology analysts needed a framework to value the alternative Web portals and e-commerce companies, most of which lacked a history of earnings or cash flows. For these firms, analysts needed to creatively assess the value of the expected revenue flows that could be reasonably associated with a given visitor to a Web site. Consequently, such measures as the "revenues per eyeball" and "revenues per page view" emerged.

A final relative valuation method is the market price per share–to–book value per share ratio (P/Book value). This metric indicates the rel-

Exhibit 1.2   Relative Valuation Methods: Average Industry Multiples

| | Average Multiples* | | |
Industry	P/E	P/Sales	P/Book Value
Automobile	11.3	0.4	1.6
Beverage	20.8	1.9	5.3
Chemical	12.2	0.8	2.1
Computer	42.2	2.4	9.2
Semiconductor	44.4	6.4	7.4

*As of September 2000. P/E is price-to-earnings; P/Sales, price-to-sales; and P/Book value, price–to–book value.

ative premium that investors are willing to pay over the book value of their equity in a firm. Unfortunately, the measure "book value per share" is highly sensitive to accounting conventions and changes, as well as to the many accounting policy decisions that the management of a target firm is called upon to make. For this reason, the P/Book value metric is used very selectively, and realistically, it is neither a valid nor viable valuation framework for most firms.

Exhibit 1.2 presents relative P/E, P/Sales, and P/Book value data for a variety of industries. Note the high variance in the multiples between those industries considered "high growth," such as the computer and semiconductor manufacturing industries, versus those industries considered "slow growth," such as the automobile manufacturing or chemical industry. (Compare, for instance, the shaded values in Exhibit 1.2.)

Direct Valuation Methods

Unlike the relative valuation approaches, direct valuation methods provide investors with an *explicit* share value or price objective. Moreover, they are superior to the relative valuation methods because the direct valuation approaches explicitly value what really matters to investors — expected cash flows. Preeminent among this group of frameworks is the discounted cash flow approach.

Discounted cash flow analysis (DCFA) is premised on one of the most fundamental tenets of corporate finance: The value of an asset today is equal to the present value of the (uncertain) future cash flows expected to be provided by the asset over its economic life. Under this framework, the operating value of a business is defined as the sum of the present value of a target firm's expected operating cash flows during a specific forecast period, plus the present value of the target firm's continuing value thereafter. Central to this framework is the development of realistic pro forma financial statements representing an assessment of a firm's expected future operations. The equity value of the target firm — that is, the value accruing to the common (or voting) shareholders of the entity — is given by the operating value of the firm less the value of any claims on the company's cash flows by debtholders, preferred shareholders, minority interest shareholders, and any contingent claimants.

DCFA is a highly effective method of firm valuation, particularly when the capital structure of a target firm is expected to remain stable over time. Some acquisitions, however, are predicated on material modifications in capital structure, as in the case of a leveraged buyout. In these situations, it is often advisable to use a variant of DCFA, namely, the adjusted present value (APV) approach.

Under the APV framework, the value of a target firm is decomposed into two components: the value of the firm assuming that it is financed entirely with equity capital, and the value of the tax shield provided by a firm's actual (or expected) debt financing. As the capital structure of a firm changes, so too does its weighted average cost of capital — the rate at which a target firm's cash flows should be discounted. Furthermore, since interest is tax deductible, the use of debt financing (leverage) implicitly increases a firm's operating cash flow by reducing its cash outflow for income taxes. Hence, as a firm's capital structure changes over time, the value of the firm likewise changes, and the APV framework is an effective way for analysts to gauge firm value in the presence of a changing capital structure.

A final direct valuation framework is the economic value (EV) approach. A central tenet of this framework is that a firm that produces positive economic income will create incremental shareholder wealth and consequently will be rewarded with a higher share price. Economic value analysis focuses on the measurement of periodic economic income instead of operating cash flows (although the two are closely related). As in DCFA and APV analysis, the future periodic economic income flows produced by a firm are discounted back to the present to derive the firm value.

As we will see in Chapter 4, the three methods — DCFA, APV, and EV — can yield equivalent results. Just which method an analyst chooses is usually a question of capital structure stability and analyst preference. Exhibit 1.3 compares the three methods.

Exhibit 1.3   Comparison of Operating Firm Value
              Using Direct Valuation Methods

Discounted Cash Flow Analysis	Adjusted Present Value Approach	Economic Value Approach
Present value of operating cash flows during the specific forecast period	Present value of operating cash flows assuming an equity-financed firm	Present value of economic income during the specific forecast period
—	Present value of interest tax shield from debt financing	Capital invested
Present value of a firm's continuing value	Present value of a firm's continuing value	Present value of a firm's continuing value

Summary

In this chapter, we considered the principal reasons why companies merge or acquire one another, the size and reasoning behind the presence of takeover premiums in merger and acquisition transactions, the typical steps followed in a merger and acquisition transaction, and the mainstream methods for assessing firm value.

In Chapter 2, we begin to take a closer look at the methods and techniques of firm valuation by focusing on the important processes of financial review and pro forma statement development. In Chapter 3, we examine in depth the traditional valuation frameworks of earnings multiples analysis and DCFA. Chapter 4 investigates those valuation frameworks that have emerged in the past decade — APV analysis, EV analysis, and revenues multiples valuation. In Chapter 5, we examine a number of accounting and reporting dilemmas that equity analysts must resolve as part of the valuation process. In Chapter 6, we investigate the issues of taxation and consolidated reporting as they relate to merger and acquisition transactions. And in Chapter 7, we offer some final thoughts.

Notes

1. Modigliani and Miller (1961) are credited with providing the foundation for most valuation methods. They suggested that the value of a firm consisted of two components: the steady-state value of a firm's current operations and the value of its future operations.

2. Berger and Ofek (1995) report that the conglomerate discount averages about 15 percent; however, many analysts believe that the magnitude of this discount is declining with the increasing use of such valuation frameworks as the "break-up" method and the "sum of the parts" method, which enable a conglomerate to be valued as the aggregate of its parts.

3. Other studies questioning the economic value of acquisitions include Ravenscraft and Scherer (1987), Kaplan and Weisbach (1992), and Healy, Palepu, and Ruback (1997).

4. In general, debt capital is less expensive than equity capital, in part because interest charges on debt capital are tax deductible whereas dividends on equity capital are not; debt is also less risky and thus less costly. As a consequence, a firm financed with part debt and part equity should (ceteris paribus) generate higher shareholder returns than an all-equity-financed firm.

2 Financial Review and Pro Forma Analysis

The Quaker Oats Company's $1.7 billion purchase of Snapple in late 1994 stands as one of that decade's worst acquisitions. With Snapple's poor operating performance dragging the consolidated operating results down, Quaker's stock price stagnated while the Dow Jones industrial average moved up by more than 70 percent. So now that Quaker has sold the beverage company, should Quaker shareholders celebrate?

Mourning would be more appropriate. The price Quaker paid for its soft-drink misadventure goes well beyond the $1.4 billion in losses directly associated with the sale of Snapple to Triarc Company for just $300 million. In addition, Quaker absorbed more than $100 million in cash losses and charges related to Snapple from 1994 to 1997. And since the deal damaged its balance sheet, Quaker's credit rating suffered, raising its cost of capital.

Another cost: Quaker helped pay for the acquisition by selling its petfood and candy businesses that had given it a larger scale, steady earnings, and international reach. It also paid punishing capital-gains taxes on those sales.

The total losses associated with the Snapple acquisition may well exceed the original acquisition price.

Adapted from G. Burns, "What Price the Snapple Debacle?" *Business Week,* 14 April 1997, 42.

• • •

Why did more than 50 percent of the major mergers and acquisitions in the United States completed in the 1990s, according to *Business Week* magazine, erode shareholder value? And why did more than 77 percent of those transactions, according to *Forbes* magazine, not earn a rate of return at least equivalent to the cost of the capital necessary to finance them? The answer to both questions is often the same: overestimation of target firm value.

The process of valuing a firm presents innumerable opportunities for error, and analysts and executives frequently tend to err on the positive side when assessing firm value. This predisposition to "focus on the good side of things" has been referred to as the **winner's curse,** in that winning a bidding war for an acquisition target may actually mean losing.[1]

This chapter begins our exploration of the process of valuing a firm. We assume that a target company has been identified and that the acquisition appears desirable from a strategic standpoint. Hence, we enter the valuation process at the point when the question is raised, "What does the future hold for the target company?" The answer necessitates a review of the recent past and the development of various scenarios about the future. In this chapter, we formalize the historical review of an acquisition target by means of **financial review,** and we articulate the alternative future scenarios by means of **pro forma analysis.**

Specifically, this chapter addresses the following key questions:

- How should the historical financial review of a target company be organized?

- Which financial ratios should be calculated?

- How can forward-looking pro forma financial statements be developed?

- How can the sensitivity of the pro forma scenarios to key forecast assumptions be evaluated?

Financial Review

Financial review is the process of analyzing, evaluating, and describing the financial history of a company; it is a key element of the process of **due diligence** that precedes any acquisition offer. Financial review serves four key functions when an acquisition candidate is being valued. First, it provides the necessary information for an acquirer to confirm that a target company is a financially appropriate and desirable acquisition. Second, it identifies the target company's financial strengths and weaknesses, and hence those factors that will enhance or detract from future consolidated results. Third, it helps the executive or analyst gain an understanding of the fundamental business model of a target and identify the key revenue and cost drivers of the business. Finally, it provides a set of benchmark relationships the analyst needs to build a realistic set of pro forma financial statements. As we will see below, the common-size statements and ratios developed as part of the historic financial review often provide the key percentage estimates and relationships used for building pro forma financial statements.

The techniques of financial review are many and varied, hence, we limit our consideration to those techniques most relevant to the valuation process: ratio analysis and cash flow analysis. (For further details, see Lev 1974; Ferris, Tennant, and Jerris 1992; Stickney and Brown 1999; and Haskins, Ferris, and Selling 2000.)

Ratio analysis is the process of investigating the relationship between various balance sheet, income statement, and cash flow statement accounts. Analysts may use ratios to investigate these relationships across multiple time periods through what is commonly called **trend analysis** or between various alternative target companies in what is traditionally labeled **cross-section analysis.** In addition to comparing ratios over time for a given target, or between alternative targets, it is often advisable for an analyst to compare a target company's ratios to industrywide indices. Standard & Poor's, Moody's Investors Service, Value Line, Dun & Bradstreet, and *The Financial Times,* among others, provide industry statistics that permit comparisons of a company's performance against the average performance of all companies within a given industry. This type of comparison enables the executive or valuation analyst to assess the relative performance of a target candidate against a set of comparable companies.

Cash flow analysis refers to the process of identifying the various sources and uses of cash flows of a target company. This analysis enables the following questions to be addressed:

- Is the target company generating a positive **cash flow from operations** (CFFO), and if so, is it generating a positive **discretionary cash flow?**[2]

- How has the target company been using its available cash resources — to retire debt, to repurchase shares, to pay dividends, or
  to replace property, plant, and equipment?

- How has the target company been financing its capital expenditures — from debt, equity placements, operations, or the liquidation of noncurrent assets?

- Is the target company likely to need a cash infusion after the
  acquisition?

As cash is the primary investment attribute of interest to investors, the
analysis of cash flows is particularly significant in the process of financial
review.

Ratio Analysis

Professional analysts have always faced the problem of deciding how
to organize a financial review of a target company. It is commonly ac-
knowledged that the five key areas of interest are firm profitability, effective asset management, liquidity, solvency, and shareholders' returns.
But a coherent framework linking these key areas has been elusive. (For
an international perspective, see Choi et al. 1985.)

One framework that has been successfully implemented is the
DuPont Model, so named for the company in which it was developed.
This model successfully integrates the areas of **profitability** and **asset
management,** featuring a company's return on assets (ROA) as the quin-
tessential measure of firm and managerial performance. One advantage
of the DuPont Model (see Exhibit 2.1) is that it highlights the important
interplay between effective asset management and firm profitability,
namely, that a company's ROA can be positively affected by

- increasing the net profit margin on each individual sale transaction,

- increasing the volume of sales transactions (i.e., increasing turnover), or

- some combination of increasing profit margins and increasing
  turnover.

In essence, the DuPont Model focuses on evaluating earnings and a
company's investment in assets — that is, its business or operational risk.
It focuses on the income statement and the asset side of the balance sheet.
Unfortunately, the model ignores the important issue of how a company
has financed its investment in assets (i.e., its financial risk) — with debt or
equity, and if with debt, whether short-term or long-term debt.

Exhibit 2.1   The DuPont Model

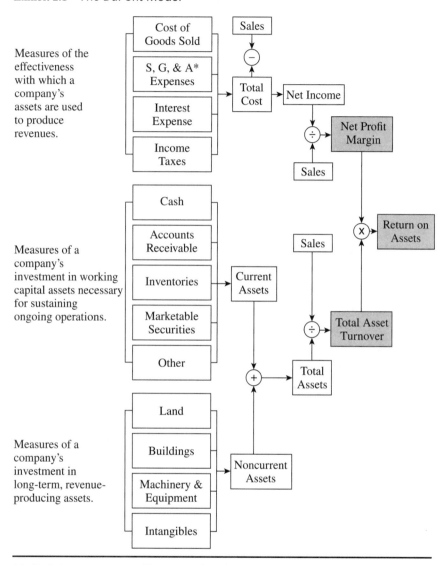

Measures of the effectiveness with which a company's assets are used to produce revenues.

Measures of a company's investment in working capital assets necessary for sustaining ongoing operations.

Measures of a company's investment in long-term, revenue-producing assets.

*S, G, & A expenses are selling, general, and administrative expenses.

To overcome this limitation, many analysts have turned to an extension of the DuPont Model known as the **ROE Model,** or the **return on shareholders' equity model.** The strength of the ROE Model is that not only does it integrate all five areas of analysis, but it is also premised on the widely held notion that the *principal goal of management is to maxi-*

mize shareholder wealth. In essence, the ROE Model is broader in scope than the DuPont Model, considering the operating, investing, and financial decisions of a business.

The cornerstone of the ROE Model is a single shareholder-focused index of firm performance called the **return on equity,** or ROE:

$$\text{ROE} = \frac{\text{Net Income after Taxes } - \text{ Preferred Stock Dividends}}{\text{Average Common Shareholders' Equity}}$$

ROE measures the rate of return generated by a company for its owners — the voting (or common) shareholders.[3] This return largely depends on two factors: (1) How profitably a company is able to use the assets that it has at its disposal, and (2) the relative size of the owners' investment in the firm. Clearly, the more profitably a company uses its assets, the greater the returns to the owners. A second way that the owners' returns can be maximized, however, is through the use of **financial leverage,** or borrowing. If a company can generate a return on its borrowed assets that exceeds its cost of borrowing, then the company can enhance its ROE by leveraging the owners' investment. Thus, the ROE Model highlights the fact that corporate management can affect shareholder wealth through *both* its operating decisions *and* its financing decisions.

These relationships become apparent by decomposing ROE into its two principal components — profitability and financial leverage:[4]

$$\text{ROE} = \text{Profitability} \times \text{Financial Leverage}$$

$$= \frac{\text{Net Income after Taxes}}{\text{Average Total Assets}}$$

$$\times \frac{\text{Average Total Assets}}{\text{Average Common Shareholders' Equity}}$$

Notice that the first component of ROE is nothing more than a company's ROA, the cornerstone of the DuPont Model. **ROA** tells us about a firm's profitability, whereas the second component, financial leverage, tells us how the company has been financed and how successfully management has been able to lever the owners' investment. It is important to observe that leverage, or the extent to which a company is able to borrow, is a double-edged sword: Leverage will enhance a company's ROE only as long as the cost of borrowing is *less* than the returns generated on the borrowed assets; thereafter, leverage will reduce a firm's ROE and destroy shareholder value.

ROE can be further decomposed by examining the individual factors that contribute to a company's profitability. Firm profitability, as measured by ROA, can be seen to depend on two factors: (1) the relative profitability of each sale that a company generates — that is, its net profit margin, and (2) the number of sales, or turnover, that a company is able to generate given its existing asset base. These relationships are observable by decomposing ROA into its component elements — net profit margin and asset turnover:[5]

$$\text{Profitability} = \text{Net Profit Margin} \times \text{Asset Turnover}$$

$$= \frac{\text{Net Income after Taxes}}{\text{Net Sales}} \times \frac{\text{Net Sales}}{\text{Average Total Assets}}$$

Decomposing ROA into its individual components highlights the two principal ways that management can enhance shareholders' returns through its operating decisions. The above equation reveals, for example, that shareholders' returns can be positively affected either by increasing a company's net profit margin or by increasing the number (or volume) of its sales transactions. That is, the higher a company's net profit margin, the greater will be the shareholders' returns on any given sale; and the higher the number of sales that are generated for a given investment in assets, the greater a firm's overall profitability.

Returning to our cornerstone ratio and incorporating these latest concepts yields the following equation:

$$\text{ROE} = (\text{Net Profit Margin} \times \text{Asset Turnover}) \times \text{Financial Leverage}$$

This equation reveals that the three principal drivers of shareholders' returns are (1) the relative profitability of each sale transaction, (2) the number of sale transactions generated given a company's investment in operating assets, and (3) the extent to which a company has been able to successfully lever the shareholders' investment. Exhibit 2.2 presents an illustration of how the ROE Model both builds on and extends the DuPont Model.

To illustrate the relationship of these performance drivers, consider the financial data for Nokia Corporation, one of the world's leading telecommunications companies, headquartered in Finland. Using data from the company's summary of selected financial information, performance ratios for the period 1994–1997 can be calculated to reveal the trend in Nokia's shareholders' returns (see the shaded area in Exhibit 2.3). In

Exhibit 2.2   The Return on Shareholders' Equity (ROE) Model

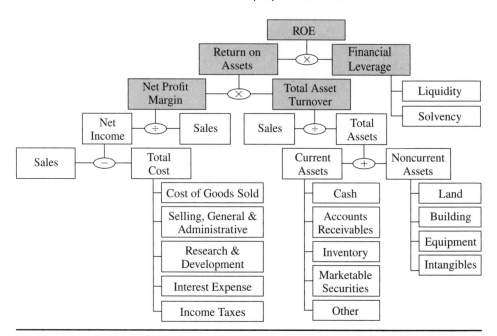

Exhibit 2.3   Nokia Corporation Return on Equity Analysis

Performance Measure	1994	1995	1996	1997
Net profit margin	8.6%	3.2%	6.5%	10.4%
Asset turnover	1.20×	1.21×	1.19×	1.40×
ROA	10.3%	3.9%	7.8%	14.6%
Financial leverage	2.67×	2.31×	2.22×	2.00×
ROE	27.5%	9.0%	17.2%	29.3%

ROA is return on assets; and ROE, return on equity.

1997, Nokia's ROE was 29.3 percent, up from 9.0 percent in 1995 and 17.2 percent in 1996. (See Appendix 2A for the Nokia data used in this analysis.)

To understand the causal factors of this growth, Nokia's ROE for 1997 can be decomposed as follows:

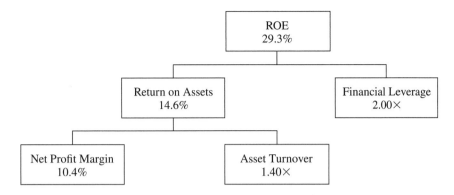

Considering the company's trend data in Exhibit 2.3, we see that the growth in Nokia's ROE has largely come from its increasing net profit margin, up from 3.2 percent in 1995 to 10.4 percent in 1997, and its asset turnover, which increased from 1.21 times in 1995 to 1.40 times in 1997. The company's financial leverage declined from its 1994 high of 2.67 times to 2.00 times in 1997.

Decomposition Analysis

Just as it is possible to decompose ROE into its three key drivers of profit margin, asset turnover, and financial leverage, so is it possible to decompose each of these three key drivers into their subcomponents. **Decomposition analysis** is the process of segmenting a component of ROE into its principal subcomponents and in so doing enabling the analyst to begin the process of identifying the *specific* causes of change in each of the key ROE drivers.

Decomposing Profit Margin. A company's net profit margin reveals the relative profitability of its basic operating activity. For the valuation analyst to be able to identify just which components of operations were responsible for generating an increase (or decrease) in profitability, it is instructive for him or her to decompose the net profit margin into the various subratios that, collectively, comprise this ratio.

The most effective way of decomposing a company's net profit margin into its subcomponents is by means of **common-size income statements.** In common-size financial statements, all amounts are expressed as a percentage of some base financial statement item. For example, in common-size income statements all amounts are expressed as a percentage of net sales. (In common-size balance sheets, all amounts are

Exhibit 2.4   Nokia Corporation Common-Size Income Statements

	1994	1995	1996	1997
Net sales	100.0%	100.0%	100.0%	100.0%
Cost of goods sold	(67.1)	(67.1)	(69.6)	(63.1)
Gross profit	32.9	32.9	30.4	36.9
Research and development expense	(5.9)	(5.0)	(6.2)	(6.7)
Selling, general, and administrative expense	(11.8)	(9.3)	(7.7)	(8.9)
Operating profit	15.2	18.6	16.5	21.3
Share of results of associated companies	0.1	0.2	0.1	0.1
Net financial income	1.7	1.6	1.4	1.5
Exchange gains and losses	1.5	0.0	0.1	0.2
Profit before interest, tax, depreciation, and minority interest	18.5	20.4	18.1	23.1
Interest expense	(1.9)	(2.0)	(2.5)	(1.9)
Depreciation/amortization expense	(3.3)	(5.0)	(5.7)	(5.3)
Income tax expense	(3.1)	(2.1)	(2.2)	(4.3)
Minority interest	(0.3)	(0.2)	(0.0)	(0.2)
Profit from continuing operations	9.9	11.1	7.7	11.4
Discontinued operations	—	(6.4)	0.6	0.5
Net profit	9.9	4.7	8.3	11.9
Preferred stock dividends	(1.3)	(1.6)	(1.8)	(1.5)
Net profit margin	8.6	3.2	6.5	10.4

expressed as a percentage of total assets.) Trend analysis of common-size income statements permits an analyst to assess how a company's income statement accounts are changing over time relative to sales, and thus how the various income statement items contribute to the net profit margin. Exhibit 2.4, for example, presents the common-size income statement data for Nokia Corporation, 1994–1997.

The data in Exhibit 2.4 reveal the following:

- Nokia's net income as a percentage of net sales grew from 3.2 percent in 1995 to 10.4 percent in 1997.

- Nokia's cost of goods sold declined from 67.1 percent to 63.1 percent over the four years, accounting for most of the company's increase in profitability.

- Research and development costs increased slightly from 5.0 percent in 1995 to 6.7 percent in 1997.

- Selling, administrative, and general expenses declined from 11.8 percent in 1994 to 8.9 percent in 1997, accounting for approximately 21 percent of Nokia's increase in profitability.

- Interest expense generally increased over the four years until 1997 when it declined to 1.9 percent, whereas income taxes increased from 3.1 to 4.3 percent.

As the above analysis of Nokia's common-size income statement data reveals, decomposing the net profit margin enables the analyst to address the following questions:

- Is the target company's net profit margin changing over time? If so, what factors are causing the changes: cost of goods sold, research and development outlays, selling and administrative costs, interest costs, income taxes, or what?

- How well is the target company management managing its cost of doing business? Has the company reached sufficient volume levels to gain any economies of scale? In what areas, if any, does the company seem to be overspending?

Decomposing Asset Turnover. Asset turnover, or what is sometimes called "asset management," refers to the degree of productivity that a company is able to achieve with respect to its operating assets. It is a measure of the effectiveness with which a company's management is able to employ the valuable resources provided by creditors and owners alike. Not surprisingly, a strong link exists between the effective use of a company's assets and the degree of profitability that a company is able to achieve. Whereas the net profit margin focuses on the *rate* at which profit is generated from each unit of sales, the asset turnover ratio focuses on the *volume* of sales generated from a given investment in operating assets. Thus, in Exhibit 2.3, we see that in 1997 Nokia Corporation generated 0.104 Finnish markka (FIM) in net profit from each markka of sales revenue, while generating 1.40 FIM in sales revenue from each markka invested in operating assets. It can be readily seen from this data that Nokia can increase its return to shareholders *either* by increasing the rate of profit per markka of sales or by increasing the number of sales markkas generated from its existing investment in operating assets.

The decomposition of asset turnover traditionally focuses on two groups of assets that are closely linked to the operations of a company:

the working capital assets, which include cash, trade receivables, and inventory; and the noncurrent revenue-producing assets such as property, plant, and equipment. For most companies, analysts usually calculate the following ratios when determining how effectively corporate management has used a company's key operating assets:

Working Capital Ratios:

$$\text{Current Asset Turnover} = \frac{\text{Net Sales}}{\text{Average Current Assets}}$$

A measure of the value of net sales generated from a given investment in current assets.

$$\text{Accounts Receivable Turnover} = \frac{\text{Net Sales}}{\text{Average Accounts Receivable}}$$

A measure of the number of receivable collection cycles (i.e., credit sale $\rightarrow$ accounts receivable $\rightarrow$ cash collection) occurring in a given period of time (usually one quarter or one year).

$$\text{Receivable Collection Period} = \frac{365 \text{ Days}}{\text{Receivable Turnover}}$$

A measure of the number of days, on average, required for collecting an outstanding account receivable, calculated on an annual (or quarterly) basis.

$$\text{Inventory Turnover} = \frac{\text{Cost of Goods Sold}}{\text{Average Ending Inventory}}$$

A measure of the number of production cycles (i.e., inventory production $\rightarrow$ sale) occurring in a given period of time (usually one quarter or one year).

$$\text{Days' Inventory on Hand} = \frac{365 \text{ Days}}{\text{Inventory Turnover}}$$

A measure of the quantity of inventory on hand, expressed in terms of the number of days needed to sell the existing inventory, calculated on an annual (or quarterly) basis.

$$\text{Accounts Payable Turnover} = \frac{\text{Cost of Goods Sold}}{\text{Average Accounts Payable}}$$

A measure of the number of account payment cycles (i.e., buy inventory on credit $\rightarrow$ sell inventory $\rightarrow$ payment on account) occurring in a given period of time (usually one quarter or one year).

$$\text{Days' Payable Period} = \frac{365 \text{ Days}}{\text{Payable Turnover}}$$

A measure of the number of days, on average, required for paying an outstanding account payable, calculated on an annual (or quarterly) basis.

Noncurrent Asset Ratios:

$$\text{Noncurrent Asset Turnover} = \frac{\text{Net Sales}}{\text{Average Noncurrent Assets}}$$

A measure of the value of net sales generated for a given investment in noncurrent assets.

$$\begin{array}{c}\text{Property, Plant, and} \\ \text{Equipment Turnover}\end{array} = \frac{\text{Net Sales}}{\begin{array}{c}\text{Average Property, Plant,} \\ \text{and Equipment}\end{array}}$$

A measure of the value of net sales generated for a given investment in property, plant, and equipment.

Exhibit 2.5 Nokia Corporation Asset Turnover Decomposition Analysis

Performance Measure	1994	1995	1996	1997
Asset turnover	1.20×	1.21×	1.19×	1.40×
Current asset turnover	1.75×	1.69×	1.62×	1.84×
Accounts receivable turnover	4.29×	4.24×	3.85×	4.45×
Receivable collection period (days)	85	86	95	82
Inventory turnover	3.39×	2.94×	3.34×	4.83×
Days' inventory on hand (days)	108	124	109	76
Accounts payable turnover	2.88×	2.83×	2.74×	2.64×
Days' payable period (days)	127	129	133	138
Noncurrent asset turnover	3.79×	4.33×	4.51×	5.89×
Property, plant, and equipment turnover	6.12×	6.57×	6.68×	8.84×

Several observations about the preceding ratios are noteworthy. First, in most cases, the denominator of each ratio is an average. The purpose of averaging a beginning-of-period and an end-of-period balance is to try to eliminate the effects of any significant increases or decreases in a given account. For example, it would distort the inventory turnover ratio to divide a company's cost of goods sold by its ending inventory if the firm had experienced either a dramatic increase or decrease in inventory at year end; in either case, the inventory turnover ratio would be biased by the end-of-period contraction/expansion in inventory. Second, not all of the above ratios are relevant for all companies. For example, an enterprise such as The McDonald's Company, a worldwide chain of fast-food restaurants, maintains an insignificant balance in accounts receivable. Few, if any, of the company's customer sales are undertaken on a credit basis. Thus, the analysis of receivable turnover for a company like McDonald's is unnecessary. Third, some of the ratios are merely transformations of other ratios. For example, the days' inventory-on-hand ratio is merely a transformation of the inventory turnover ratio. It is often unnecessary for analysts to calculate both ratios, although many do. Fourth, it is probably obvious that in almost all cases a high rate of turnover is to be preferred to a lower rate.[6] This generality will hold except in those cases in which management is liquidating its revenue-producing assets — a dangerous situation for any company in the long term. Finally, the above set of ratios should not be considered to be exhaustive; analysts frequently add to and subtract from the above list.

    To illustrate the use of these ratios, consider Exhibit 2.5, which shows the asset turnover ratios for Nokia. The data in Exhibit 2.5 reveal the following:

- In 1997, Nokia generated 1.84 FIM in net sales for each markka invested in current assets, up 14 percent from 1.62 FIM in 1996.

- Nokia's receivable turnover cycle vacillated from a low of 3.85 times in 1996 to a high of 4.45 times in 1997. This increase in the number of receivable collection cycles is reflected in Nokia's declining receivable collection period, which was down nearly thirteen days between 1996 and 1997.

- Nokia's inventory turnover cycle count remained relatively stable (i.e., 2.94 times to 3.39 times) from 1994 to 1996 but increased markedly in 1997 to 4.83 times. The higher the rate of inventory turnover, the higher the returns to shareholders, unless the higher turnover is achieved by means of price reductions (and hence reduced profit margins). Although Nokia's 4.83 inventory turns is quite respectable, it lags the industry average of 6.2 turns, indicating that there is still room for improvement. The increase in inventory turnover count is also reflected in a reduced days' inventory-on-hand ratio, which declined from a high of 124 days in 1995 to 76 days in 1997. This 48-day reduction undoubtedly contributed to Nokia's improved profitability in 1997.

- Nokia's accounts payable turnover declined from 2.88 times in 1994 to 2.64 times in 1997. This decline is reflected in an increase in Nokia's accounts payable period from 127 days to 138 days. When contrasted with Nokia's average receivable collection period of 82 days in 1997, this suggests that Nokia is managing its working capital flows very efficiently.

- Nokia's property, plant, and equipment (PP&E) turnover grew steadily from 6.12 FIM for each markka invested in PP&E in 1994 to 8.84 FIM in 1997. This indicates that Nokia increased its efficiency with respect to PP&E: The company was able to generate a 44 percent higher volume of sales for an equivalent investment in PP&E.

The decomposition analysis of Nokia's asset turnover suggests that the increase in the company's asset turnover from 1994 to 1997 almost certainly resulted from an improvement in the company's management of all key operating asset categories: receivables, inventory, and PP&E.

Decomposing Financial Leverage.   Financial leverage refers to the ability of a company to increase its asset base through borrowing.

Financial leverage can be a powerful tool for enhancing shareholders' returns, but the effectiveness of leverage in maximizing shareholders' returns is directly linked to the spread between a company's cost of borrowing and the returns on those borrowed funds. As this spread declines, the ability of financial leverage to enhance shareholders' returns also declines.

The ability of financial leverage to enhance shareholders' returns can thus be seen to be a function of a firm's cost of borrowing and its return on borrowed assets (which we ignore for the moment). Furthermore, a firm's cost of borrowing is directly linked to its ability to service its existing debt — what is commonly called **financial risk.** A company with low financial risk (i.e., a high ability to repay debt and debt service charges) will be able to borrow at a lower cost than a company with higher financial risk. For this type of company, increases in the amount of leverage will be more effective in enhancing shareholders' returns than will increases in leverage for a company with high financial risk. Hence, one way that analysts evaluate the extent and effectiveness of financial leverage is by evaluating a company's current financial riskiness.

The analysis of financial leverage usually focuses on two dimensions of financial riskiness: short-term risk, or **liquidity,** and long-term risk, or **solvency.** For most companies, the following ratios are calculated when financial risk is analyzed:

Short-Term Risk:

$$\text{Quick Ratio}^7 = \frac{\text{Cash} + \text{Marketable Securities} + \text{Trade Receivables}}{\text{Current Liabilities}}$$

A measure of the highly liquid current assets available for repaying short-term liabilities.

$$\text{Operating Cash Flow Ratio} = \frac{\text{Cash Flow from Operations}}{\text{Current Liabilities}}$$

A measure of the cash flow from operations available for repaying short-term liabilities.

Long-Term Risk:

$$\text{Total Liabilities–to–Equity Ratio} = \frac{\text{Total Liabilities}}{\text{Common Shareholders' Equity}}$$

A measure of the relative investment of creditors versus common shareholders in a company.

$$\text{Long-Term Debt–to–Equity Ratio} = \frac{\text{Long-Term Debt}}{\text{Common Shareholders' Equity}}$$

A measure of the relative investment of long-term creditors versus common shareholders in a company.

$$\text{Interest Coverage Ratio} = \frac{\text{Income before Taxes} + \text{Interest Expense}}{\text{Interest Expense}}$$

A measure of the extent to which current operations can support current debt service charges.

Two observations about the above ratios are useful. First, a company's short-term obligations can be repaid with cash generated from a variety of sources: future operations, existing liquid assets (as reflected by the current asset section of the balance sheet), the sale of assets, the sale of stock, or new borrowings. The short-term liquidity ratios focus on the two sources of liquid resources that are immediately available to managers: cash from operations and cash (or other highly liquid current assets) on hand. Second, the long-term solvency ratios themselves focus on two separate aspects of risk: (1) the ability of a company to cover the current cost of debt from the income generated by existing operations, and (2) the existing level of financial leverage that currently characterizes a company. If a company is already highly leveraged (i.e., already has a high proportion of assets from creditors), then further financial leverage will not be as effective in enhancing shareholders' returns. As stated above, as the degree of leverage increases, so too does a firm's riskiness, and lenders will charge commensurately higher interest costs, thereby reducing the utility of additional leverage.

Exhibit 2.6 Nokia Corporation Financial Leverage Decomposition Analysis

Performance Measure	1994	1995	1996	1997
Financial leverage	2.67×	2.31×	2.22×	2.00×
Short-term liquidity				
Quick ratio	115.8%	86.1%	123.7%	135.9%
Operating cash flow ratio	22.5%	−4.0%	55.8%	55.5%
Long-term solvency				
Total liabilities–to–equity ratio	119.8%	134.2%	108.8%	93.0%
Long-term debt–to–equity ratio	28.6%	18.7%	15.2%	7.6%
Interest coverage ratio	6.90×	6.62×	4.04×	8.32×

To illustrate the use of these ratios, consider Exhibit 2.6, which shows a decomposition analysis of Nokia Corporation's financial leverage ratios. The data in Exhibit 2.6 reveal the following:

- Nokia's use of financial leverage steadily declined from its high of 2.67 times in 1994 to 2.00 times in 1997. This decline in the use of financial leverage is reflected in the significant increases in Nokia's liquidity and solvency over the same period.

- With respect to liquidity, the quick ratio increased from 115.8 percent in 1994 to 135.9 percent in 1997, and the operating cash flow ratio increased from −4.0 percent in 1995 to 55.5 percent in 1997. Both ratios indicate improved levels of liquidity, and hence a reduced use of short-term leverage.

- With respect to solvency, the total liabilities–to–equity ratio declined from 119.8 percent in 1994 to 93.0 percent in 1997, and the long-term debt–to–equity ratio declined from 28.6 percent in 1994 to 7.6 percent in 1997. The interest coverage ratio generally increased from 6.90 times in 1994 to 8.32 times in 1997. The decline in Nokia's debt–to–equity ratios and the significant improvement in the interest coverage ratio indicate a material decline in Nokia's reliance on long-term leverage.

Overall, the decomposition analysis of Nokia's financial leverage indicates a dramatic reduction (i.e., more than 25 percent) in the use of financial leverage.

Analytical Framework: Putting It All Together

Exhibit 2.7 presents a composite framework for the ratio analysis of a target company. The framework is premised on the notion that the principal goal of corporate management is to maximize shareholders' wealth.

Exhibit 2.7   ROE Model for Financial Review

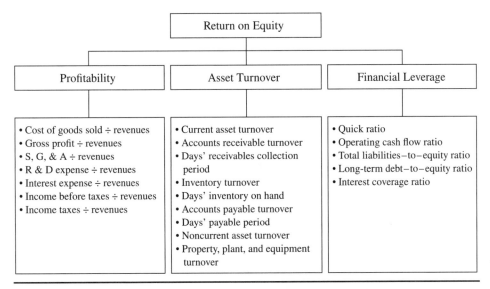

S, G, & A is selling, general, and administrative; and R & D, research and development.

As such, the cornerstone of the model is the return on common share-holders' equity, or ROE. As discussed above, ROE can be decomposed into the three key drivers of profitability, asset turnover, and financial leverage. And each of the three key drivers can themselves be decomposed into various subcomponents, as depicted in Exhibit 2.7.

Cash Flow Analysis

With the exception of the operating cash flow ratio, all of the ratios discussed thus far are derived from income statement and balance sheet data. Given that cash is the one asset that a company cannot operate without, and that it is the investment attribute of principal interest to investors, the analysis of cash flows is an important component of any financial review. Since the demand for cash flow data has become widespread, most countries now require the presentation of a statement of cash flows (SCF). Where an SCF is not presented, the valuation analyst must have the necessary skills to prepare one. (Appendix 2B presents a methodology for the preparation of an SCF from balance sheet and income statement data.)

The structure of the SCF worldwide has evolved into a fairly consistent presentation composed of three categories:

- Cash flows from operating activities (CFFO)

- Cash flows from investing activities (CFFI)

- Cash flows from financing activities (CFFF)

The CFFO represents the cash generated from the sale of goods or the provision of services, less the cash paid for operations — in essence, net income on a modified cash basis. The CFFI, on the other hand, represents the cash paid for intercorporate investments (both short- and long-term), the cash paid for new capital investments, and the cash received from the sale or disposal of noncurrent assets. Finally, the CFFF represents the cash generated from the sale of stock and from long- and short-term borrowings, less the cash paid for retiring outstanding debt, repurchasing treasury stock, or paying dividends.

Cash flow analysis enables the analyst to address a variety of key questions, such as the following:

- Is the target company generating a positive CFFO, and if so, is it also generating a positive discretionary cash flow?

- What types of strategic investments has the target company been making?

- How has the target company been financing its operations and its strategic investments?

- How has the target company financed its dividend payments?

To illustrate this type of analysis, consider Exhibit 2.8, which contains the SCF for the Nokia Corporation for 1995–1997; this data reveals the following:

- Nokia generated a positive CFFO of 10.201 billion FIM in 1997, an increase of about 23 percent over 1996. The company also generated a positive discretionary cash flow of 3.782 billion FIM, calculated as follows:

CFFO		10.201 billion
Less	Dividend payments	(1.061)
	Debt retirements	(2.007)
	Capital and research and development expenditures	(3.351)
Discretionary cash flow		3.782 billion

- Nokia's 1997 CFFI was a negative 2.972 billion FIM. The company made significant investments in new PP&E (2.402 billion),

Exhibit 2.8   Nokia Corporation Cash Flow Analysis:
Consolidated Statements of Cash Flows*

	1995	1996	1997
Operating activities			
Net income	1,747	3,263	6,259
Depreciation/amortization	1,825	2,236	2,762
Deferred income taxes	(333)	195	640
Equity income, net of dividends	(85)	(37)	(54)
Other items	1,566	(331)	(283)
Net change in operating assets and liabilities	5,351	2,993	877
Net cash provided by operating activities	(631)	8,319	10,201
Investing activities			
Acquisitions and investments	(96)	(175)	(552)
Proceeds from disposals of investments and other assets	2,305	(277)	425
Purchases of property, plant, and equipment	(3,299)	(2,028)	(2,402)
Proceeds from disposals of property, plant, and equipment	396	293	506
Capitalized research and development costs	(742)	(677)	(949)
Net cash used in investing activities	(1,436)	(2,864)	(2,972)
Financing activities			
Retirement of debt (short- and long-term)	1,222	(433)	(2,007)
Payment from affiliates	145	(605)	355
Share issuances	37	—	72
Purchases of treasury shares	—	(210)	—
Dividends	(789)	(901)	(1,061)
Net cash used in financing activities	615	(2,149)	(2,641)
Effect of exchange rate changes on cash and cash equivalents	(87)	25	114
Net increase (decrease) during the year	(1,452)	3,306	4,588
Balance at beginning of year	5,268	4,214	7,545
Balance at end of year	3,729	7,545	12,247

*This data has been reformatted. Values are for year ended 31 December, in millions of Finnish markka.

research and development (0.949), and key equity investments (0.552) such as Ipsilon Networks, Inc. These investment outlays were partially offset by the proceeds generated from disposing of select investments (0.425) and certain fixed assets (0.506).

- Nokia's 1997 CFFF was a negative 2.641 billion FIM, largely because of the company's continuing program of debt reduction (2.007 billion) and dividend payments (1.061 billion).

As we shall see in Chapter 3, the link between the SCF and firm value will take on particular meaning as we define a company's free cash flows in terms of its CFFO. With the historical financial review complete, we now turn to the task of generating realistic scenarios about a company's future operating performance.

Pro Forma Analysis

After completing the historical financial review, the valuation analyst is ready to begin developing forward-looking pro forma financial statements. **Pro forma financial statements** are an analyst's best guess as to how a target company will perform in the future. These estimates reflect the likely cost reductions and synergies, as well as revenue enhancements, that an acquiring company can reasonably expect once an acquisition is completed.[8] Inherent in the process of developing pro forma financial statements is the necessity of the analyst making numerous assumptions about events that have yet to occur. If the valuation analyst is to avoid the winner's curse — that is, overpricing a successful acquisition — it is imperative that he or she base all assumptions on sound logic and reasoning. When such assumptions are not well conceived, the cost to an acquiring firm can be quite significant, as the Quaker Oats vignette at the beginning of this chapter reveals.

The preparation of pro forma statements is typically a six-step process:

1. *Forecast revenues for the target company.* The projection of future revenues is, without question, the single most important step in the pro forma process. As this is the starting point, a mis-estimation at this stage will be compounded into a multitude of other forecasted values. In general, sales are usually forecasted for three to five years, and possibly as long as ten years. Most professional analysts, however, are considerably reluctant to forecast beyond five years, in large measure because of the high probability of error in such long-term forecasts.[9] As most businesses will have a continuing value beyond the final forecast year, the analyst must also project a value of the business for all years subsequent to the final forecast year. This value is known as the **continuing, terminal,** or **exit value,** and the process of estimating this value is discussed in Chapter 3.

2. *Forecast operating expenses (excluding acquisition financing costs)*. The projection of operating expenses includes the preparation of forecasts for cost of goods sold, research and development costs, selling and administrative expenses, and other continuing income and expense items. These forecasts should include the effects of any anticipated cost reductions or economies of scale expected to arise as a consequence of an acquisition. Some operating expenses are relatively easy for an analyst to forecast because they are either fixed in amount or vary as a function of revenues, whereas others are more difficult to project because they are neither strictly fixed nor strictly variable. A good source of information for help in forecasting operating expenses is the historical common-size income statements (see Exhibit 2.4). For those operating expenses that vary in a relatively constant relationship with sales, as revealed by a multiyear common-size statement analysis, the common-size percentage may be a useful way for an analyst to forecast these expenses in future periods.

3. *Forecast the change and composition of total assets on the balance sheet*. There are two approaches to forecasting assets: (1) Forecast *total* assets and then allocate this total among the individual asset accounts using common-size balance sheet relationships (and potentially other assumptions), and (2) forecast the *individual* asset accounts and then sum the accounts to arrive at a value for total assets. The first approach is most frequently used largely because of its ease in application. It is usually undertaken by assuming that most companies maintain a relatively constant relation between revenues and total assets (i.e., a constant total asset turnover ratio). The individual asset accounts are then forecasted by reference to various assumptions about the growth (or decline) in the various asset accounts and to a target company's most recent common-size balance sheet.

   The second approach to forecasting assets is more complex but somewhat more refined. For example, it is reasonable to expect that the PP&E turnover ratio would decline with small increases in revenues, whereas the current asset turnover ratio would remain relatively fixed. These expected relationships are more easily incorporated in the pro forma balance sheet with the second approach.

4. *Set total equities equal to total assets (from step 3) and forecast the cost of financing the acquisition transaction and the target company's long-term financing in general.* As part of this step, the analyst will need to forecast any net proceeds from the issuance and repurchase of capital stock, any net proceeds from the issuance and retirement of long-term debt, any changes in non−interest-bearing liabilities (i.e., accounts payable and accrued expenses), and the target company's future dividend policy, if any. At this juncture, it is also appropriate for the analyst to deal with the question of cash surpluses (deficits) relative to the balance forecasted in step 3. As most companies maintain bank lines of credit, one useful assumption is adjusting the amount of short-term interest-bearing debt for any cash deficit (or surplus) relative to the step 3 forecast.[10]

5. *Complete the pro forma income statement and balance sheet by forecasting interest costs and income taxes.*

6. *Derive the pro forma SCF from the pro forma income statements and balance sheets.*

Embedded in the above six-step process are a number of subtle decisions that are best illustrated by considering an actual situation — to which we now turn. (Appendix 2D contains alternative approaches to forecasting the various income statement and balance sheet accounts.)

Developing Pro Forma Financial Statements: An Illustration

To illustrate the types of forecasting and modeling decisions inherent in the preparation of pro forma financial statements, we begin with Exhibit 2.9, which contains the condensed historical income statements and balance sheets of Nokia Corporation for 1996 and 1997. The task at hand is the development of projected financial statements for 1998.

Nokia's annual report discloses that the company's five-year annual average growth rate for revenues has been approximately 24 percent, although the growth rate from 1996 to 1997 was 34 percent. Standard & Poor's forecast for growth in the global communications equipment industry was 13 percent, whereas BT Alex.Brown, Inc., forecasted net operating revenue growth for Nokia of 25 percent in 1998.[11] BT Alex.Brown's higher growth rate reflects the company's "global leadership, strong management, and financial flexibility." [12] For the purposes of our illustration, we begin by adopting BT Alex.Brown's operating revenue forecast for 1998 and apply it to the data in Exhibit 2.9 (see the

Exhibit 2.9 Nokia Corporation Historical and Projected Financial Statements Forecasting Revenues, Operating Expenses, and Asset Mix

	Historical				Projected*	
	1996	**%**	**1997**	**%**	**1998**	
Income statement						
Net sales	39,321	100.0	52,612	100.0	65,765	(Step 1)
Cost of goods sold	(27,360)	(69.6)	(33,194)	(63.1)	(41,493)	(Step 2)
Gross profit	11,961	30.4	19,418	36.9	24,273	
Research and development expenses	(2,446)	(6.2)	(3,539)	(6.7)	(4,424)	(Step 2)
Selling, general, and administrative expenses	(3,013)	(7.7)	(4,663)	(8.9)	(5,829)	(Step 2)
Operating profit	6,502	16.5	11,216	21.3	14,020	
Share of results of associated companies	37	0.1	54	0.1	68	(Step 2)
Net financial income	534	1.4	763	1.5	954	(Step 2)
Exchange gains	27	0.1	106	0.2	133	(Step 2)
Profit before interest, tax, depreciation, and minority interest	7,100	18.1	12,139	23.1	15,174	
Interest expense	(966)	(2.5)	(1,006)	(1.9)		
Depreciation/amortization expense	(2,236)	(5.7)	(2,762)	(5.3)		
Income tax expense	(856)	(2.2)	(2,274)	(4.3)		
Minority interest	2	—	(99)	(0.2)		
Profit from continuing operations	3,044	7.7	5,998	11.4		
Discontinued operations	219	0.6	261	0.5		
Net profit	3,263	8.3	6,259	11.9		
Balance sheet						
Intangible assets (net)	1,455	4.4	2,061	4.9	2,576	(Step 3)
Property, plant, and equipment (net)	5,662	17.0	6,240	15.0	7,800	(Step 3)
Investments	901	2.7	789	1.9	986	(Step 3)
Other noncurrent assets	391	1.2	355	0.9	444	(Step 3)
Total noncurrent assets	8,409		9,445		11,806	
Inventories	6,423	19.3	7,314	17.5	9,143	(Step 3)
Accounts receivable (net)	10,898	32.8	12,732	30.5	15,915	(Step 3)
Short-term investments	5,886	17.7	9,363	22.4	11,704	(Step 3)
Cash and cash equivalents	1,659	5.0	2,884	6.9	3,605	(Step 3)
Total current assets	24,866		32,293		40,366	
Total assets	33,275	100.0	41,738	100.0	52,173	(Step 3)

(continued)

Exhibit 2.9   Nokia Corporation Historical and Projected Financial Statements
              Forecasting Revenues, Operating Expenses, and Asset Mix (*continued*)

	Historical				Projected*
	1996	**%**	**1997**	**%**	**1998**
Share capital	1,498		1,499		
Other restricted equity	5,298		5,542		
Treasury shares	(657)		(654)		
Untaxed reserves	1,516		1,279		
Retained earnings	8,270		13,858		
Total shareholders' equity	15,925		21,524		
Minority interests	29		195		
Long-term debt	2,117		1,348		
Other long-term liabilities	297		295		
Total long-term liabilities	2,414		1,643		
Short-term borrowing	3,404		3,008		
Current portion of long-term debt	555		285		
Accounts payable and accrued expenses	10,610		14,541		
Advance payments	338		542		
Total current liabilities	14,907		18,376		
Total liabilities	17,321		20,019		
Total equities	33,275		41,738		

Values are in millions of Finnish markka.
*All values are rounded to the nearest whole number.

shaded area, which presents the forecasted outcomes from steps 1, 2, and 3 above). To forecast Nokia's operating expenses (i.e., step 2), we use the common-size income statement percentages from 1997. Although this assumption is likely to be incorrect in that it presumes that *all* of Nokia's operating expenses move in a constant proportion to changes in net revenues, it is valid for at least some of Nokia's operating expenses. For the purposes of step 3, we use the common-size percentages from the 1997 balance sheet after assuming that total assets will change in direct proportion to net revenues (i.e., a constant total asset turnover ratio); thus, total assets were first projected at a growth rate of 25 percent, and then the individual asset account balances were distributed on the basis of Nokia's 1997 common-size percentages.

For forecasting Nokia's long-term financing (step 4), the following assumptions were adopted:

- The company's 1998 dividend payments remain approximately the same amount (1,061 million FIM) as in 1997.

- The company issues no new shares; any new financing will be undertaken with lower costing debt.

- The balance of treasury shares remains unchanged.

- The company's 1998 non−interest-bearing debt remains the same percentage of total equities (i.e., 34.8 percent) as in 1997.

- The company maintains constant levels of advance payments, current portion of long-term debt, long-term debt, and other long-term liabilities.

For completion of Nokia's pro forma income statement (step 5), two final items need to be forecasted — interest expense and income taxes. The company's annual report reveals that income taxes average approximately 27 percent, and hence this figure is used to forecast 1998 income taxes (unless a higher or lower rate is anticipated). With respect to interest expense, an equation is needed to calculate this expense, as follows:

$$\text{Interest Expense} = I_{St}\left(\frac{\text{STD}_B + \text{STD}_E}{2}\right) + I_{Lt}\left(\frac{\text{LTD}_B + \text{LTD}_E}{2}\right)$$

where I_{St} is short-term average cost of debt, I_{Lt} is long-term average cost of debt, STD is short-term debt, and LTD is long-term debt (including current maturities).

This equation assumes that Nokia's interest expense is a function of the company's beginning and ending balances of debt, which are averaged in the above equation. Nokia's annual report indicates that the company's weighted average cost of debt was 7.2 and 6.5 percent for short-term and long-term debt, respectively, during 1997. Given forecasts of relatively stable interest rates for 1998, these same rates were adopted for the 1998 forecast. Plugging this data into the equation above for the 1998 interest expense yields

$$\text{Interest Expense} = 7.2\%\left(\frac{3{,}008 + \text{STD}_E}{2}\right) + 6.5\%\left(\frac{1{,}633 + 1{,}633}{2}\right)$$

and reveals that the year-end balance of short-term debt (STD_E) is still unknown.[13] Finding STD_E and the interest expense that satisfy the above equation with sufficient precision can be conveniently handled by the iterative calculation feature on a spreadsheet program. (See Appendix 2C for the EXCEL™ spreadsheet formulas associated with Exhibit 2.10.)

Exhibit 2.10 presents the final results of our pro forma analysis for 1998 for Nokia.[14] With an expected revenue growth of 25 percent, our

Exhibit 2.10 Nokia Corporation Historical and Projected Financial Statements Forecasting Net Income and Shareholders' Equity

	Historical		Projected*	
	1997	%	1998	
Income statement				
Net sales	52,612	100.0	65,765	(Step 1)
Cost of goods sold	(33,194)	(63.1)	(41,493)	(Step 2)
Gross profit	19,418	36.9	24,273	
Research and development expenses	(3,539)	(6.7)	(4,424)	(Step 2)
Selling, general, and administrative expenses	(4,663)	(8.9)	(5,829)	(Step 2)
Operating income	11,216	21.3	14,020	
Share of results of associated companies	54	0.1	68	(Step 2)
Net financial income	763	1.5	954	(Step 2)
Exchange gains	106	0.2	133	(Step 2)
Profit before interest, taxes, depreciation, and minority interest	12,139	23.1	15,174	
Interest expense	(1,006)	(1.9)	(286)	(Step 5)
Depreciation/amortization expense	(2,762)	(5.3)	(3,320)	(Step 5)
Income tax expense	(2,274)	(4.3)	(3,090)	(Step 5)
Minority interest	(99)	(0.2)	(124)	(Step 5)
Profit from continuing operations	5,998	11.4	8,354	(Step 5)
Discontinued operation	261	0.5	—	(Step 5)
Net profit	6,259	11.9	8,354	(Step 5)
Balance sheet				
Intangible assets (net)	2,061	4.9	2,576	(Step 3)
Property, plant, and equipment (net)	6,240	15.0	7,800	(Step 3)
Investments	789	1.9	986	(Step 3)
Other noncurrent assets	355	0.9	444	(Step 3)
Total noncurrent assets	9,445		11,806	
Inventories	7,314	17.5	9,143	(Step 3)
Accounts receivable (net)	12,732	30.5	15,915	(Step 3)
Short-term investments	9,363	22.4	11,704	(Step 3)
Cash and cash equivalents	2,884	6.9	3,605	(Step 3)
Total current assets	32,293		40,366	
Total assets	41,738	100.0	52,173	

(continued)

projected results reveal a 33 percent increase in Nokia's after-tax income, reflecting the presence of certain economies of scale at these higher volume levels. Nokia's ROE for 1998 is forecasted to increase slightly to 30.1 percent. The ratios indicate a continuing decline in Nokia's use of financial leverage, whereas the ROA is projected to be up slightly at

Exhibit 2.10 Nokia Corporation Historical and Projected Financial Statements Forecasting Net Income and Shareholders' Equity (*continued*)

	Historical		Projected*	
	1997	**%**	**1998**	
Share capital	1,499		1,499	(Step 4)
Other restricted equity	5,542		5,542	(Step 4)
Treasury shares	(654)		(654)	(Step 4)
Untaxed reserves	1,279		1,279	(Step 4)
Retained earnings	13,858		21,151	(Step 6)
Total shareholders' equity	21,524		28,817	(Step 6)
Minority interests	195		195	(Step 4)
Long-term debt	1,348		1,348	(Step 4)
Other long-term liabilities	295		295	(Step 4)
Total long-term liabilities	1,643		1,643	(Step 4)
Short-term borrowing	3,008		2,515	(Step 6)
Current portion of long-term debt	285		285	(Step 4)
Accounts payable and accrued expenses	14,541	34.8	18,176	(Step 4)
Advance payments	542		542	(Step 4)
Total current liabilities	18,376		21,518	(Step 6)
Total liabilities	20,019		23,161	(Step 6)
Total equities	41,738		52,173	(Step 4)

Values are in millions of Finnish markka.
Shaded areas are forecasted figures for the pro formas.
* All values are rounded to the nearest whole number.

16.1 percent because of a modest increase in the net profit margin to 11.5 percent. The total asset turnover remains constant as a consequence of our assumptions at step 3.

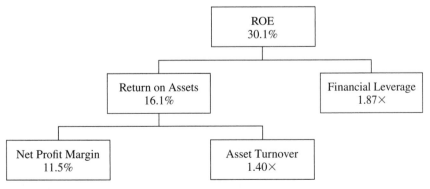

Having completed the preparation of Nokia's 1998 pro forma income statement and balance sheet, it is now possible for a pro forma SCF to

Exhibit 2.11   Nokia Corporation 1998 Pro Forma
               Statement of Cash Flows

Operating activities	
Net profit	8,354
Depreciation/amortization	3,320
Equity income	(68)
Accounts receivables	(3,183)
Inventories	(1,829)
Accounts payable and accrued expenses	3,635
Cash flow from operations	10,230
Investing activities	
Investments	(130)
Property, plant, and equipment (net)	(4,880)
Intangible assets (net)	(515)
Short-term investments	(2,341)
Other noncurrent assets	(89)
Cash flow from investing	(7,955)
Financing activities	
Short-term borrowing	(493)
Dividends	(1,061)
Cash flow from financing	(1,554)
Change in cash and cash equivalents	721

Values are in millions of Finnish markka.

be prepared. Some analysts prefer to actually project a company's SCF; we believe that it is preferable to develop the statement from existing pro forma income statement and balance sheet data. The latter approach eliminates the need for separately forecasting the effects of exchange rate movements and acquisitions/divestitures. Exhibit 2.11 presents Nokia's 1998 pro forma SCF and reveals that

- Pro forma 1998 CFFO should total approximately 10.230 billion FIM, providing discretionary cash flows of 4.289 billion FIM:

CFFO		10.230 billion
Less	Dividend payments	(1.061)
	Debt retirements	—
	Capital expenditures	(4.880)
Discretionary cash flow		4.289 billion

- Pro forma CFFI is expected to be a negative 7.955 billion FIM, and pro forma CFFF is projected to be a negative 1.554 billion

FIM, largely because of the assumption of continued dividend payments.

Although Exhibit 2.11 presents the CFFO and CFFI separately, some analysts combine the two cash flow categories for the purposes of preparing the pro forma SCF. Two arguments are usually cited for not distinguishing between operating and investing cash flows. First, the distinction between the CFFO and CFFI is not always informative. For example, the fixed asset investments needed for maintaining a company's existing productive capacity are arguably an operating cash flow. Second, there may not be sufficient information for a clear distinction to be made between the two values in the pro forma SCF. For example, in the development of pro forma data, we often do not estimate the depreciation or amortization expense. Consequently, these values are often unavailable for adjusting either the CFFO or the CFFI.[15] Hence, the analyst has two reasonable alternatives: (1) Combine the CFFO with the CFFI and not worry about projecting these noncash items, or (2) project the noncash items when individual values for the CFFO and CFFI are desired. The latter alternative was followed in the Nokia illustration.

As we will see in Chapter 3, separately forecasting the CFFO and CFFI makes the calculation of free cash flows a relatively straightforward exercise and hence is the option we prefer.

Sensitivity Analysis: Alternative Scenarios

Nokia's 1998 pro forma results presented in Exhibit 2.10 reflect a set of assumptions about a series of events that have yet to occur. Given that an analyst cannot know with certainty what the future will hold, it is often instructive for him or her to develop a series of alternative pro forma scenarios. For example, for the purposes of Exhibit 2.10, we used the BT Alex.Brown forecast of net operating revenues of 25 percent. If this estimate proves incorrect, our projected 1998 value for Nokia also will be incorrect. As a consequence, most valuation analysts try to build a range of *probable* values for an acquisition target based on a series of pro forma scenarios. For example, we might want to recalculate our pro forma analysis using a forecast of operating revenues that is somewhat lower and higher than 25 percent, perhaps 13 percent for a lower boundary (Standard & Poor's forecast) and 34 percent for a higher boundary (the growth achieved between 1996 and 1997). Rerunning the spreadsheet program enables the valuation analyst to assess the effect of these alternative rates of sales growth:

Rate of Growth in Sales	Pro Forma Sales	Pro Forma Net Income
13%	59,452	7,597
20%	63,134	8,038
25%	65,765	8,354
30%	68,396	8,669
34%	70,500	8,921

Thus, we can see that for each 1 percent change in the rate of sales growth, there is an approximate 526 million FIM change in sales and 63 million FIM change in net income.

It is also instructive to revisit some of the other key assumptions inherent in our original pro forma analysis to assess the sensitivity of the company's valuation to alternative assumptions. For example, our equation for the estimation of Nokia's interest expense for 1998 was premised on the assumption that short- and long-term interest rates from 1997 would persist through 1998. The valuation analyst might reestimate the company's pro forma results assuming an interest rate increase of, say, fifty basis points (i.e., one-half of 1 percent), and for a similar decrease. Rerunning the spreadsheet analysis reveals that there is an approximate 11 million FIM decline in net income for each fifty-basis-point increase in the short-term interest rate, and only a 6 million FIM decline in net income for a similar increase in the long-term rate.

Rerunning the pro forma analysis for multiple values of the various key assumptions can be time-consuming. As a consequence, some analysts prepare only three separate scenarios involving the key assumptions: a "most likely" scenario, an "optimistic" scenario, and a "pessimistic" scenario. This strategy is certainly less time intensive in that it requires only three iterations of the forecast model; however, it is not always costless, in that the dynamic interaction of the key assumptions cannot be rigorously explored. For this reason, analysts are increasingly turning to Monte Carlo simulation analysis to fully explore the effect of the key pro forma assumptions. Let's illustrate how we can simulate our forecast with @Risk, a widely used simulation package.

The key assumptions of our model are the sales growth and the short-term and long-term interest rates. In our sensitivity analysis, we chose 13 percent as a lower boundary and 34 percent as an upper boundary for the growth rate, and we assumed that interest rates could increase (or decrease) by fifty basis points. We might want to investigate how net sales and net profits change when the sales growth rate varies between 13 and 34 percent and, simultaneously, the short-term and long-term interest rates increase or decrease by fifty basis points.

Before simulating, the distributions of the sales growth rate and the short-term and long-term interest rates must be defined. For sales growth, we choose a triangular distribution, with a minimum of 13 percent, a most likely value of 25 percent, and a maximum of 34 percent. For the short-term interest rate, we use a uniform distribution, with a minimum of 6.7 percent and a maximum of 7.7 percent. Similarly, for the long-term interest rate, we choose a uniform distribution, with a minimum of 6 percent and a maximum of 7 percent.[16] The results of the Monte Carlo simulation reveal that

- Nokia's net sales varies between 59,570 and 70,441 million FIM, whereas net profits vary between 7,608 and 8,915 million FIM.

- The tornado graph[17] (not presented) indicates that the effect of the growth in sales on forecasted sales and profit is high, as the correlation is close to 1. On the other hand, the effect of short-term and long-term interest rates on forecasted sales and profit is low. It is positive for sales, whereas it is negative for profit (an increase in interest rates leads to a decrease in profit).

Although reviewing the sensitivity of assumptions inherent in a pro forma analysis can be tedious, it provides the valuation analyst with critical insight regarding the relative importance of each of his or her assumptions. The exercise also enables the analyst to build a range of pro forma values that will have the highest likelihood of occurring and, in so doing, will provide the highest probability of the analyst avoiding the winner's curse.

Summary

In this chapter we considered the related processes of financial review and pro forma analysis. Financial review refers to the process of analyzing, evaluating, and describing the financial history of a target and is an integral part of the due diligence investigation that should precede any acquisition. Financial review also provides essential inputs for the preparation of pro forma financial statements that are necessary for firm value to be assessed. Although much is made about selecting an appropriate valuation multiple or discount rate, *nothing* is more important in assessing firm value than a complete and accurate modeling of a target's operations.

In Chapter 3, we link the construction of pro forma financial statements to our ultimate goal of assessing firm value.

Notes

1. See Varaiya and Ferris (1989). The winner's curse has also been referred to as the "performance extrapolation hypothesis," which suggests that bidders overextrapolate past performance when assessing the value of a potential acquiree.

2. Discretionary cash flows (DCF) are defined as follows:

DCF = CFFO − Dividend Payments − Debt Retirement
          − Capital Expenditures to Replace Used-Up Capacity

In essence, a company's DCF is that amount remaining from the cash flow from operations (CFFO) after all required cash outflows are deducted. It represents the surplus cash flow that management has at its disposal to undertake some discretionary act — retire debt early, retire stock, acquire another company — without relying on incremental external funding. We differentiate between a firm's discretionary cash flows and its free cash flow, which will be defined in Chapter 3.

3. Preferred stock dividend distributions are not tax deductible in most countries. In those countries (e.g. Germany) in which preferred stock dividends (PD) are tax deductible, a tax adjustment of 1 minus the effective tax rate (tx) must be incorporated into the calculation of ROE as follows:

$$ROE = \frac{\text{Net Income After Taxes} - PD\,(1 - tx)}{\text{Average Common Shareholders' Equity}}$$

4. For convenience, we assume from this point forward that our sample firm has only common stock outstanding, and hence preferred stock dividends are ignored.

5. Some analysts question the internal consistency of ROA as a measure of profitability. Their concern stems from the fact that the traditional accounting income statement deducts an opportunity cost for debt capital (i.e., "interest expense") but makes no similar deduction for the opportunity cost of equity capital. These analysts believe that a more consistent measure of firm profitability is given by unlevered ROA, or UROA:

$$UROA = \frac{\text{Net Income After Taxes} + \text{Interest Expense}\,(1 - tx)}{\text{Average Total Assets}}$$

where tx is effective tax rate.

UROA is a measure of firm profitability before interest charges. The adjustment for taxes is designed to recognize the tax benefit resulting from the interest expense deduction. Another refinement some analysts use is to replace average total assets with the sum of shareholders' equity and interest-bearing debt — that is, to eliminate those assets obtained through non–interest-bearing debt. This refinement creates a measure called return on net assets (RONA):

$$\text{RONA} = \frac{\text{Net Income After Taxes} + \text{Interest Expense} \, (1 - tx)}{\text{Shareholders' Equity} + \text{Debt}}$$

6. It is not true, however, that a high rate of payable turnover is always preferred to a lower rate.

7. A close variant of the quick ratio is the current ratio, measured as current assets divided by current liabilities. The quick ratio is generally preferred to the current ratio because the current ratio includes all current assets, some of which (e.g., inventory and prepaid expenses) are not always liquid.

8. For most acquirers, the preparation of pro forma financial statements is executed in two phases: Phase one involves the preparation of a "base case" forecast of a target, ignoring any cost reductions, synergies, or revenue enhancements that are likely to result as a consequence of the merger. This benchmark forecast is usually a simple extrapolation of recent operating results, on an "as is" basis. Phase two involves the preparation of pro formas for any value-enhancing consequences related to cost reductions, synergies, and/or revenue enhancements that the acquirer hopes to realize after the successful acquisition and integration of the target. Total firm value is then the aggregate of the two separate forecasts.

9. HOLT Value Associates, Inc., a valuation consulting company, prepares forecasts of up to forty years for potential acquisitions. The company has achieved considerable success using a mean-reversion model for its forecast periods beyond ten years.

10. Forecasting the balance sheet is usually more challenging than the income statement because it rarely balances. For instance, forecasted total assets exceeding the sum of forecasted total liabilities and shareholders' equity indicates a need for additional financing for covering a forecasted growth in assets. The easiest way for coping with this imbalance is to create a "line-of-credit" account — in essence, a plug figure. If the line-of-credit account requires a positive (credit) balance for balancing the balance sheet, it implies that the company needed additional financing; on the other hand, if the line-of-credit account requires a negative (debit) balance, the company will presumably produce excess liquid funds that can be used to pay off other interest-bearing debt. In either case, it will be necessary for the analyst to include the line-of-credit account in calculating interest charges in step 5 of the pro forma development process to ensure a correct forecast of interest charges.

11. Standard & Poor's, Industry Surveys: Communications Equipment, 16 October 1997.

12. BT Alex.Brown, "The Information Age Goes Wireless," 18 September 1997.

13. Nokia's long-term debt of 1,633 is the sum of the company's "current position of long-term debt" (285) and "long-term debt" (1,348).

14. As a reality check for our pro forma financial statements, Nokia reported the following actual results for 1998:

Net sales	79,231
Net profits	10,408
Total assets	59,660
CFFO	10,029

Thus, with the exception of the CFFO, our 1998 forecast was quite conservative.

15. Projecting the depreciation and amortization expense can be easily undertaken although several additional assumptions are required. For example, it is necessary to assume an average remaining life for the asset category, a method of depreciation and amortization (usually straight-line), salvage value (usually zero), and the acquisition date for any additions to the asset category (usually a half-year convention).

16. As we do not know what the distributions for sales growth and short-term and long-term interest rates are, we prefer to use a distribution that does not require strong assumptions, such as the normal distribution. The triangular distribution seems appropriate for sales growth as it assumes that the possible values range between a minimum (13 percent) and a maximum (34 percent), with a high probability for the most likely value (25 percent) to be observed. The uniform distribution seems more appropriate for the short-term and long-term interest rates, as they are allowed to vary between a minimum and a maximum, with equal probability.

17. A tornado graph allows one to study the effect of each input on the output.

Appendix 2A
Nokia Corporation
Financial Data

Consolidated Profit and Loss Account*

	1993	1994	1995	1996	1997
Net sales	23,697	30,177	36,810	39,321	52,612
Cost of goods sold	(16,662)	(20,234)	(24,703)	(27,360)	(33,194)
Gross profit	7,035	9,943	12,107	11,961	19,418
Research and development expense	(1,332)	(1,766)	(1,834)	(2,446)	(3,539)
Selling, general, and administrative expense	(3,242)	(3,572)	(3,436)	(3,013)	(4,663)
Operating profit before interest, tax, and depreciation	2,461	4,605	6,837	6,502	11,216
Share of results of associated companies	28	22	85	37	54
Net financial income	637	514	591	534	763
Exchange gains and losses	(134)	450	(10)	27	106
Profit before interest, tax, depreciation, and minority interests	2,992	5,591	7,503	7,100	12,139
Interest expense	(850)	(580)	(745)	(966)	(1,006)
Depreciation/amortization expense	(996)	(1,009)	(1,825)	(2,236)	(2,762)
Income tax expense	(299)	(932)	(769)	(856)	(2,274)
Minority interests	(80)	(75)	(77)	2	(99)
Profit from continuing operations	767	2,995	4,087	3,044	5,998
Discontinued operations	—	—	(2,340)	219	261
Net profit	767	2,995	1,747	3,263	6,259
Preferred stock dividends	(78)	(388)	(571)	(699)	(774)

Shares (as of 31 December 1997):
Common	Number	78,687,000		
		Price per share	390 FIM	
Preferred	Number	221,165,000		
		Price per share	387 FIM	
Earnings per share	21.17 FIM			
Dividend per share	7.50 FIM			

*Data were prepared using international accounting standards (IAS) and have been reformatted. Values are for year ended 31 December, in millions of Finnish markka.

Consolidated Balance Sheet*

	1993	1994	1995	1996	1997
Assets					
Intangible assets (net)	590	541	1,581	1,455	2,061
Property, plant, and equipment (net)	4,770	5,097	6,109	5,662	6,240
Investments	2,258	1,976	837	901	789
Other noncurrent assets	376	329	520	391	355
Total noncurrent assets	7,994	7,943	9,047	8,409	9,445
Inventories	5,129	6,803	9,982	6,423	7,314
Accounts receivable (net)	6,227	7,835	9,518	10,898	12,732
Short-term investments	2,201	3,989	2,888	5,886	9,363
Cash and cash equivalents	1,096	1,279	1,326	1,659	2,884
Total current assets	14,653	19,906	23,714	24,866	32,293
Total assets	22,647	27,849	32,761	33,275	41,738
Shareholders' equity					
Share capital†	1,378	1,498	1,498	1,498	1,499
Other restricted equity	3,329	5,494	5,455	5,298	5,542
Treasury shares	(348)	(437)	(470)	(657)	(654)
Untaxed reserves	1,717	1,727	1,873	1,516	1,279
Retained earnings	435	4,136	5,450	8,270	13,858
Total shareholders' equity	6,511	12,418	13,806	15,925	21,524
Minority interests	536	555	422	29	195
Liabilities					
Long-term debt	3,397	3,071	2,121	2,117	1,348
Other long-term liabilities	683	486	457	297	295
Total long-term liabilities	4,080	3,557	2,578	2,414	1,643
Short-term borrowing	3,435	2,453	4,332	3,404	3,008
Current portion of long-term debt	139	278	187	555	285
Accounts payable and accrued expenses	5,976	8,086	9,388	10,610	14,541
Advance payments	534	502	396	338	542
Provision for discontinued operations	1,436	—	1,652	—	—
Total current liabilities	11,520	11,319	15,955	14,907	18,376
Total liabilities	15,600	14,876	18,533	17,321	20,019
Total equities	22,647	27,849	32,761	33,275	41,738
†Includes preferred share capital	556	777	951	999	1,106

*Prepared using international accounting standards (IAS). Values are for year ended 31 December, in millions of Finnish markka.

Appendix 2B
Preparation of
Statement of
Cash Flows

The demand for cash flow data has become so prevalent that most countries now require a statement of cash flows (SCF). Some countries, however, require the presentation of an SCF only for publicly traded companies (i.e., Argentina, Denmark, and Japan) or for large companies (Finland, Hong Kong, Ireland, Norway, Singapore, Sweden, and the U.K.), and the list of countries *not* requiring an SCF (i.e., Belgium, France, Germany, India, Italy, Luxembourg, The Netherlands, and Switzerland) is dwindling. Nonetheless, the valuation analyst must be prepared to develop an SCF from available financial data either when an SCF is not presented or when a statement of fund flows (SFF) is presented instead. In this appendix, a methodology for coping with these situations is presented.

Cash Flow Fundamentals

To prepare an SCF, the analyst needs the following data: (1) an income statement for the current period, and (2) the balance sheets as of the beginning and the end of the accounting period. With only these three financial statements, the analyst can prepare an approximate SCF using the four-step process outlined below. A more complete SCF is possible where detailed data are given in the footnotes to the financial statements.

To begin, recall that the fundamental accounting equation for the balance sheet is given as

$$Assets = Liabilities + Owners' Equity, or$$

$$A = L + OE$$

Substituting the major components of a company's assets, liabilities, and shareholders' equity into this equation yields the following:

$$CA + NCA = CL + NCL + CS + RE$$

53

where CA is current assets, NCA is noncurrent assets, CL is current liabilities, NCL is noncurrent liabilities, CS is capital stock, and RE is retained earnings.

Decomposing the current asset category into cash (C) and all other current assets (OCA) yields yet another version of the fundamental accounting equation:

$$C + OCA + NCA = CL + NCL + CS + RE \qquad \textbf{(2B.1)}$$

At this juncture, it is helpful to recognize that an SCF is nothing more than a formal explanation of the positive and negative changes to a company's cash account. The SCF merely lists where a company's cash inflows came from and how the various cash amounts were used. Having access to a company's internal accounting records would make the preparation of an SCF a simple exercise; it would involve merely listing the various inflows and outflows to the company's cash account. Such access is rarely available, however, and thus a methodology is needed so that the analyst can estimate this data from available financial information.

Because an SCF is merely a listing of the various changes in a company's cash account, it can be expressed in its simplest form by the following equation:

$$\text{Cash}_E - \text{Cash}_B = \Delta\text{Cash} \qquad \textbf{(2B.2)}$$

where B is the beginning of the accounting period, E is the end of the accounting period, and Δ is change.

Using a few basic algebraic concepts, it is possible to redefine Equation 2B.2 in terms of Equation 2B.1. Putting the subscripts B and E on the elements of Equation 2B.1 yields

$$C_B + OCA_B + NCA_B = CL_B + NCL_B + CS_B + RE_B$$

and

$$C_E + OCA_E + NCA_E = CL_E + NCL_E + CS_E + RE_E$$

Isolating C_B and C_E on the left-hand side of these two equations yields

$$C_E = CL_E + NCL_E + CS_E + RE_E - (OCA_E + NCA_E)$$

and

$$C_B = CL_B + NCL_B + CS_B + RE_B - (OCA_B + NCA_B)$$

Subtracting the second from the first equation above yields

$$C_E - C_B = (CL_E - CL_B) + (NCL_E - NCL_B) + (CS_E - CS_B) + (RE_E - RE_B)$$
$$- (OCA_E - OCA_B) - (NCA_E - NCA_B) \qquad \textbf{(2B.3)}$$

Equation 2B.3 is a more explicit, formalized version of Equation 2B.2, and thus both are representations of the SCF. More importantly, Equation 2B.3 provides a very simple approach to the preparation of an SCF: In words, it tells us that an SCF can be prepared by merely listing the changes in all of the balance sheet accounts.

From this observation, we can now formulate a four-step procedure for creation of a basic but instructive SCF:

1. Identify the change in the cash and cash equivalents account.* This figure represents the "bottom line" of the SCF: All increases and decreases in cash *must* net to this figure. It is a check figure for verifying the accuracy of the cash flow analysis.

2. Calculate the change in all balance sheet accounts by subtracting the beginning balance *from* the ending balance.

3. Identify each balance sheet account with the activity most closely related to it: operations (O), investing (I), or financing (F). As a general rule, the following associations are usually made, although exceptions will exist:

    Operations: RE, OCA, CL

    Investing: NCA

    Financing: NCL, CS

4. Place each of the individual balance sheet accounts (except cash) under one of three activity categories and identify whether the change in the account balance involved a cash inflow or outflow. (Recall that the total sources and uses of cash must aggregate to the check figure identified in step 1.)

An Illustration

To illustrate the four-step process for building an SCF, we consider the financial statements of Worldwide Enterprises, Inc. (WWE), presented in Exhibits 2B.1 and 2B.2. Exhibit 2B.1 presents WWE's comparative balance sheets for 1999 and 2000, and Exhibit 2B.2 presents WWE's income statement for 2000.

1. The check figure for WWE's SCF is a decrease of 45.6 million (i.e., 34.5 − 80.1). Thus, WWE's cash outflows must have exceeded its inflows by 45.6 million.

2. Calculate the change in all balance sheet accounts by subtracting the beginning (1999) balance from the ending (2000) balance; these values are presented in Exhibit 2B.1 under the column headed by the Δ.

3. Identify the activity category associated with each individual balance sheet account (this is done in the far right column of Exhibit 2B.1). It is important to note that judgment calls are necessary at this step. For example, even though most current liabilities, such as accounts payable

---

*Cash equivalents are short-term (i.e., three months or less), risk-free (i.e., local government–issued) securities.

Exhibit 2B.1　Worldwide Enterprises, Inc., Comparative
Balance Sheets (in millions)

| | As of 31 December | | | Activity |
	2000	1999	Δ	Category*
Assets				
Cash and cash equivalents	34.5	80.1	(45.6)	
Marketable securities	100.8	0.9	99.9	I
Receivables	299.7	240.3	59.4	O
Inventories	286.2	765.9	(479.7)	O
Total current assets	721.2	1,087.2		
Investments	1,549.5	1,872.3	(322.8)	I
Property and equipment (net)	582.6	571.2	11.4	I
Goodwill (net)	17.7	18.0	(0.3)	I
Other assets	204.3	501.9	(297.6)	I
Total assets	3,075.3	4,050.6		
Liabilities and shareholders' equity				
Notes payable and current long-term debt	162.6	435.3	(272.7)	F
Other current liabilities	457.5	828.3	(370.8)	O
Total current liabilities	620.1	1,263.6		
Long-term debt	1,090.2	1,752.6	(662.4)	F
Deferred income taxes	148.8	107.1	41.7	O
Other debt	24.6	27.3	(2.7)	F
Total noncurrent liabilities	1,263.6	1,887.0		
Shareholders' capital	883.8	862.2	21.6	F
Retained earnings	307.8	37.8	270.0	O
Total shareholders' equity	1,191.6	900.0		
Total equities	3,075.3	4,050.6		

*O is operations; I, investing; and F, financing.

Exhibit 2B.2　Worldwide Enterprises, Inc.,
2000 Income Statement (in millions)

Net revenues	1,737.9
Less operating expenses*	(1,341.9)
Income from continuing operations	396.0
Equity in loss of unconsolidated subsidiary	(75.0)
Net income	321.0
Less dividends paid	(51.0)
Transferred to retained earnings	270.0

*Includes depreciation expense of 30.

Exhibit 2B.3   Worldwide Enterprises, Inc., Preliminary Statement of Cash Flows (in millions)*

Operating activities	
Retained earnings	270.0
Receivables	(59.4)
Inventories	479.7
Other current liabilities	(370.8)
Deferred income taxes	41.7
Cash flow from operations	361.2
Investing activities	
Marketable securities	(99.9)
Investments	322.8
Property and equipment (net)	(11.4)
Goodwill	0.3
Other assets	297.6
Cash flow from investing	509.4
Financing activities	
Notes payable and current long-term debt	(272.7)
Long-term debt	(662.4)
Other debt	(2.7)
Contributed capital	21.6
Cash flow for financing	(916.2)
Change in cash and cash equivalents	(45.6)

*Figures in parentheses denote a cash outflow.

and accrued liabilities payable, are typically associated with a company's operations, some current liabilities (e.g., the current portion of long-term debt) are more correctly considered to be related to financing. Similarly, marketable securities, a current asset, may be considered related to operations in some company settings but related to investing in others. Without specific knowledge of the transactions that gave rise to a particular account, it is difficult to be certain of an account's proper classification. A misclassification of an account will not lead to an unbalanced SCF but merely a misspecification of the relative totals of the three activity categories.

4. Exhibit 2B.3 contains the preliminary SCF, derived from changes in the balance sheet accounts organized under the three activity categories. Remember that an increase (decrease) of an asset is a use (source) of cash, whereas an increase (decrease) of a liability is a source (use) of cash. Note that the total of the three activity categories equals the change in the cash account (i.e., a decrease of 45.6 million), and this ensures that the analysis was performed correctly.

We can conclude from the preliminary SCF in Exhibit 2B.3 that WWE generated cash flows from operations (CFFO) of 361.2 million and cash flows from investing (CFFI) of 509.4 million, while spending 916.2 million on financing activities (principally the retirement of debt). For many financial analyses, the preliminary SCF will be sufficient; however, in other circumstances, a more exacting estimate of a company's SCF is desirable and can be prepared using other available information. In the preparation of Exhibit 2B.3, only WWE's balance sheet data were used, and this SCF can be refined by incorporating the income statement data from Exhibit 2B.2. For example, Exhibit 2B.2 reveals that WWE's 2000 net income was 321.0 million and dividends paid amounted to 51.0 million. Note that these two amounts net to the change in the retained earnings account on the balance sheet (i.e., 321.0 − 51.0 = 270.0). Thus, by substituting these two new figures for the retained earnings figure in our initial SCF in Exhibit 2B.3, we are able to produce a refined measure of the company's cash flows. The restated figures are as follows:

	Original	Adjustment	Revised
Operations	361.2	−270.0 in retained earnings	
		+321.0 2000 net income	412.2
Investing	509.4		509.4
Financing	(916.2)	−51.0 2000 dividend payments	(967.2)
Change in cash	(45.6)	0	(45.6)

Observe that the inclusion of the additional income statement data did not change the check figure — a decrease in cash of 45.6 — but did result in a restatement of the CFFO and the cash flows from financing (CFFF). Our restated figures suggest that the CFFO was actually 412.2 million, as opposed to 361.2 million, and the CFFF was a negative 967.2 million instead of a negative 916.2 million. This refinement did not change the CFFI.

Another common refinement that the analyst should undertake involves depreciation and amortization. It is well known that depreciation is an accrual accounting concept in which the original cost for acquiring a depreciable asset is allocated over the many periods that one is expected to benefit from the asset. Thus, depreciation expense is the portion of an asset's cost allocated to a given accounting period; it represents neither a current cash inflow nor a current cash outflow but merely an allocation of a cash expenditure made in a prior period.

Since depreciation is one of the largest expense items deducted in arriving at periodic net income, it is usually necessary for the analyst to adjust net income for this item in order to avoid understating the actual cash flow from operations. Exhibits 2B.1 and 2B.2 reveal the change in property and equipment, net of accumulated depreciation, and current depreciation expense, respectively. Using T-accounts to help visualize the events that led to these ending balances, we can assess the cash flow effects of these accounts as follows:

	Property and Equipment (net)		2000 Depreciation Expense
12/31/99 Balance	571.2		
			30.0
2000 Purchases	41.4		
		30.0	
12/31/00 Balance	582.6		

Without reference to the current depreciation charge of 30.0 million, our initial conclusion from Exhibit 2B.3 was that 11.4 million was spent for new property and equipment (i.e., an outflow of cash). By including the depreciation expense, we see that the actual cash expended for new capital equipment was 41.4 million, and with these two figures we are able to further refine our preliminary SCF from Exhibit 2B.3:

		Adjustment	Revised
Operations	412.2	+30.0 2000 depreciation expense	442.2
Investing	509.4	−30.0 additional 2000 purchases	479.4
Financing	(967.2)		(967.2)
Change in cash	(45.6)	0	(45.6)

The inclusion of the depreciation expense does *not* change the bottom-line check figure of 45.6 but does result in a modification of the CFFO and the CFFI. Our restated figures suggest that the CFFO was 442.2 and the CFFI was 479.4. This refinement did not affect the CFFF.

A final modification to our preliminary SCF is possible by incorporating the fact that WWE's 2000 net income of 321.0 million includes 75.0 million representing WWE's "equity in loss of unconsolidated subsidiary." To obtain an accurate estimate of only WWE's CFFO, analysts frequently remove those income or loss items relating to affiliated or associated companies. In this instance, the 75.0 million reduction in WWE's net income should be removed and transferred to the investing activities section as an adjustment to the "investments account." This modification produces the following restated amounts:

		Adjustment	Revised
Operations	442.2	+75.0 equity in subsidiary loss	517.2
Investing	479.4	−75.0 adjustment to "investments"	404.4
Financing	(967.2)		(967.2)
Change in cash	(45.6)	0	(45.6)

Exhibit 2B.4   Worldwide Enterprises, Inc., Statement
of Cash Flows (in millions)

Operating activities	
Net income	426.0[1]
Receivables	(59.4)
Inventories	479.7
Other current liabilities	(370.8)
Deferred income taxes	41.7
Cash flow from operations	517.2
Investing activities	
Marketable securities	(99.9)
Investments	247.8[2]
Property and equipment (net)	(41.4)[3]
Goodwill	0.3
Other assets	297.6
Cash flow from investing	404.4
Financing activities	
Notes payable and current long-term debt	(272.7)
Long-term debt	(662.4)
Other debt	(2.7)
Contributed capital	21.6
Dividends	(51.0)
Cash flow for financing	(967.2)
Change in cash and cash equivalents	(45.6)

[1] Net income = 321.0 + 30.0 + 75.0 = 426.0
[2] Investments = 322.8 − 75.0 = 247.8
[3] Property and equipment (net) = (11.4) − (30.0) = (41.4)

Incorporating these three modifications into Exhibit 2B.3 provides the final version of WWE's SCF, which is presented in Exhibit 2B.4.

The above three examples involving retained earnings (net income and dividends), property and equipment (depreciation and purchases), and equity in the earnings of a subsidiary readily illustrate the benefit of extending the preliminary SCF when additional data are available. The inclusion of income statement and footnote data enables the analyst to build a relatively accurate estimate of a company's SCF.

Direct versus Indirect Methods.   Although no additional information is available for further refinement of WWE's SCF, a final consideration involves the presentation *format* of the operations section of the SCF. Two alternative approaches exist for presenting the CFFO: the **direct method** and the **indirect method**.

Although these two approaches to formatting the operations section of the SCF originated in the United States, they have gained widespread acceptance in those countries that require the presentation of an SCF as a basic financial statement. Most companies that present an SCF usually prefer the indirect method, which is the format adopted in Exhibit 2B.4; however, most professional analysts prefer to use the direct method because of the additional insights that this format provides regarding a company's operations.

To illustrate how a direct-method version of the CFFO would be constructed, we begin with the major elements of WWE's income statement (see Exhibit 2B.2) and then adjust these elements for the various balance sheet accounts that relate to them. Thus, for example, operating revenues would be adjusted for the change in receivables, and operating expenses for the change in inventory, deferred income taxes, other current liabilities, and, of course, depreciation expense:

	Accrual Income Statement	Adjustment	Direct Method
Net revenues	1,737.9		
	(59.4)	Increase in receivables	
Cash flow from operating revenues			1,678.5
Operating expenses	1,341.9		
	(479.7)	Decrease in inventory	
	370.8	Decrease in other current liabilities	
	(41.7)	Increase in deferred income taxes	
	(30.0)	Depreciation expense	
Cash flow for operating expenses			(1,161.3)
Cash flow from operations			517.2

Note that under either the direct or the indirect method, WWE's CFFO remains the same (i.e., 517.2 million); however, under the direct method, the rearrangement of data allows us to identify two additional cash flow items: cash flow from operating revenues (1,678.5) and cash flow for operating expenses (−1,161.3). These two figures can be quite revealing about a company's internal operations. For example, the relationship of cash operating revenues to accrual operating revenues (i.e., 1,678.5/1,737.9) reveals the rate at which cash is produced for each dollar of sales — in this case, about 96.6 percent. Analysts often use this ratio to assess the quality of a company's revenue recognition policy. In general, the higher the relationship between cash and accrual revenues, the higher the quality of a company's revenue recognition policy. In this case, the relationship is quite strong — it approaches 100 percent — and thus we would conclude that WWE's revenue recognition policies were appropriate and could be relied upon in forecasts of future revenues. When the relation is low (i.e., approaching 70 percent or less), it often indicates that the company is using an aggressive revenue recognition policy and consequently may be recording accrual sales in advance of the receipt of cash on those sales. When this occurs, it is referred to as **front-end loading** and may indicate that current revenues are an inappropriate basis for forecasting future revenues.

The relationship between cash operating expenses and accrual operating expenses can similarly be used for evaluation of a company's expense recognition policy. For most companies, the relation of its cash to accrual operating expenses (i.e., 1,161.3/1,341.9) will be less than 1, in large measure because of the adjustment for such noncash expenses as depreciation, amortization, and the change in deferred income taxes; however, where this relation is substantially greater than 1, it may be indicative of **rear-end loading**. Rear-end loading occurs when a company incurs significant cash expenditures that are accounted for as assets rather than expenses. In some instances, the capitalization of such expenditures to the balance sheet is justified, whereas in others it may not be. In any case, when the relation of cash operating expenses to accrual operating expenses is large, most professional analysts see a "red flag" requiring further investigation.

The topics of front-end loading and rear-end loading are important due diligence considerations as the valuation analyst reviews the accounting policies an acquisition target uses. We will return to these issues again in Chapter 5.

Converting the SFF

In a number of countries, accepted accounting practice calls for the presentation of a statement of fund flows (SFF) instead of an SCF. This is *not* problematic for the valuation analyst because the SFF frequently contains all of the necessary information for preparation of an SCF. Whereas the SCF presents and reconciles the various changes to a company's cash account, the SFF presents and reconciles the various changes to a company's net working capital (i.e., current assets minus current liabilities) or some similar measure of "funds." The SFF is, thus, just a more broadly defined financial statement; the SCF is more narrowly defined, considering only cash flows. Since the SFF considers a broader definition of "funds flow," a company's cash flows are captured within this broader definition, and the analyst's task is to "tease" the cash flow information from the SFF.

To illustrate the conversion of an SFF to an SCF, we consider the data presented in Exhibit 2B.5. Part A of this exhibit presents the consolidated statement of sources and applications of funds for Pirelli S.p.A., an Italian manufacturer of vehicle tires; Part B presents the same information reorganized into an indirect-method SCF. As always, the preparation of Pirelli's SCF requires that certain assumptions be made (e.g., the "changes in other provisions" relates to operating activities), and the transformation from an SFF to an SCF requires a reinterpretation of the sign of certain account balances (e.g., the decrease in in-

Exhibit 2B.5   Pirelli S.p.A.

A. Consolidated Statement of Sources and Applications of Funds (in millions of lire)	1993	1992
Sources		
Net loss for the year	(95,839)	(154,008)
Depreciation and amortization	557,099	531,080
Changes in provisions relating to personnel	36,832	(57,190)
Disposal of investments	424,171	292,854
Net book value of fixed assets disposed of	203,728	231,685
Changes in other provisions	(115,840)	(19,570)
Total sources	1,010,151	824,851
Applications		
Increase in property, plant, and equipment	358,964	293,847
Increase in intangible assets	15,602	35,576
Increase in financial assets	—	4,978
Increase (decrease) in inventories	(86,810)	(172,837)
Increase (decrease) in trade and other accounts receivable/payable	142,914	277,240
Other applications (including exchange differences in the year)	38,779	111,437
Total applications	469,449	550,241
	540,702	274,610
Financed by		
Share capital increase	117,369	518,621
Increase (decrease) in short-term financial payables	(366,343)	(366,488)
Increase (decrease) in long-term financial payables	(602,477)	(789,779)
Decrease (increase) in cash and cash equivalents	310,749	363,036
	(540,702)	(274,610)

(continued)

ventories is reported as a negative balance in Part A but a positive balance in Part B). The preparation of Pirelli's SCF requires only a reorganization of existing figures.

Pirelli's SCF in Part B shows several new facts that were disguised by the SFF presentation in Part A:

- Despite net losses in both 1992 and 1993, Pirelli generated a positive CFFO in both years.

- The debt reduction (short- and long-term) observable in both Parts A and B was financed by a combination of cash flow from new share issuances and from operations.

- The proceeds from Pirelli's disposal of investments and fixed assets was largely used to fund new capital investment.

Exhibit 2B.5   Pirelli S.p.A. (*continued*)

B. Statement of Cash Flows (in millions of lire)	1993	1992
Cash flows from operating activities		
Net loss for the year	(95,839)	(154,008)
Depreciation and amortization	557,099	531,080
Increase (decrease) in inventories	86,810	172,837
Increase (decrease) in trade and other accounts receivable/payable	(142,914)	(277,240)
Changes in provisions relating to personnel	36,832	(57,190)
Changes in other provisions	(115,840)	(19,570)
Cash flow from operations	326,148	195,909
Cash flows from investing activities		
Disposal of investments	424,171	292,854
Net book value of fixed assets disposed of	203,728	231,685
Increase in property, plant, and equipment	(358,964)	(293,847)
Increase in intangible assets	(15,602)	(35,576)
Increase in financial assets	0	(4,978)
Other applications (including exchange differences)	(38,779)	(111,437)
Cash flow from investing	214,554	78,701
Cash flow from financing		
Share capital increase	117,369	518,621
Increase (decrease) in short-term financial payables	(366,343)	(366,488)
Increase (decrease) in long-term financial payables	(602,477)	(789,779)
Cash flow from financing	(851,451)	(637,646)
Decrease (increase) in cash and cash equivalents	(310,749)	(363,036)

- The positive CFFO in 1992 and 1993 resulted largely from the add-back of depreciation and a net decrease in trade and other receivables, and not from the company's basic operations. (Pirelli reported a net loss from operations in both years.)

Summary

The purpose of this appendix has been to present a simple four-step process to help analysts prepare an SCF. A thorough financial analysis would be incomplete without a review of a company's cash flows. Valuation analysts must have the skill to prepare a pro forma SCF from pro forma balance sheet and income statement data as the pro forma cash flow data will be central to any target firm valuation, as we will see in Chapter 3.

Appendix 2C
Displayed Formulas
for EXCEL™
Spreadsheet

	A	B	C	D
1	Short-term debt interest rate	0.072		0.072
2	Long-term debt interest rate	0.065		0.065
3	Tax rate	.27		.27
4	Sales growth	.25		.25
5				
6	**Income statement**	**1997**	**Common-size**	**Projected 1998**
7	Net sales	52,612	= B7/B7	= B7 · (1 + B4)
8	Cost of goods sold	33,194	= B8/B7	= C8 · D7
9	Gross profit	19,418	= B9/B7	= D7 − D8
10	R&D expense	3,539	= B10/B7	= C10 · D7
11	S, G, & A expenses	4,663	= B11/B7	= C11 · D7
12	Operating profit	11,216	= B12/B7	= D9 − D10 − D11
13	Share of results	54	= B13/B7	= C13 · D7
14	Net financial income	763	= B14/B7	= C14 · D7
15	Exchange gains	106	= B15/B7	= C15 · D7
16	EBITDA	12,139	= B16/B7	= D12 + D13 + D14 + D15
17	Interest	1,006	= B17/B7	= B1 · (B50 + D50)/2 + B2 · (B47 + D47)/2
18	Depreciation/amortization	2,762	= B18/B7	= 0.32 · (D28 + D29)
19	Income tax	2,274	= B19/B7	= B3 · (D16 − D17 − D18 − D20)
20	Minority interest	99	= B20/B7	= C20 · D7
21	Profit	5,998	= B21/B7	= D16 − D17 − D18 − D19 − D20
22	Discontinued operations	261	= B22/B7	= 0
23	Net profit	6,259	= B23/B7	= D21
24	Dividends	1,061		= B24
25	Transfer to retained earnings	5,198		= D23 − D24
26				

	A	B	C	D
27	**Balance Sheet**			
28	Intangible assets	2,061	= B28/B38	= C28 · D38
29	PP&E (net)	6,240	= B29/B38	= C29 · D38
30	Investments	789	= B30/B38	= C30 · D38
31	Other noncurrent	355	= B31/B38	= C31 · D38
32	Total noncurrent	9,445	= B32/B38	= SUM(D28:D31)
33	Inventories	7,314	= B33/B38	= C33 · D38
34	Accounts receivable	12,732	= B34/B38	= C34 · D38
35	Short-term investments	9,363	= B35/B38	= C35 · D38
36	Cash and equivalent	2,884	= B36/B38	= C36 · D38
37	Total current	32,293	= B37/B38	= SUM(D33:D36)
38	Total assets	41,738	= B38/B38	= B38 · D7/B7
39				
40	Share capital	1,499		= B40
41	Other capital	5,542		= B41
42	Treasury stock	654		= B42
43	Untaxed reserves	1,279		= B43
44	Retained earnings	13,858		= B44 + D25
45	Total owners' equity	21,524		= D40 + D41 − D42 + D43 + D44
46	Minority interest	195		= B46
47	Long-term debt	1,348		= B47
48	Other long-term debt	295		= B48
49	Total long-term debt	1,643		= D47 + D48
50	Short-term borrowings	3,008		= D56 − D45 − D46 − D49 − D51 − D52 − D53
51	Current maturities	285		= B51
52	Accounts payable	14,541	= B52/B56	= C52 · D38
53	Advance payment	542		= B53
54	Total current	18,376		= SUM(D50:D53)
55	Total debt	20,019		= D49 + D54
56	Total equities	41,738		= D38

R&D is research and development; S, G, & A, selling, general, and adminstrative; EBITDA, earnings before interest, taxes, depreciation, and amortization; and PP&E, property, plant, and equipment.

Appendix 2D
Account Forecasting Alternatives

Account	Basis for Forecast
• Sales revenue	• Historical trend; third-party forecast; historical trend adjusted for industry outlook and/or inflation rate.
• Cost of goods sold	• Constant percentage of sales revenue (i.e., from common-size income statement); percentage of sales revenue adjusted for expected economies (or diseconomies) of scale; historical growth rate adjusted for inflation.
• Depreciation expense	• Constant (i.e., a fixed cost); gross PP&E divided by average expected life (see footnotes to the financial statements) plus one-half of new capital expenditures for PP&E divided by average expected life (i.e., assuming straight-line depreciation and half-year convention).
• Amortization expense	• Constant (i.e., a fixed cost); gross intangible assets divided by average expected life plus one-half of new intangible asset investment divided by average expected life.
• Selling, general, and administrative expenses	• Constant percentage of sales revenue; percentage of sales revenue adjusted for expected decrease (increase) in spending, as revealed in annual report or other public sources of information; historic growth rate adjusted for inflation.
• Interest expense	• Weighted-average cost of short-term debt times average outstanding balance of short-term debt plus weighted-average cost of long-term debt times average outstanding balance of long-term debt.
• Income tax expense	• Net income before taxes times statutory tax rate (i.e., federal, state, and local); net income before taxes times average effective tax rate as revealed in annual report or other public sources.

Account	Basis for Forecast
• Dividends	• Constant; constant dividend payout ratio; historical dividend payout ratio adjusted for expected stock sales and repurchases; historical growth rate.
• Cash	• Constant percentage of total assets; historical growth rate.
• Trade receivables	• Constant percentage of total assets; historical receivable turnover or historical growth rate (if forecasted individually).
• Inventory	• Constant percentage of total assets; historical inventory turnover.
• Prepaid and other current assets	• Constant percentage of total assets.
• Investments	• Constant; constant percentage of total assets; constant adjusted for any publicly disclosed future acquisitions or divestitures.
• Property, plant, and equipment	• Constant; constant percentage of total assets; constant PP&E turnover ratio; constant adjusted for any publicly disclosed capital expenditures or divestitures.
• Intangible assets	• Constant; constant percentage of total assets.
• Total assets	• Constant total asset turnover; constant adjusted for publicly disclosed expenditures (divestitures) of specific assets; historic growth rate.
• Trade payables	• Constant percentage of total assets; historic payable turnover.
• Short-term debt	• Constant percentage of total assets; a plug for balancing forecasted balance sheet.
• Current maturities of long-term debt	• Constant; constant adjusted for repayment schedule if revealed in footnotes to the financial statements.
• Accrued expenses payable	• Constant; constant percentage of total assets or total current assets.
• Long-term debt	• Constant; constant adjusted for change in current maturities; a plug for balancing forecasted balance sheet (when short-term debt is not plug).
• Contributed capital	• Constant; constant adjusted for publicly disclosed stock placements; historic growth rate.
• Retained earnings (ending)	• Beginning balance plus forecasted earnings less forecasted dividends.
• Treasury stock	• Constant; constant adjusted for publicly disclosed stock buybacks.
• Adjustments to equity	• Constant; constant adjusted for publicly available information on foreign exchange movements.

PP&E is property, plant, and equipment.

3 Traditional Valuation Models

MARKET VIEW
Air Products and Chemicals, Inc.—
The Risk of Cross-Border Mergers

In August 1999, Air Products and Chemicals, Inc., of the United States and Air Liquide SA of France agreed to jointly acquire their U.K. rival The BOC Group Plc for £7.2 billion ($11.03 billion). Intraindustry acquisitions, however, frequently require the approval of regulatory authorities, in this instance in both the European Union (EU) and the United States. After receiving assurances from its legal counsel that the acquisition would receive the necessary regulatory approvals, Air Products began purchasing British sterling, the currency that it would need to execute the purchase transaction.

In May 2000, Air Products publicly disclosed that despite EU regulatory approval, the U.S. Federal Trade Commission had denied approval of the acquisition on antitrust grounds.* As part of the announcement, Air Products also disclosed that it would record a $300 million after-tax charge for currency losses as a result of the failed acquisition attempt. Over the ten-month period of August 1999 through May 2000, the British sterling collapsed in value relative to the U.S. dollar. Had the acquisition transaction been completed as planned, Air Products would have paid less than the $11 billion agreed on in

*S. Lipin and B. Bahree, "Failure of Deal for BOC Hurts Air Products," *The Wall Street Journal,* 11 May 2000, A3.

August 1999, as a result of the currency decline, which would have offset any currency losses associated with its accumulation of British sterling.

Analysts pointed to the collapse of the acquisition, and to the disclosed currency losses, as a classic example of the risks of cross-border acquisitions.

● ● ●

Valuation analysts have historically relied on two time-tested approaches to valuation:

- Earnings multiples analysis
- Discounted cash flow analysis (DCFA)

In the 1990s, however, a variety of alternative valuation models evolved, in part in response to the emergence of the "new economy" and in part as analysts sought ways to improve upon or extend the traditional models. These alternative valuation approaches, which are largely extensions of the discounted cash flow approach, are reviewed in Chapter 4. This chapter addresses the following key questions:

- What are adjusted earnings multiples and how can they be used for valuation of a company?
- What is DCFA and how can it be effectively implemented?
- What is the weighted average cost of capital (WACC) and how is it calculated?
- What is the continuing value of a target company and how can it be estimated?

Earnings Multiples Analysis

Perhaps the most commonly used form of valuation analysis involves the use of price-to-earnings (P/E) multiples. For example, brokerage firm account executives frequently advise their clients to buy (or sell) a security if its P/E multiple falls below (or rises above) some normal trading range, suggesting some form of market mispricing. This type of ad hoc valuation is typical of the small share–block segment of the securities industry but also has proponents in the "market for control" or the large share–block market segment. (We distinguish between the market for control and the small share–block market because the cost of obtaining majority control of an entity almost always necessitates the payment of a premium above current market value.)

Earnings valuation multiples can be calculated for a variety of earnings-based metrics but are most often calculated for earnings after taxes (P/E), earnings before interest and taxes (P/EBIT), and earnings before interest, taxes, depreciation, and amortization (P/EBITDA). Regardless of which multiple is used, "earnings" should be defined with reference to a company's **permanent earnings,** that is, its *recurring* operating earnings *excluding* such one-time items as discontinued operations, extraordinary items, and one-time write-offs and charges. The specific multiple used is usually a matter of industry convention; however, when analysts are conducting a valuation analysis using both earnings multiples and discounted cash flows, the P/EBITDA multiple appears to be the metric of choice because of its close proximity to a company's cash flows from operations (CFFO).

Earnings multiples can also be calculated for a variety of time periods. A **trailing multiple,** for example, is obtained by dividing the recent closing market price per share by the historical earnings per share (EPS) reported for the most recently completed accounting period (i.e., the quarter or fiscal year). A **forward multiple,** on the other hand, is the current closing price per share divided by forecasted EPS. As one of the principal reasons for using an earnings multiples valuation approach is to avoid the time-consuming process of modeling a target firm's operations, forecasted EPS figures may be obtained from such market data services as Zacks Investment Research, Institutional Brokers Estimate System, and First Call/Thomson Financial. Forward multiples are sometimes adjusted upward (or downward) to reflect changes in market sentiment or for certain positive (negative) information about a company's future performance that is anticipated to affect its share price (e.g., additional earnings growth associated with new product introductions).[1]

Regardless of the particular earnings multiple chosen, it is important to remember that such multiples are only *relative* measures of value that are highly *industry dependent.* For example, on 1 March 1999, the S&P 500 P/E multiple averaged 33; however, Fidelity Investments, Inc., reported the following industry P/E averages for the same period:

Industry	Average P/E
Technology	50–60
Pharmaceutical	40–50
Consumer products	35–45
Telephone	25–30
Banks	20–25
Automobile manufacturers	8–10

Exhibit 3.1   Comparable Company Earnings Multiples Analysis

Company	Closing Share Price at 1 June 1998	Trailing Price-to-Earnings Ratio	Forward Price-to-Earnings Ratio*	
			1998	1999
NL Industries, Inc.	$19.69			
Albemarle Corporation	24.69	16.5×	15.8×	15.1×
The General Chemical Group Inc.	24.56	10.0	9.4	8.6
Geon Company	21.31	14.2	14.7	12.5
Georgia Gulf Corporation	25.06	9.7	12.9	12.4
Lyondell Petrochemical	29.19	6.8	12.5	11.4
Millennium Chemicals Inc.	33.19	11.1	16.1	13.3
TETRA Technologies, Inc.	20.56	20.4	13.7	10.7
Wellman, Inc.	24.56	18.1	15.9	14.3
Median		12.7	14.2	12.4
Average		13.3	13.9	12.3
Adjusted average†		13.3	14.3	12.4

*Forward earnings-per-share forecasts based on First Call consensus estimate.
†Excludes the highest and lowest values.

Once an appropriate multiple — both metric and time frame — has been selected, it can then be used for calculation of a future price objective (or value) for a target company. For example, to implement the earnings multiples framework, first identify a group of companies comparable to the target company in terms of product line and risk characteristics. Then obtain the individual P/E ratios for each firm in the set of comparable companies. Next, calculate an average P/E ratio across the set of comparable firms and multiply that figure by the EPS of the target firm to obtain an estimate of the target's share price. To illustrate, consider the comparable company earnings multiples data reported in Exhibit 3.1. The nine companies listed operate in the chemical and specialty chemicals industry, largely in the United States, and are considered to be "comparable" in terms of size and principal line of business.

If the valuation objective is, for instance, to establish a fair value for the shares of NL Industries, valuation analysts would typically calculate an *adjusted* industry average multiple — that is, one that excludes the high and low outlier values that may bias the analysis. The adjusted industry average multiple would then be multiplied by the target's estimated *forward* earnings to arrive at NL's price objective, as follows:

Basis	Adjusted Industry Average Multiple	Forecasted Consensus Earnings per Share	Price Objective
Price to forward (1998) earnings multiple	14.3	1.62	23.17
Price to forward (1999) earnings multiple	12.4	2.60	32.24

Assuming that markets are efficient and share prices reflect the future earnings of a company, a target price range of $23.17 to $32.24 per share appears appropriate for NL's shares. Given the importance of the selected multiple to the inferred share value, analysts frequently build a sensitivity table to assess how much the valuation is affected by slight changes in the selected multiple. For example, consider the following sensitivity data:

Basis/Scenario	Adjusted Industry Average Multiple	Forecasted Consensus Earnings per Share	Price Objective
Price to forward (1998) earnings multiple			
Conservative scenario	13.8	1.62	22.36
Most likely scenario	14.3	1.62	23.17
Optimistic scenario	14.8	1.62	23.98
Price to forward (1999) earnings multiple			
Conservative scenario	11.9	2.60	30.94
Most likely scenario	12.4	2.60	32.24
Optimistic scenario	12.9	2.60	33.54

The sensitivity data reveal that if the adjusted industry average multiple is overestimated (underestimated) by 0.5, NL's price objective will be biased by $0.81 per share if based on 1998 forward earnings and by $1.30 per share if based on 1999 forward earnings. These per-share amounts can be multiplied by the target's actual number of shares outstanding for assessment of the total cost of a potential acquisition mispricing, which in this instance would be approximately 4 percent above (below) the "most likely" scenario price objective.

The principal limitation of earnings multiples valuation is that it assumes that the riskiness of a target's earnings is constant over time and that such earnings are sustainable indefinitely — assumptions that are almost certain to be incorrect. A second limitation is that reported accounting earnings may not be (and often are not) a good proxy for the long-term sustainable operating cash flows of a company: Cash flows from operations may be greater than or less than the reported earnings of a company. Third, the method works best when a highly comparable group of firms is available; the method's efficacy declines as comparability declines. Finally, as most mergers and acquisitions destroy shareholder value, some analysts are concerned that any type of comparable company valuation analysis — comparable transaction analysis or, to a lesser extent, comparable earnings multiples analysis — may contribute to or perpetuate this undesirable phenomenon. Stated alternatively, if an entire industry sector is mispriced, so too will be the target under this methodology.

The principal advantage of earnings multiples analysis lies in its ease and speed of application. But where millions of dollars of investment capital are involved, ease and speed do not always equate with an accurate assessment of firm value. Consequently, when an acquirer is contemplating a large acquisition, a more thorough valuation analysis involving a complete modeling of a target's operations, as provided by DCFA, is usually warranted.

Discounted Cash Flow Analysis

Discounted cash flow analysis is premised on one of corporate finance's most fundamental notions: *The value of an asset (or bundle of assets) today is equal to the present value of the future cash flows expected to be provided by the asset over its economic life.* DCFA is thus largely founded on concepts and methods of evaluating capital budgeting projects. Hence, as applied to a business entity, DCFA suggests that the value of an enterprise today is the sum of the various future (but uncertain) cash flows to be generated by the entity's operations, discounted at some rate that reflects the riskiness (or uncertainty) of those cash flows.

Although relatively straightforward in its exposition, a number of operational dilemmas and questions are associated with the implementation of DCFA. For instance, "Over what time period should an analyst try to predict the future cash flows of an acquisition target?"; "What is

the appropriate way of measuring a target's cash flows from operations?";
and "What is the appropriate discount rate to use for the purposes of discounting a target's future cash flows (assuming that they can be effectively
modeled)?"

The answers to these questions, and others, are seldom unequivocal.
In the following sections, we consider a number of alternatives.

Forecasting an Uncertain Future. One of the first dilemmas
valuation analysts face when implementing DCFA is deciding on the
length of the forecast period. Most analysts resolve this initial dilemma
by addressing the question, "For how many periods can I *reliably* prepare pro forma financial statements?" The answer depends, in part, on
such factors as the expected stability of the target's industry in general
and the stability of the target's operations in particular; the expected stability of such macro-level factors as inflation, interest rates, and tax rates;
and the analyst's own level of experience in preparing such forecasts. Although the answer will vary greatly from one analyst to another, it typically ranges from one to ten periods, and may be as high as forty periods.
Once the analyst resolves this issue, he or she can then begin to opera-
tionalize the discounted cash flow model by defining **firm operating value**
as follows:

$$
\begin{array}{l} \text{Firm} \\ \text{Operating} \\ \text{Value} \end{array} = \begin{array}{c} \text{Present Value of} \\ \text{Operating Cash Flows} \\ \text{during the Specific} \\ \text{Forecast Period} \end{array} + \begin{array}{c} \text{Present Value of} \\ \text{Operating Cash} \\ \text{Flows Thereafter} \end{array} \quad \textbf{(3.1)}
$$

The second term of this expression is commonly referred to as the **continuing value (CV)** of a business, or alternatively, as its **terminal** or **exit
value.** Hence, firm operating value may be respecified as

$$
\begin{array}{l} \text{Firm} \\ \text{Operating} \\ \text{Value} \end{array} = \begin{array}{c} \text{Present Value of} \\ \text{Operating Cash Flows} \\ \text{during the Specific} \\ \text{Forecast Period} \end{array} + \begin{array}{c} \text{Present Value of} \\ \text{the Firm's CV} \end{array} \quad \textbf{(3.2)}
$$

Determining the length of the specific forecast period involves an
important trade-off between the effect of the two components of target
firm operating value: the forecast of the periodic operating cash flows
and the forecast of the firm's CV. The longer the forecast period selected,
the smaller will be the effect of the CV on firm operating value. At the
extreme, the effect of the CV can be virtually eliminated by forecasting

operating cash flows for twenty or more years, largely as a consequence of the discounting process. Where operating cash flows are highly uncertain, the forecast period will, of necessity, be short, causing the CV to constitute the majority (and possibly all) of a target's total operating value.

Defining Operating Cash Flows. Although various definitions may be used depending on the explicit goal of the valuation analysis, a widely accepted definition of **operating cash flows** is *the CFFO available to all capital providers — both debt holders and equity holders — net of the required capital expenditures necessary to (1) cover the replacement cost of the firm's productive capacity consumed, and (2) support future incremental revenue-generating activities.*

In valuation work, this measure is usually referred to as a target's **free cash flows** (FCFs) and can be readily calculated from the pro forma financial statements (see Chapter 2) as follows:

$$FCF = CFFO + \text{Interest Charges} \ (1 - tx)$$
$$- \text{Net Capital Investment} \qquad \textbf{(3.3)}$$

where tx is the effective tax rate.

Since FCF is a measure of the operating cash flows available to *all* stakeholders in an entity, the analyst must adjust the CFFO for any interest charges accruing to debt holders (the second term in Equation 3.3) that are deducted in the calculation of an entity's earnings. (Notice that the FCF also ignores the dividends paid to equity holders.) This adjustment effectively "unlevers" the CFFO and treats the returns to debt holders and equity holders equivalently. As defined above, the FCF is a measure of the after-tax operating cash flows, assuming that a business is all equity financed. The amount of the interest add-back is simply the amount of interest deducted against earnings on the pro forma income statement, net of income taxes to avoid double counting the cash flow effect of the tax deductibility of interest (i.e., the interest tax shield).[2]

An adjustment for a firm's investment in new capital assets and for the consumption of productive capacity is also necessary (see the last term in Equation 3.3). The real income and cash flows of an entity can be calculated only after the cost of the productive assets consumed in a given period has been recovered; that is, drawing on the economic (as opposed to accounting) definition of "income," any excess wealth after leaving an entity as well-off as it was as of the beginning of the period constitutes the entity's real income. Failure to adjust the CFFO for the value of productive capacity consumed — or what some analysts call "maintenance capital expenditures" — would cause the FCF to be overstated. Similarly, the analyst must also subtract the cost of the capital investment necessary to support a company's future incremental revenue-generating activities if such revenue growth is forecasted in the pro forma scenarios. Both expenditures represent cash outflows that will be unavailable for distribution to stakeholders.

Various metrics may be used to proxy for the value of the net capital investment, often simply referred to as **CapEx** (capital expenditure). In most instances, the proxy is based on the actual or expected value of net property, plant, and equipment (PP&E) investment in a given period. For example, CapEx may be proxied by

1. The estimated net capital expenditures (i.e., total capital expenditures less total retirements) obtained from the pro forma statement of cash flows.

2. A multiyear average of actual and pro forma capital expenditures obtained from the historical and pro forma statement of cash flows.

3. A company's expected capital expenditures as reported in the management discussion and analysis section of the annual report.

4. The periodic depreciation expense deducted on the pro forma income statement.

Because the periodic depreciation expense often fails to accurately reflect the higher expected replacement cost of the productive capacity consumed, as well as the required capital investment for future incremental revenue flows, the best proxies are those obtained from the historical and/or pro forma statement of cash flows involving actual or expected net purchases of PP&E, or as reported in a company's management discussion and analysis.

A final word on the calculation of FCF. Many authors define an entity's FCF with reference to its EBITDA and working capital; for instance, a commonly used definition is as follows:

$$FCF = EBITDA - CapEx - \text{Change in Working Capital} - \text{Cash Taxes Paid}$$

This measurement is *precisely* equivalent to the definition of FCF in Equation 3.3. The calculation of CFFO (see Appendix 2B) includes the change in any working capital accounts (except those, such as the "current portion of long-term debt," that are related to financing), the income taxes actually paid, and an adjustment for such noncash charges as depreciation and amortization expense. The only item excluded from EBITDA but not the CFFO is the after-tax interest charges, which are separately added back in Equation 3.3 to unlever the CFFO. We prefer the definition of FCF given in Equation 3.3 because it clearly and explicitly links the measurement of FCF to the development of the pro forma financial statements.

The Appropriate Discount Rate.   A widely accepted principle in corporate finance is that the cost of capital of an investment is the rate of return required by the investors in a project. If suppliers of capital do not receive a fair rate of return to compensate them for the risk they are taking, they will move their capital in search of better returns. As a minimum, the cost of capital must equal the investors' opportunity cost (i.e., the rate that could be earned on other risk-equivalent investments) *and* the investors' cost of funds. This minimum rate of return is sometimes referred to as a **hurdle rate,** in that it represents that threshold return which must be earned in order to justify the investment from the investor's perspective (i.e., to have a positive net present value).

In the case of an acquisition, there are two schools of thought as to the appropriate discount rate to use when a target company is being valued: (1) the target company's **weighted average cost of capital (WACC),** and (2) the acquirer's hurdle rate. Proponents of the target's WACC argue that it is necessary to use that rate which best reflects the riskiness of the target's cash flows; it is the rate the capital market uses, for instance, to assess a firm's current share price. Proponents of the acquirer's hurdle rate, on the other hand, argue that investment capital is a scarce resource and the acquirer must choose only those acquisitions providing a rate of return at least as great as the acquirer's WACC. Although this latter rate is not theoretically defensible, acquirers frequently use it when valuing target firms.

The Target's WACC.   The WACC is defined as follows:[3]

$$WACC = (E/V) \times r_e + (D/V) \times (1 - tx) \times r_d$$

where

E = the market value of equity of the target company, measured by its total market capitalization.

D = the market value of debt of the target company, usually proxied by the market value of any outstanding long-term bonds.[4]

V = the total market value of the target (i.e., $E + D$).

E/V = the proportion of total firm value represented by equity.

D/V = the proportion of total firm value represented by debt.

tx = the target's corporate tax rate, defined as the ratio of the income tax expense divided by pretax income, obtained from the pro forma income statement.

r_e = the target's cost of equity funds, calculated using the Capital Asset Pricing Model (CAPM):

$$r_e = r_f + \beta_e \times (r_m - r_f)$$

where

r_f = the current risk-free rate of return, proxied, for example, for U.S. acquisitions by the current yield to maturity of the U.S. ten-year treasury bond.[5]

β_e = a measure of the systematic risk of the target, proxied by the firm's equity beta, available from any commercial data service, such as Value Line, Disclosure/Worldscope, or Standard & Poor's.[6,7]

r_m = the current market rate of return for a well-diversified portfolio of equity securities, proxied, for example, for U.S. acquisitions by the return on the S&P 500 index, or approximately 13.2 percent, which is the average return for the seventy-two-year period 1926–1998.

$(r_m - r_f)$ = the equity risk premium required by "the market" on a well-diversified portfolio of equity securities; this measure is usually assumed to be 7.5 percent in the United States, which is the average risk premium over the seventy-two-year period 1926–1998.[8]

r_d = the target's current cost of debt financing, typically proxied by the target's current yield to maturity on its outstanding debt or by the current yield to maturity for equivalent credit risk–rated companies.

In words, a target's WACC is its cost of equity funds weighted by the proportion of total firm market value attributed to equity holders, plus its cost of debt funds weighted by the proportion of total firm market value attributable to debt holders. The cost of debt is calculated on an

Exhibit 3.2   Calculating the Weighted Average Cost of Capital (WACC)

Assume that the following information is known about the Thunderbird Corporation, a U.S.-based entity:

Risk premium on a well-diversified portfolio	7.5%
Equity beta	1.3
Pretax cost of debt, based on credit rating of outstanding bonds	10.0%
Effective income tax rate	30%
Market value of equity	$900 million
Market value of debt	$500 million

WACC calculation:

1. r_e $= r_f + \beta_e \times (r_m - r_f)$
   $= 6.5\% + 1.3 \times (7.5\%)$
   $= 6.5\% + 9.75\% = 16.25\%$

2. D/V $= 500/(900 + 500) = 0.357$
   E/V $= 900/(900 + 500) = 0.643$

3. $\text{WACC} = (E/V) \times r_e + (D/V) \times (1 - tx) \times r_d$
   $= (0.643 \times 16.25\%) + [0.357 \times 10.0\% \times (1 - 30\%)]$
   $= 12.95\%$

after-tax basis (i.e., r_d is multiplied by $[1 - tx]$) to reflect the tax shield provided by the tax deductibility of interest expense (but not dividends) in most countries. The target's WACC is the rate most analysts prefer when valuing a potential acquisition as a stand-alone enterprise. Equity analysts also prefer it when assessing a firm's current fair market value. Indeed, the use of the target's WACC is intuitively appealing because of the consistency it affords: The target's cash flows are discounted at a rate reflecting the average riskiness of those cash flows even though various projects of the firm may entail different risks. Exhibit 3.2 illustrates the calculation of a target's WACC.

Implicit in the above discussion is the assumption that a target's capital structure, and hence WACC, remains relatively constant over time.[9] Theoretically, when material changes in capital structure occur, it is appropriate for the WACC to be recalculated after each change. Indeed, debt capital is cheaper than equity capital because it has a more senior claim on assets and because the interest expense associated with it is tax deductible. As more debt is added to a company's capital structure, the cost of debt increases, and the WACC will (paradoxically) decline with the increased use of leverage until the benefits of the interest tax shield from debt are outweighed by bankruptcy risk. Material changes in capital structure are likely to occur in highly leveraged transactions and in acquisitions to be followed by restructuring. Practically, recalculation of the WACC after each change in capital structure results in a problem of circular logic: The market value of equity is required for recalculation of the WACC, but the reason the WACC is needed is for assessment of the future market value of equity. Consequently, when changes in capital structure are expected to be immaterial, or are assumed to be unknown by virtue of the assumptions made in the preparation of pro forma financial statements leading to the calculation of a target's FCFs, analysts usually make the simplifying assumption of a constant WACC. An alternative to recalculation of the WACC in the presence of material changes in capital structure is the adjusted present value approach, which is discussed in Chapter 4.

The Acquirer's Hurdle Rate. From the perspective of many acquirers, the appropriate discount rate to use when discounting a target's FCFs and CV is the acquirer's required hurdle rate. The hurdle rate may be the acquirer's WACC or some desired rate of return. This viewpoint reflects the capital budgeting notion that a project's cash flows should be discounted at the investor's required rate of return for assessment of the suitability (and price) of an investment to the investor. Although not theoretically defensible, this view is widely held among many acquisition-oriented firms and implicitly reflects the reality that investors have a limited supply of investable capital. It also reflects the notion that most acquirers prefer to select those projects with the highest net present value, not just those with positive net present values. This view, for instance, is commonly embraced by venture capitalists as they evaluate alternative investment opportunities.

When a target and an acquirer operate in the same or a related industry, the target's WACC and the acquirer's WACC are likely to converge considerably; consequently, just which rate is used may be relatively immaterial to final target firm value. When a target and an acquirer operate in different industries, however, with corresponding differences in the riskiness of firm/industry cash flows, these rates of return may diverge considerably, with a material variance in assessed firm value.

Acquirers frequently justify the use of their own WACC (or hurdle rate) on the grounds that shareholder value will be created only when its capital is invested at rates of return at least as great as its own cost of capital. Implicit in this practice is the assumption that capital markets are not always efficient and that the acquirer wants to act like a "value investor," selecting only undervalued targets.[10] A likely consequence of this practice, however, is that the acquirer will tend to select targets with relatively riskier cash flow streams. Exhibit 3.3 illustrates this phenome-

Exhibit 3.3   Comparison of Discount Rates: The Target's Weighted Average Cost of Capital (WACC) versus the Acquirer's Hurdle Rate

One of the dilemmas involved in implementing the discounted cash flow approach to firm valuation is the selection of an appropriate discount rate. Academicians usually recommend the use of a target's WACC in order to best match the riskiness of the firm's operating cash flows with the riskiness implied by the discount rate. Acquisition analysts, however, frequently use a hurdle rate based on the acquirer's WACC or some desired rate of return. (See also Appendix 3B.)

To illustrate the consequences of this latter decision, consider the following data:

Target's WACC		12%	
Target's free cash flows		Nominal Value	Present Value at 12%
$t = 1$		$100,000	$82,286
$t = 2$		150,000	119,579
$t = 3$		175,000	124,561
Target's continuing value at $t = 3$		200,000	142,356
Present value of target at $t = 0$			$475,782
Acquirer's hurdle rate	8%	12%	15%
Present value of target	$518,880	$475,782	$446,947

If an acquirer's hurdle rate approximates the target's WACC (i.e., 12 percent), the valuation results using either the target's WACC or the acquirer's hurdle rate will be equivalent ($475,782 in the above example). If, on the other hand, an acquirer's hurdle rate exceeds the target's WACC (i.e., 15 percent), it is unlikely that the acquisition transaction will take place, as the acquirer will consistently undervalue the target (i.e., $446,947 versus $475,782), and hence any tender offer is likely to be rejected. Finally, if the acquirer's hurdle rate is less than the target's WACC (i.e., 8 percent), the acquirer will tend to overpay for the target (i.e., $518,880 versus $475,782) and thus will destroy shareholder value.

Analysis: When an acquirer's hurdle rate is used that is greater than a target's WACC, the acquirer will tend to accept only those acquisitions in which the implied riskiness of the target's cash flows exceeds the riskiness implied by the target's WACC, unless, of course, some form of market mispricing is present. Alternatively, when an acquirer's hurdle rate is less than a target's WACC, the acquirer will tend to overpay for such acquisitions, providing yet another case of the winner's curse.

---

non and reveals that when an acquirer's hurdle rate is used that is greater than the target's WACC, the acquirer will tend to accept only those acquisitions in which the implied riskiness of the target's cash flows exceeds the riskiness implied by the target's WACC; alternatively, when an acquirer's hurdle rate is less than a target's WACC, the acquirer will tend to fall victim to the winner's curse.

Calculating the Continuing Value. As noted above, one of the methodological dilemmas facing the valuation analyst when implementing DCFA is the question, "For how many periods can I reliably forecast pro forma financial statements?" Most analysts routinely prepare one-to three-year forecasts, and some for even longer periods. Whatever the length of the forecast period, however, the decision ultimately involves a trade-off between the effect and importance of the two components of target firm value: the periodic estimates of FCFs and the estimated CV of the firm.

The continuing or terminal value of a firm is an assessment of the future FCFs for a target for all periods beyond the specific forecast period. It is the value that an acquirer can reasonably expect to receive if the target is sold at the end of the forecast period. It is a proxy for the aggregate future FCFs that the analyst feels unable to forecast or uncomfortable forecasting on a period-by-period basis. And like each of the individual forecasted periodic FCFs, the continuing or terminal value is also discounted back to the present to arrive at the total estimated operating value of the firm.

As a practical matter, the longer the specific forecast period for the FCFs, the smaller will be the assigned CV, largely as a consequence of the discounting process. For very short forecast periods, or when a target's FCFs are small or negative, the CV may constitute the majority (or even all) of a target's total value. This situation would be characteristic, for example, of a start-up venture with zero or negative CFFOs.

A number of approaches are available for estimating CV, but the two most widely used are

- The exit multiple method
- The FCF growth method

Both methods suffer from the same limitation: They assume that the riskiness and sustainability of a target's earnings are constant over time, and that assumption is likely to be incorrect.

Exit Multiple Method. Under the exit multiple method, the analyst uses a multiplier — for instance, the forward P/E multiple — to multiply the final period estimate of a target's permanent earnings to arrive at the estimated CV or exit value. The exit value is an estimate of the value that the acquirer could reasonably expect to receive if the target were resold at the end of the specific forecast period. This estimated value is then discounted back to the present using the selected discount rate. The multiple can be adjusted upward (or downward) to reflect any enhancements (or decrements) to target firm value that the acquirer is expected to create during the forecast period.

The exit multiple method is commonly implemented with any of the following metrics:

- P/E multiple: the final period estimate of permanent earnings multiplied by a forward P/E multiple

- P/EBITDA multiple: the final period estimate of EBITDA multiplied by a forward P/EBITDA multiple

- Price-to-FCF multiple: the final period estimate of FCF multiplied by a forward P/FCF multiple

- Price-to-sales multiple: the final period estimate of net sales multiplied by a forward P/Sales multiple

Just which exit multiple is used is typically a function of industry norms; however, the P/Sales multiple is commonly used when the final period estimate of earnings or cash flow is expected to be negative.

To illustrate the exit multiple method, suppose that pro forma financial statements are prepared for five years and that the target's fifth-year FCF is estimated to be $50,000. Furthermore, assume that the average forward P/FCF multiple for firms in this industry is 10 but in this instance is adjusted upward to 13 to reflect the higher revenue growth rate that is expected to arise after the target's product mix and marketing are refocused. Finally, assume that the target's WACC is 12 percent. The forecasted CV using the exit multiple method is

$$CV_5 = P/FCF \times FCF_5$$

$$CV_5 = 13 \times \$50,000 = \$650,000$$

And the present value (PV) of the CV is given by

$$PV(CV) = CV_t/(1 + r)^t$$

$$PV(CV) = \$650,000/(1.12)^5 = \$368,827$$

where t is the number of years and r is the hurdle rate.

Representative exit multiples are typically estimated from historical data from a target's home country and industry; however, given the importance of the exit multiple to overall firm value, most analysts build a sensitivity table to assess by how much firm value is affected by slight changes in the selected multiple. For example, consider the following sensitivity data:

Scenario	Exit Multiple	Continuing Value	Present Value
Conservative	11	550,000	312,085
Most likely	13	650,000	368,827
Optimistic	15	750,000	425,570

If the exit multiple is biased by plus or minus 15 percent (i.e., a multiple of 11 or 15), the CV will be biased by $100,000, a 15 percent difference from the most likely CV, and the present value of the CV will be biased by $56,742. Whether or not this amount is material to the total firm value largely depends, of course, on the length of the specific forecast period, as well as on the present value of the FCFs.

FCF Growth Method. Under the FCF growth method, a target's FCF is assumed to grow at some constant annual rate, g, in perpetuity. The growth rate of the target's FCF may be calculated from the actual FCFs generated in the pro forma analysis or can be extrapolated from the actual historical growth rate of FCF. Most analysts, however, are unwilling to assume that such growth rates are sustainable in the long term and consequently (arbitrarily) adopt a lower growth rate.[11] The CV is then given by the following equation:[12]

$$CV_t = FCF_{t+1}/(WACC - g)$$
$$= FCF_t(1 + g)/(WACC - g)$$

Using the data from the above example, if g is assumed to be 7 percent, then the CV is

$$CV_5 = \$50,000(1 + 0.07)/(0.12 - 0.07)$$
$$= \$1,070,000$$

and the present value is

$$PV(CV) = \$1,070,000/(1.12)^5 = \$607,147$$

The FCF growth method is highly sensitive to the selection of g. For instance, if g were actually 6 percent rather than 7 percent, the CV in our illustration above would be $883,333, with a present value of $501,227, for an estimation error of about 21 percent.[13]

Measuring the Equity Value of a Firm.   Once the above DCFA dilemmas have been resolved and a firm's operating value estimated (see Equation 3.2), it is possible for the **total firm value** of a target company to be estimated as follows:

$$\begin{matrix} \text{Total} \\ \text{Firm Value} \end{matrix} = \begin{matrix} \text{Firm} \\ \text{Operating Value} \end{matrix} + \begin{matrix} \text{Market Value of Any} \\ \text{Nonoperating Assets} \end{matrix} \quad \textbf{(3.4)}$$

Companies frequently invest in other corporate entities for diversification or strategic purposes unrelated to current operations. These investments are usually accounted for using the equity method, and their cash flow effects are normally excluded from the calculation of a target's CFFO; consequently, the CV of these nonoperating assets will not be reflected in either the present value of the target's FCFs or its CV. Thus, to avoid understating the total value of the firm, analysts must add the market value of these (and any other) nonoperating assets to firm operating value to arrive at the total firm value.[14] Among the "other non-operating assets" that should be added to firm operating value are those nonoperating assets carried on the balance sheet, the value of any unrecorded intangible assets unrelated to continuing operations, and the after-tax value of any overfunded pension plan assets carried off the balance sheet.

The **equity value** of the target company may now be calculated by subtracting from the total firm value the value of all other claimholders, to include the market value of all debt (except working capital debt, which is explicitly reflected in the CFFO), any minority interest, the market value of any equity-related securities having claims senior to the common shareholders' claims (e.g., preferred stock), and the value of any contingent claims:

$$\begin{matrix} \text{Firm} \\ \text{Equity Value} \end{matrix} = \text{Total Firm Value} - \begin{matrix} \text{Market Value of Debt,} \\ \text{Minority Interest,} \\ \text{Preferred Stock, and} \\ \text{Contingency Claims} \end{matrix}$$

Among the debt instruments that should be subtracted from total firm value are the current maturities of long-term debt, long-term debt, convertible debentures, capitalized leases, the capitalized value of operating leases, and the after-tax amount of any unfunded pension or post-retirement benefit liabilities.[15] Also deductible, along with the market value of any outstanding preferred stock, is the fair value of any out-

Exhibit 3.4   Calculating the Equity Value of a Target Company

Firm operating value	$114,000
+ Market value of unconsolidated investments	24,000
+ Market value of other nonoperating assets	4,000
Total firm value	$142,000
− Market value of	
Current maturing portion of long-term debt	(2,500)
Long-term debt	(20,000)
Convertible debentures	(12,000)
Capitalized leases	(8,000)
Capitalized value of operating leases	(4,000)
After-tax value of unfunded pension and postretirement liabilities	(13,000)
− Market value of minority interest	(7,500)
− Market value of	
Stock options	(3,000)
Preferred stock	(22,000)
Equity value of the company	$50,000
Equity value per share	$25.00

standing employee stock options or warrants. Finally, deductible as a contingent claim is the estimated value of any lawsuits and government actions. Exhibit 3.4 illustrates the calculation of the equity value for a hypothetical firm.

Once the equity value of a target has been calculated, it can then be placed on a per-share basis by dividing by the number of shares outstanding. The equity value per share thus represents an analyst's best estimate of target firm value per share. In most instances this per-share estimate will represent the upper bound of value that an acquirer should be willing to pay for a target — paying a higher value will lower the acquirer's expected rate of return below the discount rate used.

For evaluation of the reliability of the estimated equity value per share, it is possible to calculate an **implied P/E ratio** as follows:

$$\text{Implied P/E Ratio} = \frac{\text{Estimated Equity Value Per Share}}{\text{Current Earnings Per Share}}$$

The implied P/E can be used as a validity check by comparing it to the adjusted industry average P/E ratio on a forward EPS basis for a set of comparable companies. If a target's implied P/E ratio is above the adjusted industry average, it may indicate the possibility of forecast errors in the pro forma analysis and may suggest that the analyst should revisit his or her pro forma assumptions.

A Survey of Best Practices.   A recent survey of leading U.S. companies and their financial advisers provides evidence of the "best practices" successful companies are using for valuation purposes (see Bruner and Eades 1998). The survey found the following:

- The dominant valuation technique is DCFA.

- The principal discount rate used in DCFA is the target's WACC, with the relative weighting of a target's debt and equity components assessed with the use of market (not book) values.

- The principal approach used for estimating a company's cost of equity is the Capital Asset Pricing Model (CAPM).

- When the cost of equity is being calculated, the risk-free rate is usually proxied using the ten-year (or greater) U.S. treasury bond rate (largely because the yield curve is relatively flat beyond ten years).

- Despite the fact that the CAPM calls for the use of a forward-looking beta (to reflect the uncertainty surrounding a target's *future* cash flows), most companies use a beta derived from historical data.[16]

- When estimating the equity market risk premium (i.e., $r_m - r_f$), financial advisers used an estimate of 7.0 to 7.4 percent, whereas acquirers used an estimate of 4.0 to 6.0 percent, causing the cost of capital estimates of financial advisers to frequently exceed those of the acquiring companies they advise.

- When a multidivisional target is being valued, each division is valued separately using a distinct WACC and then aggregated to arrive at a target's total value.

The survey found that despite considerable agreement in valuation practices, "best practices companies can expect to estimate their WACC with an accuracy of no more than plus or minus 100 to 150 basis points."

Cross-Border Considerations.   When an acquisition involves entities from different countries, an additional set of considerations arises: foreign currency risk, country or political risk, blocked funds risk, and expropriation risk, among others. These risks create additional uncertainty surrounding a target's cash flows, so the valuation analyst must consider them *explicitly.* (See, for instance, the Air Products and Chemicals, Inc., vignette at the beginning of this chapter.)

Cross-border acquisitions usually involve the added complexity of the need for two sets of pro forma financial statements — one for the acquirer and one for the target (or project). The target's pro formas are prepared using the target's functional currency, with explicit consideration given to expropriation risk. **Expropriation risk** refers to the probability that a target's assets and operations will be taken over by a foreign government. The acquirer's pro formas are then prepared after the subsidiary's pro formas are translated into the functional currency of the acquirer. This computation requires an assumption with respect to the movement of exchange rates and thus an explicit consideration of **currency exchange rate risk.** At this stage, some consideration of repatriation constraints, or **blocked-funds risk,** can also be incorporated into the valuation analysis.

Blocked funds — either partial or full — may have considerable value to an acquirer if the funds can be reinvested at favorable rates of return in the foreign country or if the acquirer's objectives are market share oriented. A classic example of this was the decision by the McDonald's Company to invest $40 million in the former Soviet Union in the early 1990s. The company's multimillion dollar investment was made with the full realization that existing Republic of Russia laws prevented the repatriation of any profits. Obviously, the Russian investment of McDonald's was predicated on a long-term view of global market growth, and not on short-run cash flow repatriation.

The acquirer's translated FCFs can then be calculated and discounted. Determination of the appropriate discount rate, however, is an issue of considerable debate among analysts. In theory, the discount rate should be the risk-adjusted cost of capital of the target. As noted above, however, many acquirer's use their own WACC or some desired (or required) rate of return (hurdle rate) for the purposes of discounting the target's cash flows. But international acquisitions have additional uncertainties. Consequently, many analysts believe that the appropriate way to account for these added risks is by adding a risk premium to the discount rate. For instance, some multinational acquirers tack on international risk premiums as high as 10 percentage points above their normal domestic hurdle rate.[17] One objection to this approach is that it assumes that the degree of risk is uniform over the life of the target. Furthermore, because of the exponential nature of discounting, a uniformly higher discount rate (because of an add-on risk premium) substantially penalizes early cash flows and may not adequately reflect the risk in later periods.

An alternative approach to addition of a risk premium to the discount rate is direct incorporation of the various risks in the pro forma financial statements, as discussed above. By preparing subsidiary pro formas first, initially in the target's functional currency, the analyst can explicitly incorporate expropriation risk as well as political risk. Furthermore, he or she can explicitly incorporate exchange rate risk when the parent's pro formas are prepared from the translated subsidiary pro formas. Given the substantial effect of the discount rate on firm value, adding a risk premium to the selected discount rate may be equivalent to "using a cannon to kill a fly."

An Illustration of DCFA.   In Chapter 2, the financial data of Nokia Corporation were analyzed and used to prepare a one-year (1998) set of pro forma financial statements (see Exhibits 2.10 and 2.11). We now return to that pro forma data to illustrate DCFA valuation.

The data necessary for estimating Nokia's FCF for 1998 can be extracted from Exhibits 2.10 and 2.11:

$$FCF_{1998} = CFFO_{1998} + \text{Interest Charges (net)}_{1998} - CapEx_{1998}$$

$$= 10{,}230 + 286(1 - 0.27) - 4{,}880$$

$$= 5{,}636 \text{ mFIM (millions of Finnish markka)}$$

To calculate the present value of Nokia's FCF as of year end 1997, one must first calculate Nokia's WACC:

	mFIM	%
Market value of common stocks	30,688	25.3
Market value of preferred stocks	85,591	70.6
Market value of long-term debt	1,643	1.4
Market value of short-term debt	3,293	2.7
Total market value at year end 1997	121,215	100.0

Yield on Finnish government ten-year bond (r_f)	5.5%
Return on a well-diversified market portfolio (r_m)	14.0%
Equity beta	1.13
Pretax cost of long-term debt (r_{dl})	6.5%
Pretax cost of short-term debt (r_{ds})	7.2%
Cost of preferred stock (r_p)	2.0%
Effective tax rate (tx)	27.0%

Nokia's cost of equity (r_e) can be estimated as follows:

$$r_e = r_f + \beta_e \times (r_m - r_f)$$

$$= 5.5\% + 1.13(14.0\% - 5.5\%)$$

$$= 5.5\% + 9.6\% = 15.1\%$$

And Nokia's WACC may be estimated as[18]

$$WACC = (E/V) \times r_e + (P/V) \times r_p + (D_l/V) \times (1 - tx) \times r_{dl}$$
$$+ (D_s/V) \times (1 - tx) \times r_{ds}$$

$$= (25.3\% \times 15.1\%) + (70.6\% \times 2.0\%)$$
$$+ [1.4\% \times (1 - 0.27\%) \times 6.5\%]$$
$$+ [2.7\% \times (1 - 27\%) \times 7.2\%]$$

$$= 3.82\% + 1.41\% + 0.07\% + 0.14\% = 5.4\%$$

The present value (PV) of Nokia's 1998 FCF can then be calculated as follows:

$$PV(FCF) = FCF_{1998}/(1 + r)^t$$

$$= 5,636/(1 + 0.054)^1$$

$$= 5,345 \text{ mFIM}$$

Since the explicit forecast period is only one year, Nokia's CV will constitute the majority of the firm's total operating value (see Equation 3.1). If Nokia's FCFs are assumed to grow at an annual rate (g) of 2 percent, the expected rate of inflation, the firm's CV can be estimated using the FCF growth model, as follows:

$$CV_{1998} = FCF_{1999}/(WACC - g)$$

$$= FCF_{1998}(1 + g)/(WACC - g)$$

$$= 5,636 (1 + 0.02)/(0.054 - 0.02)$$

$$= 166,952 \text{ mFIM}$$

The present value of the CV is

$$PV(CV) = CV_{1998}/(1 + r)^t$$

$$= 166,952/(1 + 0.054)^1$$

$$= 158,333 \text{ mFIM}$$

The firm operating value (Equation 3.2) can now be calculated:

$$\text{Firm Operating Value} = \text{PV(FCF)} + \text{PV(CV)}$$
$$= 5,345 + 158,333$$
$$= 163,679 \text{ mFIM}$$

The present value of the CV represents 96.7 percent of Nokia's operating value. Note that one of the key variables in the calculation of CV is the growth rate of the FCF. As shown below, both numerically and graphically, Nokia's operating value increases from 103,541 million FIM when the growth rate is assumed to be 0 percent to 1,270,981 million FIM when the growth rate is assumed to be 5 percent (i.e., about twelve times greater).

Assumed Growth Rate	Estimated Operating Value (mFIM)
0%	103,541
1%	126,843
2%	163,679
3%	230,665
4%	390,466
5%	1,270,981

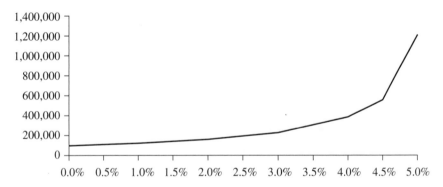

The total firm value (Equation 3.4) can now be estimated as

$$\text{Total Firm Value} = \text{Firm Operating Value} + \text{Market Value of Nonoperating Assets}$$
$$= 163,679 + (789 + 355)$$
$$= 164,823 \text{ mFIM}$$

In the absence of market value data for Nokia's investments and other noncurrent assets, the book values (i.e., 789 and 355, respectively) from Exhibit 2.10 were used as proxies for their market values.

Finally, Nokia's equity value and equity value per share can now be estimated:

$$\text{Equity Value} = \text{Total Firm Value} - \text{Market Value of Debt,}$$
$$\text{Minority Interest, and Preferred Stock}[19]$$

$$= 164,823 - 90,722$$

$$= 74.101 \text{ mFIM}$$

Equity Value Per Share $= 941.72$ FIM

Thus, using DCFA, Nokia's price objective would be approximately 942 FIM per share.

Nokia's equity value depends on the present value of 1998 FCF (i.e., on 1998 FCF and the WACC) and on the present value of the firm's CV (i.e., on 1998 FCF, the WACC, and the growth rate). To study the sensitivity of Nokia's equity value to these components, the analyst can simulate the model used to calculate the company's equity value. As in Chapter 2, the key variables for 1998 FCF are

- The sales growth, which is assumed to follow a triangular distribution; the minimum is taken to be 13 percent, the most likely value as 25 percent, and the maximum as 34 percent.

- The short-term and long-term interest rates, which are assumed to follow a uniform distribution, ranging from 6.7 percent to 7.7 percent for the short-term rate and from 6 percent to 7 percent for the long-term rate.

We also assume that the growth rate of the FCF follows a uniform distribution, ranging from 0 percent (conservative) to 4 percent (optimistic).

We use @Risk to simulate the model used for calculation of Nokia's equity value with the following results:

- Nokia's equity value varies from 7,246 million FIM (92 FIM per share) to 335,111 million FIM (4,259 FIM per share), with a mean of 100,067 million FIM (1,272 FIM per share) and a standard deviation of 75,758 million FIM (963 FIM per share).

- As we noticed before, Nokia's equity value is very sensitive to the present value of the CV and, in particular, to the assumption about the growth rate of FCF. The tornado graph (not presented) indicates that the correlation between the growth rate and the equity value is 93.9 percent. On the other hand, the correlation between sales growth and equity value is −8.5 percent, which means that as sales growth increases, equity value decreases. This result is not surprising, as an increase in sales growth leads to an increase in such assets as PP&E, which leads to a decrease in 1998 FCF and thus a decrease in Nokia's equity value. Note that Nokia's equity value is relatively insensitive to alternative interest rates.

At the end of 1997, Nokia's common shares were trading at 390 FIM. Compared with the mean equity value of 1,272 FIM, Nokia appears to be relatively undervalued. This result is confirmed by a P/E multiples analysis. In late 1997, the investment banking firm of Alexander Brown projected a twelve-month price objective of 20–24 times 1998 estimated earnings. From Exhibit 2.10, forecasted 1998 net earnings of 8,354 million FIM less estimated 1998 preferred stock dividends of 774 million FIM yields a forward EPS of 96 FIM and a forward price target of 1,920 FIM.

Summary

In this chapter, we reviewed the two leading approaches to firm valuation — earnings multiples analysis and DCFA. Although earnings multiples analysis is an acceptable approach for valuation of small share-block purchases, a more thorough analysis — as provided by DCFA — is desirable when substantial amounts of capital are involved.

The implementation of DCFA requires that the analyst resolve a number of dilemmas, including

1. For how many periods should the analyst try to forecast a target's FCFs?

2. How should the analyst calculate the target's operating cash flows and CV?

3. What discount rate should the analyst use when discounting a firm's FCF and CV?

Once these issues are resolved, the analyst should then perform a thorough modeling of a target's future operating performance.

Notes

1. Kim and Ritter (1999) report that forward P/E multiples provide more accurate valuations than trailing P/E multiples; moreover, Liu, Nissim, and Thomas (2001) report that forward P/E multiples outperform not only trailing P/E multiples but also cash flow multiples and sales multiples.

2. The effect of the interest tax shield is already reflected in the pro forma CFFO as taxes are calculated on a cash basis (i.e., adjustments are made for the change in deferred income taxes and income taxes payable).

3. This definition assumes that the target has only common equity outstanding. In the event that the target also has preferred equity outstanding, the WACC will need to be reformulated as follows:

$$\text{WACC} = (E/V) \times r_e + (P/V) \times r_p + (D/V) \times (1 - tx) \times r_d$$

where V is $E + P + D$; P, the market value of preferred equity; and r_p, the target's cost of preferred shares, equal to the dividend paid per share divided by the preferred stock market price per share.

4. The proxy for D ignores many common forms of long-term debt, such as capitalized leases, operating leases, pensions, and other postretirement benefits. Methods for incorporating these other forms of long-term debt in the calculation of WACC are discussed in Appendix 3A. When these alternative forms of debt are immaterial in amount, they may be ignored.

5. Measures for the current risk-free rate of return can be obtained from Ibbotson Associates, Inc., *Stocks, Bonds, Bills, and Inflation Yearbook*.

6. Some analysts prefer to use an estimated future value for beta rather than a historical value.

7. Because of the high variance in reported equity beta values provided by commercial data services, some analysts prefer to construct their own measures using industry data. One such method is the following:

1. Identify a set of comparable companies and collect the following variables for each company: β_e, E, D.

2. Using the collected data, calculate the asset beta (β_a) for each comparable company as follows: $\beta_a = \beta_e \times \dfrac{E}{E + D(1 - tx)}$

3. Sum the individual company asset betas and then calculate an industry average (β_{Ia}).

4. Use the industry average asset beta to estimate the equity beta (β_e) for the target firm, as follows: $\beta_e = \beta_{Ia} \times \dfrac{E + D(1 - tx)}{E}$.

A second approach is to simply use the industry beta, which is typically more stable and reliable than individual company betas. A rule of thumb some analysts follow is to use the industry beta if the individual company beta from several sources varies by more than 0.2, indicating a high degree of instability in the individual firm beta.

8. For target companies outside the United States, it is necessary for a risk-free rate and market premium representative of the target's home market to be obtained.

9. Some analysts prefer to estimate the WACC for a *target* capital structure rather than the current capital structure. This approach has the advantage of anticipating future significant changes in capital structure that may materially affect firm value. For example, if an acquirer is planning to change a target's level of debt after acquisition, the market value of the target should be calculated twice — once using the WACC assuming no debt change and once using the revised WACC reflecting the debt increase. The difference between the two values represents the potential increase in target value due to the improved use of leverage. If the additional debt can only result as a consequence of the acquisition, then the increase in value represents a potential synergistic effect.

10. Efficient market theory holds that prices reflect unbiased estimates of future cash flows. Whether capital markets are indeed efficient seems to matter little, in that many acquirers appear to act as if they are not.

11. The unwillingness of most analysts to assume an indefinitely sustainable FCF growth rate essentially reflects the concern that over time, above average rates of return gravitate to a mean value (i.e., the phenomenon of mean reversion).

12. The relevant FCF for the CV is the next year's rather than the current year's FCF. Indeed, the CV reflects all of the cash flows that the company will generate in the future. The current year's FCF has already been integrated in the firm's operating value.

13. Berkman, Bradbury, and Ferguson (1998) report that the most reliable DCFA valuation outcomes result when the CV is estimated using earnings (not FCF) with an assumption of zero growth rate.

14. When the value of such intercorporate investments and other nonoperating assets are immaterial in amount, analysts frequently use the reported book values as a proxy for their market values.

15. When the value of debt and/or minority interest is immaterial, book value may be used as an acceptable proxy for market value. When the debt and/or minority shares are publicly traded, an approximate market value may be estimated directly from the market value of the debt instrument or the minority shares.

16. The financial advisers surveyed cited the consulting firm Barra as "the best provider of beta estimates." Barra publishes beta estimates, using forward-looking values, for more than ten thousand companies worldwide.

17. See "Lowering the Bar: Make Bets on Foreign Markets When Conventional Hurdle Rates Say No?" *CFO Magazine,* August 2000, 111–113.

18. The calculation of Nokia's WACC illustrates two anomalies. First, more than 70 percent of the company's market value is embedded in its convertible

preferred stock. Second, the cost of preferred stock capital is unusually low (i.e., 2 percent), perhaps as a consequence of the conversion value of the preferred shares. These factors conspire to give Nokia a WACC of only 5.4 percent.

19. Nokia's market value of debt and minority interest was proxied by the reported book values in Exhibit 2.11:

	mFIM
Long-term debt	1,348
Current portion of long-term debt	285
Short-term borrowing	3,008
Other long-term liabilities	295
Minority interest	195
Preferred stock	85,591
	90,722

Appendix 3A
Calculating the
WACC for a Complex
Capital Structure

In most situations, the weighted average cost of capital (WACC) can be proxied by the following formula:

$$\text{WACC} = (E/V) \times r_e + (D/V) \times (1 - tx) \times r_d$$

where E is the market value of equity; D, the market value of debt; V, the total market value of the firm (i.e., $E + D$); E/V, the proportion of total firm value represented by equity; D/V, the proportion of total firm value represented by debt; tx, the effective corporate tax rate; r_e, the cost of equity funds; and r_d, the cost of debt funds.

D can be successfully proxied by the market value of a company's outstanding long-term bonds. In some situations, however, material quantities of other debt instruments may be outstanding (e.g., capitalized leases, operating leases, pensions, and other postretirement liabilities) that should be considered in the calculation of the WACC.* For these additional debt instruments, it is necessary to add additional components to the above equation to ensure that all of the debt outstanding is fully reflected in the WACC. For each of the additional debt components, the following information is needed:

1. The market value of the debt (i.e., $\tilde{D}$).

2. The yield or cost of the debt (i.e., $\tilde{r}_d$).

For most debt instruments, the reported balance sheet values will be a good proxy for market value. Operating leases, however, are carried off the balance sheet and hence will necessitate a balance sheet transformation (see Chapter 5)

---

*Some analysts include deferred income taxes in the calculation of the WACC under the argument that deferred income taxes represent an implicit form of financing provided by the government. The argument has validity although deferred income taxes should nonetheless be *excluded* from the calculation of the WACC because the "government financing" is effectively interest free.

for capitalization of the present value of the future operating lease payments to the balance sheet. This is usually accomplished by finding the present value of the future minimum lease payments as disclosed in the footnotes to the financial statements, using the firm's long-term cost of debt (or the average rate implicit in the leases, if known).

An Illustration

Assume that the following information is known about the Thunderbird Corporation, a U.S.-based entity:

Risk-free rate	6.5%
Risk premium on a well-diversified portfolio ($r_m - r_f$)	7.5%
Equity beta	1.3
Pretax cost of outstanding bonds	10.0%
Effective corporate tax rate	30.0%
Market value of equity	$900 million
Market value of outstanding bonds	$500 million

In addition, a review of Thunderbird's footnotes reveals that the company has certain operating leases, carried off the balance sheet, with an implicit cost of lease financing of 12 percent and the following future minimum lease payments:

In one year	$150 million
In two years	$140 million
In three years	$130 million
In four years	$120 million
In five years	$110 million
Thereafter	$400 million
Total	$1,050 million

The present value (PV), and hence estimated market value, of the operating leases can be calculated as follows:

PV of $150 million @ 12 percent in one year:	$150 × 0.89	=	133.93
PV of $140 million @ 12 percent in two years:	$140 × 0.797	=	111.61
PV of $130 million @ 12 percent in three years:	$130 × 0.712	=	92.53
PV of $120 million @ 12 percent in four years:	$120 × 0.636	=	76.26
PV of $110 million @ 12 percent in five years:	$110 × 0.567	=	62.42
PV of $400 million @ 12 percent in six years:	$400 × 0.507	=	202.65
		Present value	679.40

And Thunderbird's WACC can be estimated as follows:

$$r_e = r_f + \beta_e \times (r_m - r_f)$$
$$= 6.5\% + 1.3 \times (7.5\%)$$
$$= 6.5\% + 9.75\% = 16.25\%$$

$$E/V = 900/(900 + 500 + 679.40) \quad = 0.433$$
$$D/V = 500/(900 + 500 + 679.40) \quad = 0.240$$
$$\tilde{D}/V = 679.40/(900 + 500 + 679.40) = 0.327$$

$$\text{WACC} = (E/V) \times r_e + (D/V) \times r_d \times (1 - tx) + (\tilde{D}/V) \times \tilde{r}_d \times (1 - tx)$$
$$= (0.433 \times 16.25\%) + [0.240 \times 10.0\% \times (1 - 0.30)] +$$
$$[0.327 \times 12.0\% \times (1 - 0.30)]$$
$$= 11.46\%$$

If Thunderbird's outstanding operating leases had not been considered, the company's WACC would have been 12.95 percent, representing an error of 149 basis points.

Appendix 3B
Some Frequently Asked Questions and Answers About DCFA and Earnings Multiples Valuation

Firm valuation is an art to be learned. In many respects, it lacks the precision associated with valuing a debenture or other fixed-return financial asset in which the future cash flows are relatively certain. There are few absolute principles to be followed when valuing a target company; however, there are many rules of thumb. Consequently, here we address some of the frequently asked questions about the discounted cash flow analysis (DCFA) and earnings multiples valuation.

1. Which WACC should I use — the target's or the acquirer's?

The only theoretically defensible discount rate is that rate which reflects the implicit riskiness of the target's cash flows, which is presumably the target's WACC. Survey results indicate, however, that acquirers frequently use their own WACC or some hurdle rate. For example, in a survey of 392 chief financial officers, Graham and Harvey (2001) found that more than 50 percent of the respondents indicated that they "always or almost always" use a hurdle rate when deciding which acquisitions to pursue. Two potential dysfunctional consequences of this practice are (1) the possibility of overpaying for an acquisition and (2) the possibility of selecting only those acquisitions with a riskier cash flow profile than the acquirer's.

For example, entertainment industry analysts have long speculated that the use of an inappropriate hurdle rate was the principal source of problems associated with Sony Corporation's 1989 acquisition of Columbia Picture Entertainment Inc. Three years after the acquisition, Sony wrote off 80 percent of its original investment. Analysts conjecture that Sony's valuation analysts probably "ran the numbers" using Sony's much lower WACC and instead should have used a much higher discount rate reflective of the uncertain cash flows that characterize the U.S. entertainment industry. (The risk-free rate in Japan has frequently been as low as 0 percent, with corporate borrowing rates often averaging only 2 to 4 percent.)

2. What discount rate should I use to value a foreign acquisition?

The "best practices" answer is always the same: Use the discount rate that best reflects the riskiness of the entity's free cash flows. The survey results of Graham and Harvey (2001), however, are again enlightening. When asked "How frequently would your company use the following discount rates when evaluating a new project in an overseas market?," the respondents indicated "always or almost always" as follows:

Response	Percent
The discount rate of the acquirer	59
A risk-matched discount rate (considering both country and industry)	51
A discount rate for the foreign country	35

Thus, although some acquirers do apparently try to match the discount rate to the particular country/industry risk profile, many do not. The obvious question then is, "Are these companies failing to undertake appropriate acquisitions because an inappropriate discount rate is being used?"

3. How can DCFA be implemented in a multidivision company?

Ideally, the best way to implement DCFA in a multidivisional company is by modeling the future performance of each division separately, applying a distinct WACC representative of the riskiness of each division, and then accumulating the individual values to arrive at an aggregate firm value. This framework is sometimes referred to as the **break-up method** or **sum-of-the-parts method.** This analysis may be particularly instructive for conglomerates and holding companies as they try to assess whether greater shareholder value is created when the individual business units are operated as a single entity or on a stand-alone basis. Recall, however, that the existing evidence regarding the market's ability to fairly value conglomerates and holding companies is unambiguous: The average conglomerate discount is about 15 percent.*

4. Does the WACC need to be recalibrated if a company's capital structure changes?

Theoretically, yes; practically, no. Unless there are material changes to a firm's capital structure, as may occur in an acquisition followed by a restructur-

*See Berger and Ofek (1995).

ing, most analysts are comfortable using the same WACC over the forecast horizon. Trying to recalibrate the WACC after a change in capital structure leads to a problem of circular logic: The WACC is initially calculated to enable one to estimate the equity value of a firm, but to recalibrate the WACC, one needs an estimate of the future equity value of the firm (relative to total firm value). Hence, where material changes in capital structure are expected to be a concern, the analyst should consider using the adjusted present value (APV) approach (see Chapter 4).

5. When I use the Capital Asset Pricing Model (CAPM) to calculate the cost of equity, should the beta be levered or unlevered?

A company is subject to two types of risk: business risk, or the risk associated with its operations, and financial risk, or the risk associated with its capital structure (specifically, the amount of debt in its capital structure). As a consequence, it is possible to identify two different betas:

- The levered beta, or equity beta, which reflects the systematic component of a company's business risk and financial risk

- The unlevered beta, or asset beta, which reflects only the systematic component of its business risk

If a company does not have any debt in its capital structure, the asset beta and the equity beta are identical. If the company is financed with debt *and* equity, however, the equity beta will be higher than the asset beta. Indeed, the higher the amount of leverage, the higher the financial risk and, therefore, the higher the equity beta.

When an analyst wants to value a company using a direct valuation method, he or she needs to calculate the cost of equity, most often using the CAPM. For DCFA and the equity method, the appropriate discount rate is the cost of levered equity, which relies on the equity beta. For APV, however, the appropriate discount rate is the cost of unlevered equity, which relies on the asset beta. Indeed, a key feature of the APV framework is that it distinguishes between the free cash flows associated with a company's operations, discounted at the cost of unlevered equity, and the interest tax shield, discounted at the cost of debt.

Most analysts estimate the unlevered beta (β_u) by the following equation:

$$\beta_u = \frac{E}{E + D(1 - tx)} \times \beta_E$$

Although it is important to understand the distinction between the asset beta and the equity beta, the effect on firm valuation of choosing one over the other is minimal. This explains why, in practice, some analysts use the equity beta, even for APV valuation.

6. **Some research firms use the EV/EBITDA multiple to value companies. What is this multiple and how does it relate to the P/EBITDA multiple?**

Some analysts use the EV/EBITDA multiple, or the entity value or enterprise value–to–earnings before interest, taxes, depreciation, and amortization multiple, where

Entity Value = Market Value of Equity + Market Value of Debt

when the P/EBITDA multiple (where P is market price per share) is not appropriate. The difference between the P/EBITDA multiple and the EV/EBITDA multiple relates to the capital structure of a company. For example, consider two companies, A and B, with the following characteristics:

Per Share	Company A	Company B
Equity value	100	100
Debt value	0	100
EBITDA	10	10

Notice that although the P/EBITDA multiple is 10 for both companies, the EV/EBITDA multiple is different, reflecting the different capital structures. Company A is financed with 100 percent equity, whereas Company B is financed 50 percent with equity and 50 percent with debt. As a result, the EV/EBITDA multiple is 10 for Company A and 20 for Company B. If a company does not have any debt, the P/EBITDA multiple will equal the EV/EBITDA multiple.

In practice, both multiples are used. The choice between one versus the other depends on the analyst's objective. If the analyst is trying to value the equity value of a firm (i.e., how much is a stake in this company worth?), it is appropriate to use the P/EBITDA multiple, whereas if the objective is to value the entity in total (i.e., how much is the company worth?), then the EV/EBITDA is technically more appropriate.

7. **The price per share–to–earnings per share (P/E) multiple framework for firm valuation is straightforward and easy to apply. What is confusing, however, is why some firms have a higher multiple than others. Why is it often said that a high P/E multiple is indicative of high future growth?**

The future value of a company (and hence, its current share price) is essentially driven by two components: the firm's value excluding any growth opportunities and the value of its growth opportunities. Suppose that a company had invested in several capital projects that will generate a positive free cash flow in the future. According to the **dividend-growth model,** a widely used model for valuing equity securities, the present value of a company, as captured by its current share price, will equal the sum of its future dividend payments, discounted at the cost of equity:

$$PPS = \sum_{t=1}^{\infty} \frac{DPS_t}{(1 + r_e)^t} \qquad \text{(3B.1)}$$

where PPS is the market price per share; DPS_t, the dividend paid per share; and, r_e, the company's cost of equity.

In order to simplify Equation 3B.1, let's assume that in the future, the dividends paid will be constant. Thus, Equation 3B.1 represents the present value of a perpetuity and collapses to the following:

$$PPS = \frac{DPS}{r_e} \qquad \text{(3B.2)}$$

According to this equation, a company can maximize its shareholders' wealth by distributing 100 percent of its earnings as dividends. And if the company does so, the dividend per share becomes equal to the earnings per share (EPS), and Equation 3B.2 becomes

$$PPS = \frac{EPS}{r_e} \qquad \text{(3B.3)}$$

Now suppose that the company has another investment opportunity that will generate a positive net present value. As a consequence of the new project, Equation 3B.3 becomes

$$PPS = \frac{EPS}{r_e} + NPVGO \qquad \text{(3B.4)}$$

where NPVGO is the net present value of the growth (investment) opportunity. Equation 3B.4 shows that the value of the company is now being driven by two components: the value of the company excluding any new growth opportunities (EPS/r_e) and the future value of the new growth opportunity (NPVGO).

If we divide Equation 3B.4 by EPS, it becomes

$$\frac{PPS}{EPS} = \frac{1}{r_e} + \frac{NPVGO}{EPS} \qquad \text{(3B.5)}$$

The left-hand side of this equation is simply the P/E multiple; the right-hand side shows that a firm's P/E multiple is related to two elements: the firm's cost of equity and the present value of its future growth opportunities. The higher the firm's cost of equity (i.e., the higher the risk of the stock), the lower the firm's P/E multiple. On the other hand, the higher the firm's NPVGO, the higher the P/E multiple.

Thus, Equation 3B.5 helps us to understand why some companies with low earnings have a high P/E multiple (e.g., Compaq, which had an EPS of $0.20 and a P/E ratio of 72 in June 2001), whereas other companies with high earnings carry a low P/E multiple (e.g., Philip Morris, which had an EPS of $3.82 and a P/E multiple of only 12 in June 2001). The difference in the P/E multiples of Compaq and Philip Morris is not driven by the level of earnings but by the level of their future growth opportunities.

Note that, as it refers to the future, NPVGO measures the *expectation* of the market with regard to a company's growth opportunities. Therefore, it is more correct to say that a high P/E ratio means a high *expectation* of growth.

4 Alternative Valuation Models

The Risk of Alternative Valuation Metrics

In April 2000, MicroStrategy, Inc., a software company that creates programs to help businesses sift through large amounts of information about customers, disclosed that the U.S. Securities and Exchange Commission (SEC) was investigating its accounting practices. At issue was MicroStrategy's method of recognizing revenue; the company apparently booked revenues from large contracts immediately rather than over the life of the contract. Not only did the practice contradict revenue accounting principles issued by the American Institute of Certified Public Accountants, but it would cause investors and Wall Street analysts to overvalue the company when price-to-sales valuation multiples were used.

Shortly after the disclosure, MicroStrategy and its independent auditor, PriceWaterhouseCoopers, issued restated financial results. The company's 1997–1999 profit figures of $121,000, $6.2 million, and $12.6 million, respectively, were restated to a loss of $885,000, a loss of $2.3 million, and a loss of $32.5 million. Furthermore, the company's 1999 revenues were revised from $205.3 million to $151.3 million, a revision of more than 25 percent.*

*M. Schroeder, "SEC Widens MicroStrategy Investigation," *The Wall Street Journal,* 24 May 2000, C1.

Although the company's share price reached $333 per share on 10 March 2000, it eventually fell to just $22.25 per share by May 2000. Investors who purchased the stock before the revenue restatement had apparently grossly overpaid for the stock.

● ● ●

Because of limitations associated with the implementation of the traditional valuation models, the 1990s saw the development of a number of alternative valuation frameworks. For example, earnings multiples analysis requires that a company have a history of earnings; however, the emergence of the "new economy," with the rapid listing of new ventures lacking a history of earnings, forced analysts to find an alternative to earnings multiples analysis, namely, **price-to-sales analysis.** Discounted cash flow analysis (DCFA), on the other hand, assumes that the capital structure of a company is stable over time. In the case of a leveraged buyout or a debt restructuring after a merger or an acquisition, the analyst needs an alternative approach that overcomes the assumption of stable capital structure underlying DCFA, for example, the **adjusted present value (APV) method** or the **equity method.** Furthermore, shortcomings in the measurement of accounting income, and hence permanent earnings, caused some analysts to seek improved measures of firm value through such classical frameworks as **economic value analysis.** Finally, where investments are structured as sequential rounds of financing, some analysts have found it useful to model the valuation using **real options analysis.**

This chapter addresses the following key questions:

- How can the value of a company be estimated in the absence of earnings or cash flows?

- How can a company be valued when its capital structure changes?

- What is economic value analysis and how can it be used to value a target company?

- How can real options be used to value a company's equity?

Valuation in the Absence of Earnings or Cash Flows

The end of the old millennium and the start of the new witnessed a traumatic period for valuation analysts and investors schooled in the traditional methods of firm valuation. The evolution of the "new economy," with its emphasis on electronic commerce, along with a widespread attitude of "irrational exuberance" among many market participants, led to a demand for equity investments unparalleled in the United States and elsewhere for more than fifty years.

In the past, a company with little or no prior history of operating earnings had no chance of being taken public by a reputable investment banker, but this era saw entities with little more than a business model and a ".com" in their corporate name being privatized with considerable enthusiasm by the market.[1] The speculative demand for "dot.com" companies that characterized this period posed new challenges for valuation analysts — specifically, how to value an entity that had no history of earnings or cash flows and only questionable prospects of attaining profitability in the foreseeable future. Obviously, a period of considerable change and introspection had arrived in which new valuation techniques were called for.

Foremost among these new approaches was the market price–to–sales (P/Sales) or the market price–to–revenue multiple approach:

$$P/Sales = \frac{Total\ Firm\ Market\ Capitalization}{Total\ Annual\ Firm\ Revenues}$$

Under this framework, target firm value is a function of two variables: (1) an appropriate P/Sales multiple, and (2) future sustainable operating revenues. Once an appropriate P/Sales multiple is determined, often by calculating an adjusted industry average multiple for a set of comparably risky firms, it is a straightforward exercise for this multiple to be multiplied with an analyst's best estimate of future sustainable revenues to arrive at an estimate of firm value. Dividing the estimated firm value by the number of actual (or expected) shares outstanding yields a forward price objective per share.

To illustrate, consider the case of GoAmerica, Inc., a leading provider of wireless Internet services. In June 2000, U.S. Bancorp Piper Jaffray initiated coverage of GoAmerica with a "buy" rating and a $30-per-share price target. Analysts for Piper Jaffray estimated that revenues for the full year 2000 would total $15.4 million, although net income, earnings before interest, taxes, depreciation, and amortization (EBITDA), and free cash flows would all remain negative. A comparable company analysis (see Exhibit 4.1) revealed that GoAmerica's closest comparable companies were trading at an average multiple of sixty to seventy times fiscal 2000 revenue estimates. On the basis of this comparable company data and Piper Jaffray's 2000 revenue estimates of $0.325 per share, Go-

Exhibit 4.1   Comparable Company Matrix: GoAmerica, Inc.*

Comparable Company	Market Price Per Share[†]	Shares Outstanding (in millions)	Market Capitalization (in millions)	Price-to-Sales Multiple
Aether Systems	$142.75	29.5	$4,204	165.1×
Phone.com	69.38	68.9	4,778	58.7
Research In Motion	30.00	78.3	2,349	18.3
Puma Technology	23.00	31.1	715	20.1
Extended Systems	33.94	10.1	341	—
724 Solutions	37.19	35.4	1,317	68.2
Average	$56.04	42.2	$2,284	66.1
Adjusted average[‡]	42.63			41.3
GoAmerica	$5.63	47.4	$267	17.3

*Data provided by U.S. Bancorp Piper Jaffray.
[†]Closing share prices as of 30 May 2000.
[‡]Excludes highest and lowest values.

America would be fairly priced at $21.50 per share if an average compa-
rable company multiple were used (i.e., $0.325 estimated 2000 revenue
per share times 66.1, the average P/Sales multiple) and $13.50 per share if
an adjusted average multiple were used. Piper Jaffray analysts, however,
felt that "GoAmerica's strong market presence, broad sales channels,
and robust product line" should justify a higher-than-average P/Sales
multiple; hence, at $30 per share, GoAmerica would be priced at ap-
proximately ninety-two times estimated 2000 revenues.[2] As the Go-
America case illustrates, P/Sales multiples are frequently adjusted upward (or downward) to reflect changes in market sentiment or for
certain positive (negative) information about a company's current or future performance that is anticipated to affect its share price.

    Although the P/Sales valuation approach overcomes the need for
positive earnings or cash flows, it suffers from a number of limitations.
First, there is the "comparability concern" associated with any type of
comparable company analysis, namely, acceptance of the assumption
that the perceived riskiness of the set of comparable companies is equivalent to the riskiness implied by a target's business model. Second, there
is the concern that estimation of future operating revenues is a reliable
indicator of future target firm earnings and cash flows. Obviously, many
business expenses may arise that may cause a firm with very high revenues to report little or no earnings or cash flows. Finally, there is the concern that when value is based only on revenue estimates, the temptation

to inflate or overstate a firm's future prospects may be overwhelming. This latter concern ultimately led to action by the SEC.

In 2000, the SEC issued staff accounting bulletin (SAB) No. 101, *Revenue Recognition in Financial Statements.* The impetus for SAB No. 101 was concern over the aggressive revenue recognition policies of many Internet companies whose valuations largely depended on future revenue estimates. For example, some of the revenue recognition abuses drawing the scrutiny of the SEC involved booking revenues before contract or service completion, recording Web-site membership fees prematurely, and recording licensing fees prematurely. SAB No. 101 reiterated the long-standing accounting principle that revenues should not be booked until they have been substantially earned. The effect of this official pronouncement was to cause a number of Internet-related companies to adjust downward previously reported revenues, subsequently causing their revenue-based valuations to fall precipitously. (See, for instance, the MicroStrategy vignette at the beginning of this chapter.)

Acceptance of the P/Sales multiple as a valid valuation metric is based largely on the belief that it is more important for companies to grow revenues than earnings. The logic behind this belief is that revenues are a good proxy for marketplace acceptance (and hence growth in market share) and that those firms that can build market share quickly will also achieve profitability and positive free cash flows rapidly.[3] As a method for assessing intrinsic value or setting share price targets, however, the P/Sales metric is inherently flawed. Like earnings multiples valuation, P/Sales multiple valuation is a *relative* valuation approach; it doesn't indicate whether a security is fairly priced but only whether it is fairly priced relative to some peer group. Hence, it is of limited value when valuation comparisons are being made across industry groups or when entire industry groups are mispriced.

A final concern about the P/Sales multiple when used for valuing Internet companies in particular is the basis used for estimating future operating revenue. The selection of exactly which measure of expected Internet usage (or "traffic") is the best proxy for future revenues appears to be open to some debate. Although analysts have relied on many Web usage proxies, the three most common are the number of unique visitors to a Web site, the number of page views, and the number of minutes spent on a firm's Web site. The results of most research to date suggest that the number of unique visitors to a firm's Web site is the traffic proxy most consistently related to future operating revenues and share price. (See Hand 2000; Rajgopal, Kotha, and Venkatchalam 2000; Trueman, Wong, and Zhang 2000; and Dewers and Lev 2000.) Regrettably, some Internet companies have resorted to a variety of techniques to build the *quantity* of their Web traffic without also building the *quality* of that traffic, creating a considerable source of valuation error.

Most seasoned analysts consider it dangerous to use P/Sales multiples as a stand-alone valuation approach. Instead, they consider it more prudent to use such multiples in conjunction with other methods, such as DCFA, even if based on somewhat long and potentially unreliable forecast horizons.

Valuation When Capital Structure Changes

One of the major assumptions underlying DCFA is that the capital structure of a target firm is stable over the forecast horizon. Indeed, when a firm's capital structure changes, the discount rate (weighted average cost of capital, or WACC) also changes, which affects the present value of the target company. When capital structure instability is present, one option for analysts is to recalculate the WACC each time the capital structure changes. This option, however, has one major disadvantage: It leads to a problem of circularity. Specifically, the weights of equity and debt in the calculation of the WACC depend on the market values of equity and debt, but as the market value of equity is not observable, it is inferred from total firm value, which is estimated by discounting the free cash flows at the WACC; therefore, the market value of equity depends on the WACC. Although the problem of circularity can be solved by iterating the financial model used for calculating the present value of the target company, this solution increases the risk of miscalculation (see Luehrman 1997a and 1997b).

Alternatively, when the capital structure of a target company materially changes over the forecast horizon, another option is to use the APV method or equity method. We consider each of these alternatives in greater detail.

Adjusted Present Value.   Like DCFA, the APV framework is an entity method — that is, a method that values the entire target company by discounting its free cash flows. For both methods, the value of a target's equity is estimated *indirectly* as the difference between the value of the entity and the market value of its debt. Developed by Stewart Myers of MIT (see Myers 1974) the APV framework distinguishes between two categories of cash flows: (1) the "real" cash flows, or the free cash flows associated with a target's operations, and (2) the "side effects," or the cash flows associated with a target's financial policies. The major side effect for most target companies is the **interest tax shield** associated with any outstanding debt.[4] Since interest payments are tax deductible (recall that dividends are not tax deductible), the use of debt financing actually decreases a target's cash outflow for taxes and thus increases its cash flow from operations and free cash flow. The cash flow savings due to the use of debt financing is called the "interest tax shield" and is calculated as follows:

$$\text{Interest Tax Shield} = \text{Interest Expense} \times tx$$

where tx is the target's effective tax rate.

Like DCFA, APV relies on the principle of **value additivity,** as follows:

$$\text{APV} = \begin{array}{c}\text{Present Value of the}\\\text{Free Cash Flows}\end{array} + \begin{array}{c}\text{Present Value of the}\\\text{Side Effects}\end{array}$$

Because the riskiness of the two components of APV may differ, the two cash flow streams are discounted using different discount rates. The free cash flows are discounted at a rate that reflects the riskiness of the target's assets — the cost of unlevered equity (i.e., the cost of equity assuming that the target is 100 percent equity financed) — whereas the cash flows associated with the interest tax shield are usually discounted using the target's cost of debt (although alternative approaches are also possible as noted below).

The **cost of unlevered equity,** sometimes called the cost of assets, can be calculated using the Capital Asset Pricing Model (CAPM) as follows:

$$r_{eu} = r_f + \beta_{eu}(r_m - r_f) \tag{4.1}$$

where r_{eu} is the cost of unlevered equity; r_f, the risk-free rate; $(r_m - r_f)$ the market risk premium; and β_{eu}, the unlevered equity beta, also called the **asset beta,** equal to[5]

$$\beta_{eu} = \frac{\beta_e}{\left[1 + \dfrac{D}{E}(1 - tx)\right]} \tag{4.2}$$

where β_e is the (levered) equity beta; D/E, the market value of debt divided by the market value of equity; and tx, the effective tax rate.

With respect to the cash flows associated with the interest tax shield, several alternative discount rates are used in practice. (For a review of these approaches, see Ehrhardt and Daves 1999.) Most analysts assume that the risk associated with the interest tax shield is equivalent to the risk associated with a target's debt payments (interest and principal). This approach suggests that the appropriate discount rate is the cost of debt. (This is the approach proposed by Stewart Myers.) Some academics argue, however, that the risk associated with the interest tax shield is higher than the risk associated with a firm's debt payments, largely because although some companies can afford the debt payments, they cannot always benefit from the interest tax shield (because of operating losses). In this context, a second approach is to use the cost of unlevered equity.[6] Finally, a third approach is to use a discount rate somewhere in between the cost of debt and the unlevered cost of equity.

One of the major advantages of the APV method is its flexibility: It allows managers to tailor their valuation analysis by identifying and separately discounting each source of target firm value. Indeed, whereas DCFA bundles the components of value into one cash flow measure (the free cash flow) and one discount rate (the WACC), the APV method unbundles the components of value into several cash flows (the free cash flow and the side effects), discounted at several discount rates according to their riskiness (the cost of unlevered equity, the cost of debt, or some rate in between).

Thus, one of the principal differences between DCFA and APV arises from the treatment of the interest tax shield. Under DCFA, the effect of the interest tax shield is considered in the calculation of the WACC (see the equation for calculating WACC in Chapter 3 on page 78), whereas under APV, it is considered as a separate and distinct cash flow component. Hence, the APV framework frequently yields superior valuation measures compared with DCFA in two situations:

- The target's tax situation is complex (i.e., its marginal tax rate is not unique). When a company borrows funds in several countries, its tax situation becomes complex, and the cash flow effect associated with the interest tax shield will vary with the tax rate in each country. APV enables the analyst to individualize the interest tax shield associated with each source of funds, whereas DCFA does not.

- The target's interest expense is not equal to the cost of debt times the market value of debt. Although a firm's interest expense will be equal to its cost of debt times the market value of the debt for "classic" debt, this is not always the case for other instruments such as zero-coupon bonds or junk bonds. APV enables the analyst to consider the *correct* interest tax shield associated with these alternative debt instruments, whereas DCFA does not.

To illustrate the use of the APV framework, consider the data for the target firm presented in Exhibit 4.2. The calculation of firm value under the APV framework can be approached as a five-step process. The **first step** is calculating the free cash flows associated with the target company's operations. They are given in the Exhibit 4.2.

The **second step** is calculating the cost of unlevered equity. From Equation 4.2, the unlevered beta is given as

$$\beta_{eu} = \frac{3.0}{\left[1 + \frac{200}{50}(1 - 30\%)\right]} = 0.79$$

From Equation 4.1, the cost of unlevered equity can be calculated as

$$r_{eu} = 6.5\% + 0.79 \times 7.5\% = 12.42\%$$

The **third step** is to discount the target firm's free cash flows and its continuing value, using the cost of unlevered equity. We assume that after Year 5, the company will grow by 5 percent per year to perpetuity:

	Year 0	Year 1	Year 2	Year 3	Year 4	Year 5
Free cash flows		2.00	16.00	30.00	44.00	58.00
Continuing value[7]						820.64
Discount factor (12.42%)		0.890	0.791	0.704	0.626	0.557
Present value		1.78	12.66	21.11	27.55	489.30
Total present value	552.40					

The **fourth step** is calculating the interest tax shield and its continuing value and discounting these values at the cost of debt.[8] We assume that from Year 5, the target firm's capital structure is stable. As a consequence, after Year 5 the interest tax shield will grow by 5 percent per year to perpetuity:

Exhibit 4.2 Financial Data for a Target Firm

Pro forma income statement	Year 1	Year 2	Year 3	Year 4	Year 5
EBITDA	100.00	125.00	150.00	175.00	200.00
Less depreciation	(40.00)	(45.00)	(50.00)	(55.00)	(60.00)
Less interest	(16.00)	(16.74)	(16.57)	(15.57)	(14.09)
EBT	44.00	63.26	83.43	104.43	125.91
Less taxes (30%)	(13.20)	(18.98)	(25.03)	(31.33)	(37.77)
NIAT	30.80	44.28	58.40	73.10	88.14

Pro forma balance sheet	Year 0	Year 1	Year 2	Year 3	Year 4	Year 5
Current assets	75.00	95.00	115.00	135.00	155.00	175.00
Net fixed assets	225.00	275.00	325.00	375.00	425.00	475.00
Total assets	300.00	370.00	440.00	510.00	580.00	650.00
Accounts payable	50.00	80.00	110.00	140.00	170.00	200.00
Long-term debt	200.00	209.20	207.13	194.57	176.09	154.39
Shareholders' equity	50.00	80.80	122.87	175.43	233.91	295.61
Total liabilities and equity	300.00	370.00	440.00	510.00	580.00	650.00

Pro forma free cash flows	Year 1	Year 2	Year 3	Year 4	Year 5
EBIT	60.00	80.00	100.00	120.00	140.00
Less taxes	(18.00)	(24.00)	(30.00)	(36.00)	(42.00)
EBIT $(1 - tx)$	42.00	56.00	70.00	84.00	98.00
Add depreciation	40.00	45.00	50.00	55.00	60.00
CFFO	82.00	101.00	120.00	139.00	158.00
Less CapEx	(90.00)	(95.00)	(100.00)	(105.00)	(110.00)
Less change in NWC	10.00	10.00	10.00	10.00	10.00
FCF	2.00	16.00	30.00	44.00	58.00

Additional information

Equity beta	= 3.0
Risk-free rate	= 6.5%
Market risk premium	= 7.5%
Cost of debt	= 8.0%

EBITDA is earnings before interest, taxes, depreciation, and amortization; EBT, earnings before taxes; NIAT, net income after taxes; EBIT, earnings before interest and taxes; tx, effective tax rate; CFFO, cash flow from operations; CapEx, capital expenditure; NWC, net working capital; and FCF, free cash flow.

	Year 0	Year 1	Year 2	Year 3	Year 4	Year 5
Interest tax shield		4.80	5.02	4.97	4.67	4.23
Continuing value[9]						147.91
Discount factor (8.00%)		0.926	0.857	0.794	0.735	0.681
Present value		4.44	4.30	3.95	3.43	103.54
Total present value	119.67					

The **fifth step** is adding the present value of the free cash flows and the present value (PV) of the interest tax shield. Subtracting the value of debt from the aggregate entity value yields the APV value of equity, as follows:

PV of free cash flows	552.40
PV of interest tax shield	119.67
Entity value	672.07
Less debt value	(200.00)
APV equity value	472.07

As shown in Exhibit 4.3, the equity value of the target firm under DCFA is $609.78, or 1.29 times the equity value ($472.07) of the firm under APV. In this instance, DCFA leads to a biased estimate of the value of the target firm's equity for two reasons:

- DCFA assumes that the capital structure of the target firm is stable between Years 0 and 5; however, the capital structure of the company changes from one year to another. In Year 0, the capital structure is composed of 20 percent equity and 80 percent debt. By Year 5, the capital structure is composed of 66 percent equity and 34 percent debt (see the pro forma balance sheet in Exhibit 4.2). As the cost of equity is greater than the cost of debt, the WACC under DCFA is underestimated, and thus the entity value of the target firm is overestimated.

- When calculating the WACC under DCFA, we used the book values of debt and equity to estimate the proportion of equity and the proportion of debt, whereas we should have used the market values. As the market value of equity is not observable, the calculation of the WACC and the entity value often results in biased estimates.[10]

Exhibit 4.3   Valuation of a Target Firm under
Discounted Cash Flow Analysis (DCFA)

The cost of equity is

$$r_e = 6.5\% + 3.0 \times 7.5\% = 29.00\%$$

The weighted average cost of capital (WACC) is

$$WACC = 29\% \times \frac{50}{200 + 50} + 8\% \times (1 - 30\%)$$

$$\times \frac{200}{200 + 50} = 10.28\%$$

The free cash flows and continuing value, discounted using the WACC, are as follows:

	Year 0	Year 1	Year 2	Year 3	Year 4	Year 5
Free cash flows		2.00	16.00	30.00	44.00	58.00
Continuing value*						1,153.41
Discount factor (10.28%)		0.907	0.822	0.746	0.676	0.613
Present value		1.81	13.16	22.37	29.75	742.69
Entity value	809.78					
Less debt value	(200.00)					
DCFA equity value	609.78					

*Calculated using a discount rate of 10.28% (WACC) and a growth rate of 5%.

One of the strengths of APV is that it allows the analyst to tailor a valuation analysis to distinguish between the various sources of value associated with a company's operations. For instance, assume that in the forecast of the target firm's financial statements it was determined that there were two areas of potential operating improvements: (1) an increase in the company's profit margin by 10 percent per year, and (2) a decrease in the company's investment in net working capital. In the past, the target's current assets and current liabilities were assumed to be equal; however, in the future, it is anticipated that the required growth in current assets will be lower than the required growth in current liabilities; that is, an improvement in the management of inventories is possible through, for example, the introduction of new purchasing procedures. Hence, a **sixth step** is distinguishing between the value of the two categories of improvements, which is illustrated in Exhibit 4.4.

As shown in the following pie chart, the APV framework allows the valuation analyst to distinguish between the four components of value for the target firm. Of the $672.07 total entity value, 82 percent relates

Exhibit 4.4   Adjusted Present Value Valuation of a Target Firm:
Valuing the Components of Firm Value

	Year 0	Year 1	Year 2	Year 3	Year 4	Year 5
Base scenario						
EBITDA		90.91	113.64	136.36	159.09	181.82
Less depreciation		(40.00)	(45.00)	(50.00)	(55.00)	(60.00)
EBIT		50.91	68.64	86.36	104.09	121.82
Less taxes (30%)		(15.27)	(20.59)	(25.91)	(31.23)	(36.55)
EBIT $(1 - tx)$		35.64	48.05	60.45	72.86	85.27
Add depreciation		40.00	45.00	50.00	55.00	60.00
Less CapEx		(90.00)	(95.00)	(100.00)	(105.00)	(110.00)
Less change in NWC		0.00	0.00	0.00	0.00	0.00
Free cash flow		(14.36)	(1.95)	10.45	22.86	35.27
Continuing value*						499.07
Discount factor (12.42%)		0.890	0.791	0.704	0.626	0.557
PV		(12.78)	(1.55)	7.36	14.31	297.57
PV of base scenario	304.91					
Profit margin improvement						
Incremental EBITDA		9.09	11.36	13.64	15.91	18.18
Less incremental taxes		(2.73)	(3.41)	(4.09)	(4.77)	(5.45)
Incremental cash flow		6.36	7.95	9.55	11.14	12.73
Continuing value*						180.08
Discount factor (12.42%)		0.890	0.791	0.704	0.626	0.557
PV		5.66	6.29	6.72	6.97	107.37
PV of margin improvement	133.01					
NWC improvement						
Incremental NWC		10.00	10.00	10.00	10.00	10.00
Continuing value*						141.49
Discount factor (12.42%)		0.890	0.791	0.704	0.626	0.557
PV		8.90	7.91	7.04	6.26	84.36
PV of NWC improvement	114.47					

EBITDA is earnings before interest, taxes, depreciation, and amortization; EBIT, earnings before interest and taxes; $tx,$ effective tax rate; CapEx, capital expenditure; NWC, net working capital; and PV, present value.

*Continuing value is calculated with a discount rate of 12.42% (cost of unlevered equity) and a growth rate of 5%.

to the company's operations: 55 percent of the value ($304.91) comes from the base scenario, whereas 24 percent ($133.01) and 21 percent ($114.47) come from improvements in, respectively, the profit margin and net working capital; 18 percent ($119.68) relates to the interest tax shield (as calculated above).

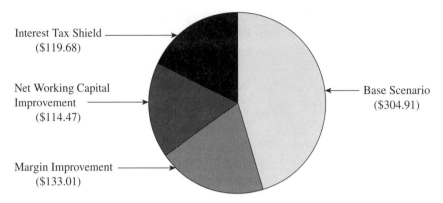

Interest Tax Shield ($119.68)

Net Working Capital Improvement ($114.47)

Margin Improvement ($133.01)

Base Scenario ($304.91)

Total Entity Value = $672.07

DCFA and APV are commonly referred to as "entity" methods. Analysts and managers use them to answer the question, "What is this company worth?" In some cases, the valuation question is not "What is the company worth?" but "What is our stake in this company worth?" This is a question that interests individual equity holders, such as venture capitalists. To answer this latter question, we now consider the equity method.

The Equity Method. Both DCFA and APV value a company's equity *indirectly,* as the difference between the market value of the entity and the market value of its debt. On the other hand, the equity method values a company's equity *directly,* focusing on the **equity cash flows,** or the cash flows available to the equity holders. The equity cash flows are equal to the difference between the free cash flows and the cash flows to the debt holders (interest and principal). Under the equity method, the equity cash flows are discounted at a discount rate that reflects the riskiness of the equity cash flows, namely, the cost of equity.

Like the APV method, the equity method is more appropriate than DCFA when a target's capital structure is changing because (1) it considers the correct interest tax shield associated with the currently outstanding debt instrument(s), and (2) it integrates the cash flow effect of the interest tax shield directly into the equity cash flow rather than into the discount rate.

Unfortunately, the equity method, like DCFA, also suffers from a problem of circularity. Indeed, the cost of equity depends on the market values of equity and debt but because the market value of equity is not observable, it is inferred from the entity value, which is estimated by discounting the free cash flows at the WACC; therefore, the market value of equity depends on the WACC and thus on the cost of equity. This cir-

cularity problem, however, can be resolved, and this resolution can be illustrated using the data for the target firm presented in Exhibit 4.2.
The **first step** is calculating the equity cash flows, as follows:

	Year 1	Year 2	Year 3	Year 4	Year 5
Net income	30.80	44.28	58.40	73.10	88.14
Add depreciation	40.00	45.00	50.00	55.00	60.00
Less CapEx	(90.00)	(95.00)	(100.00)	(105.00)	(110.00)
Less change in NWC	10.00	10.00	10.00	10.00	10.00
Cash flow available	(9.20)	4.28	18.40	33.10	48.14
Change in debt	9.20	(2.07)	(12.56)	(18.48)	(21.70)
Equity cash flow	0.00	2.21	5.84	14.62	26.44

CapEx is capital expenditure; and NWC, net working capital.

The **second step** is estimating the equity value at the end of Year 5, which is equal to the difference between the entity value and the debt value. The entity value is defined as the continuing value, discounted at the WACC. As before, we assume that (1) after Year 5, the company will grow by 5 percent per year to perpetuity, and (2) from Year 5, the company's capital structure will be stable (i.e., the WACC will be constant to perpetuity). In this context, the continuing value (CV) is given by the following expression:

$$CV_5 = E_5 + D_5 = \frac{\text{Free Cash Flow}_5 \times (1 + g)}{\text{WACC}_5 - g} \quad \textbf{(4.3a)}$$

$$CV_5 = E_5 + 154.39 = \frac{58.00 \times (1 + 5\%)}{\text{WACC}_5 - 5\%} \quad \textbf{(4.3b)}$$

where E_5 is the equity value at the end of Year 5; and WACC_5, the WACC at the end of Year 5 and is equal to

$$\text{WACC}_5 = r_{e5} \times \frac{E_5}{D_5 + E_5} + r_{d5} \times (1 - tx) \times \frac{D_5}{D_5 + E_5} \quad \textbf{(4.4a)}$$

$$\text{WACC}_5 = r_{e5} \times \frac{E_5}{154.39 + E_5} + 8\% \times (1 - 30\%) \times \frac{154.39}{154.39 + E_5} \quad \textbf{(4.4b)}$$

where r_{e5} is the cost of equity at the end of Year 5 and is given by the CAPM:

$$r_{e5} = r_f + \beta_{e5} \times (r_m - r_f) \quad \textbf{(4.5a)}$$

$$r_{e5} = 6.5\% + \beta_{e5} \times 7.5\% \quad \textbf{(4.5b)}$$

where β_{e5} is the equity beta at the end of Year 5 and equal to

$$\beta_{e5} = \beta_{eu} \times \left[1 + \frac{D_5}{E_5}(1 - tx) \right] \qquad \textbf{(4.6a)}$$

$$\beta_{e5} = 0.79 \times \left[1 + \frac{154.39}{E_5}(1 - 30\%) \right] \qquad \textbf{(4.6b)}$$

By substituting Equations 4.6b in 4.5b, 4.5b in 4.4b, and 4.4b in 4.3b, the equity value at the end of Year 5 can be estimated to be $721.93.

The **third step** is calculating the present value of the target firm's equity value. The easiest approach is to start with the equity value at the end of Year 5 and to work backward, year by year. By definition, the equity value at the end of Year 4 is equal to the equity cash flow and the equity value in Year 5, discounted at the cost of equity at the end of Year 4. Similarly, the equity value at the end of Year 3 is equal to the equity cash flow and the equity value in Year 3, discounted at the cost of equity at the end of Year 3, and so on. The results for the target firm are as follows:

	Year 0	Year 1	Year 2	Year 3	Year 4	Year 5
Equity cash flows		0.00	2.21	5.84	14.62	26.44
Entity value	602.38	669.85	731.45	786.76	835.28	876.32
Debt value	200.00	209.20	207.13	194.57	176.09	154.39
Equity value	402.38	460.65	524.32	592.19	659.19	721.93
Equity beta	1.06	1.04	1.01	0.97	0.94	0.91
Cost of equity	14.48%	14.30%	14.06%	13.78%	13.53%	13.31%

Note that the present value of the target firm's equity value given by DCFA in Appendix 4C (i.e., where the equity value is reestimated after each change in capital structure) and by the equity method are exactly equal ($402.38). This result is not surprising as both methods rely on the same set of assumptions.

When the capital structure of the target changes, APV and the equity method are more appropriate than DCFA as they quantify the effect of the change in capital structure in the cash flows of the target firm through the interest tax shield. Note that if the capital structure is stable, however, these methods still "work" and also offer a different perspective than DCFA. This explains why many analysts tend to use more than one method to value a company.[11] Another method that they use, to which we now turn, is economic value (EV) analysis. Contrary to DCFA, APV, and the equity method, EV analysis does not rely on cash flows but rather on economic income.

Economic Value Analysis

Economic value analysis is grounded in the concept of **economic income** and the proposition that a firm will build shareholder value only when its economic income is positive.[12] Under this framework, the amount of economic (or shareholder) value created is calculated by estimating a firm's economic income, as follows:

$$\text{Economic Income} = \text{Accounting Income} - \text{Cost of Equity Capital}$$

This approach correctly observes that the traditional accounting measurement of income is deficient in that while a deduction for the opportunity cost of debt capital (i.e., interest expense) is subtracted in the measurement of accounting income, an equivalent charge for the opportunity cost of equity capital is not.

A central tenet of EV analysis is that positive accounting income is a necessary but not sufficient condition for creating shareholder value; the firm must also have positive economic income. A firm that produces positive economic income will create incremental shareholder wealth and consequently will be rewarded with a higher share price. A firm that produces negative economic income, on the other hand, will destroy shareholder value, and this will be manifested in a declining share price and hence declining firm value.

For a single time period, a firm's economic income can be estimated as follows:

$$\text{Economic Income} = \text{Invested Capital} \times (\text{ROIC} - \text{WACC}) \quad \textbf{(4.7)}$$

where ROIC is a firm's return on invested capital at the beginning of the period (BOP) and is calculated as

$$\text{ROIC} = \text{EBIA} \div \text{Invested Capital}_{\text{BOP}}$$

where EBIA is a firm's net operating earnings before interest and amortization charges but after cash taxes. As ROIC, EBIA, and invested capital are accounting-based measures, they suffer from a common set of concerns: They are

- Manipulable by management
- Influenced by accounting convention and changes thereto
- Affected by inflation and currency exchange movements

To overcome some of these problems, and to move these measures closer to their economic counterparts, analysts usually undertake some adjustments, for example:

Invested Capital	Earnings before Interest and Amortization
Total assets	Unlevered operating income after cash taxes
Adjustments	**Adjustments**
Less: Accounts payable	Less: Depreciation on capitalized operating leases
Plus: Present value of operating leases	Plus:
Bad debt reserve	Increase in bad debt reserve
LIFO reserve	Increase in LIFO reserve
Cumulative amortization of goodwill	Goodwill amortization
Net R&D expenditures capitalized and amortized over five years	Increase in net capitalized R&D
Cumulative unusual losses (and gains) after taxes	Unusual loss (gain) after taxes

LIFO is last in, first out; and R&D, research and development.

Under the EV framework, the value of a firm is defined as the sum of the initial capital invested, the present value of the annual economic income calculated over the explicit forecast period, and the present value of the firm's continuing value, discounted using the target's WACC. To illustrate, consider again the financial data for the target firm in Exhibit 4.2.

The calculation of the EV of the target firm can be approached as a four-step process. The **first step** is calculating the EBIA and the invested capital for each year:

	Year 1	Year 2	Year 3	Year 4	Year 5
EBITDA	100.00	125.00	150.00	175.00	200.00
Less depreciation	(40.00)	(45.00)	(50.00)	(55.00)	(60.00)
Less cash taxes	(13.20)	(18.98)	(25.03)	(31.33)	(37.77)
EBIA	46.80	61.02	74.97	88.67	102.23
	Year 0	Year 1	Year 2	Year 3	Year 4
Total assets	300.00	370.00	440.00	510.00	580.00
Less accounts payable	(50.00)	(80.00)	(110.00)	(140.00)	(170.00)
Invested capital	250.00	290.00	330.00	370.00	410.00

EBITDA is earnings before interest, taxes, depreciation, and amortization; and EBIA, earnings before interest and amortization.

The **second step** is calculating the ROIC and the spread above the company's WACC (i.e., the difference between the ROIC and the WACC):

	Year 1	Year 2	Year 3	Year 4	Year 5
ROIC	18.72%	21.04%	22.72%	23.96%	24.93%
Less WACC	10.28%	10.28%	10.28%	10.28%	10.28%
Spread	8.44%	10.76%	12.44%	13.68%	14.65%

The **third step** is calculating the economic income using Equation 4.7:

	Year 1	Year 2	Year 3	Year 4	Year 5
Economic income	21.10	31.21	41.05	50.63	60.08

As for the other valuation frameworks, the continuing value of the target firm must be estimated. The approach many analysts use is as follows:

$$CV_5 = \frac{(EBIA_5 - IC_4 \times WACC) \times (1 + g)}{WACC - g}$$

where IC_4 is the invested capital at the end of Year 4. As before, we assume that after Year 5 the company will grow by 5 percent per year to perpetuity. Therefore:

$$CV_5 = \frac{(102.23 - 410.00 \times 10.28\%) \times (1 + 5\%)}{10.28\% - 5\%} = 1,194.73$$

The **final** step is calculating the target firm's EV equity value:

	Year 0	Year 1	Year 2	Year 3	Year 4	Year 5
Economic income		21.10	31.21	41.05	50.63	60.08
Continuing value						1,194.73
Discount factor (10.28%)		0.907	0.822	0.746	0.676	0.613
Present value		19.13	25.66	30.60	34.23	719.17
Entity value	878.93					
Less debt value	(200.00)					
EV equity value	678.93					

As a tool for valuing companies, EV-based valuations are mathematically equivalent to DCFA-based valuations. Proponents of EV, however, argue that EV is superior because it can be used simultaneously as a valuation metric and as a management tool to help in evaluating and improving firm performance. Proponents also note that the forecasted annual economic income provides a check against actual reported results, indicating whether a firm is on target to achieve an expected share price objective. Critics, on the other hand, observe that the adjustments to invested capital and EBIA are highly subjective, and therefore the forecasted EV (and hence, firm value) depends highly on them. Critics also note that EV analysis fails to explicitly consider the effects of inflation and currency movements on forecasted values. Finally, it is noteworthy that EV analysis may yield misleading results when operating profits are cyclical, when capital expenditures are changing rapidly from historical levels, and when asset values are low or significant intangibles exist. EV valuations appear most reliable for stable companies, operating in low inflation environments, with stable capital expenditures, and readily forecastable earnings.

Exhibit 4.5 presents a graphic comparison of the entity value of a firm under the DCFA, APV, and EV frameworks.

A final valuation framework is gaining in popularity and is appropriate when an investment has the characteristics of an option. This framework is called real options analysis, to which we now turn.

Real Options Analysis

An option provides its owner the right, but not the obligation, to buy (a call option) or to sell (a put option) an underlying asset at a predetermined price, called the "exercise price" or the "strike price," by a predetermined date called the "expiration date." As shown in Exhibit 4.6, the value of an option is driven by five parameters: the value of the underlying asset, the exercise price, the volatility of the value of the underlying asset, the time to expiration, and the risk-free rate of interest.[13] Some analysts have found that it is possible to consider a company's equity as a call option, wherein the underlying asset is the value of the entity and the exercise price is proxied by the market value of the company's debt. In this context, option pricing models, such as the Black-Scholes Model, can be used for valuing a target's equity. (For an application of the Black-Scholes Model to real options, see Luehrman 1998.)

Academics have studied real options for the past thirty years, but their use in merger and acquisition valuation has been limited, largely for three reasons. First, many analysts are unfamiliar with option pricing

Exhibit 4.5   Comparison of the Entity Value of a Firm

Discounted Cash Flow Analysis	Adjusted Present Value Approach	Economic Value Approach
Present value of free cash flows	Present value of interest tax shield	Present value of economic income
Discount rate: WACC	Discount rate: cost of debt	Discount rate: WACC
—	Present value of free cash flows	Invested capital (beginning of period)
—	Discount rate: unlevered cost of equity	—
Present value of continuing value	Present value of continuing value	Present value of continuing value
Discount rate: WACC	Discount rate: unlevered cost of equity	Discount rate: WACC

Exhibit 4.6   Parameters Driving Option Value

Parameter	Call Option*	Put Option*
Value of the underlying asset	+	−
Exercise price	−	+
Volatility	+	+
Time to expiration	+	+
Risk-free interest rate	+	−

*The signs indicate whether the element has a positive (+) or a negative (−) effect on the value of the option. For instance, an increase in the value of the underlying asset leads to an increase in the value of the call option and a decrease in the value of the put option.

models and argue that the use of real options is too complex. Second, it is not an easy task to value a company using real options. In practice, for example, it is too simplistic to model a target company as a single option; rather, a target must be viewed as a portfolio of options. The problem, however, is that it is difficult to estimate the parameters of each option in the "portfolio," and some of the options may interfere with each other. (For a discussion of combined options, see Copeland and Keenan 1998b.) Finally, real options analysis as a valuation framework works best when the investment occurs in stages, as in the multiple financing rounds that frequently characterize new venture financing. (For some illustrations of real options, see Copeland and Keenan 1998a.)

Appendix 4D provides an illustration of how an analyst can use real options to value a company's equity.

Summary

In this chapter we considered the P/Sales multiple valuation method, the APV approach, the equity method, the EV framework, and real options analysis. Although highly risky as a valuation approach, the P/Sales multiple may be the most reliable framework to use when a company has no current earnings or cash flows and is not expected to become profitable in the foreseeable future. APV, as well as the equity method, are appropriate valuation frameworks when a firm's capital structure is expected to change materially during the forecast horizon. EV is a valuation framework with all of the virtues of DCFA but with the added capability of also serving as a performance evaluation tool. Finally, real options analysis may be appropriate when an investment is undertaken via multiple financing rounds, as in new venture financing.

In Chapter 5, we consider a variety of accounting and reporting dilemmas that analysts must resolve *before* undertaking any valuation analysis using the valuation frameworks discussed thus far.

Notes

1. For example, Ip et al. (2000) indicate that in 1997 fewer than one-third of U.S. initial public offerings (IPOs) handled by the prestigious investment banking firm Goldman Sachs Group, Inc., involved companies with reported losses. In 2000, approximately 80 percent of the domestic IPOs handled by Goldman involved companies with reported losses.

2. As validation of their price target, analysts at Piper Jaffray also conducted a ten-year DCFA. The results of this analysis are summarized in Appendix 4A.

3. For an instructive exposition on the use of revenues as a proxy for competitive advantage and market share, see Moore (2000).

4. Luehrman (1997a) notes that other "side effects" include the costs of financial distress, subsidies, and hedges as well as issue costs.

5. Many analysts use Equation 4.2 to estimate the unlevered equity beta; however, it leads to a biased estimate of β_{eu} because it assumes that the company's debt is risk free. A precise estimate is given by

$$\beta_{eu} = \frac{\beta_e + \beta_d \times (1 - tx)}{\left[1 + \dfrac{D}{E}(1 - tx)\right]}$$

where β_d is the beta of the company's debt.

6. This is the approach used by Kaplan and Ruback (1995), which leads to the compressed APV method or capital cash flow analysis (CCFA).

7. The continuing value is calculated using the free cash flow method (see Chapter 3), with a discount rate of 12.42 percent (cost of unlevered equity) and a growth rate of 5 percent.

8. We discount these cash flow streams at the cost of debt as this is the approach most analysts use. For an illustration of capital cash flow analysis (CCFA), where the interest tax shield and its continuing value are discounted at the cost of unlevered equity, see Appendix 4B.

9. The continuing value is calculated using a discount rate of 8 percent (cost of debt) and a growth rate of 5 percent.

10. It is possible to reduce these biases by iterating the model used for calculating the present value of the company. An illustration is given in Appendix 4C.

11. Graham and Harvey (2001) indicate that a survey of 392 chief financial officers showed that fewer than 11 percent reported using APV regularly.

12. In recent years, EV analysis has been popularized by the consulting firm of Stern Stewart & Company under the name Economic Value Added, or EVA®. (See Stewart 1991.) It is noteworthy that the roots of EV analysis and EVA® can be traced to economic thought that occurred more than a century ago (see Marshall 1890) and that was previously popularized in the 1960s as the concept of "residual income." Consequently, some critics refer to EVA® as "old wine in new bottles."

13. There are two categories of options: **European options,** which cannot be exercised before their expiration date, and **American options,** which can be exercised at any time before their expiration date.

Appendix 4A
Discounted Cash
Flow Analysis:
GoAmerica, Inc.

Basic Assumptions	
Estimated revenue growth Years 4–5	25.0%
Estimated revenue growth Years 6–10	12.5%
Expected operating margin Years 4–5	27.5%
Expected operating margin Years 6–10	30.5%
Tax rate (expected)	36.0%
Depreciation rate as percentage of revenues	2.0%
Working capital as percentage of revenues	3.1%
CapEx rate as percentage of revenues	1.2%
Discount rate (WACC)	15.3%
Total debt outstanding (millions)	$5.5
Total cash on hand (millions)	$170.1
Shares outstanding (millions)	23.9
Terminal multiple-x FCF Year 10	10
Market capitalization (millions)	**$738.2**
Approximate share price	**$30.9**
Corresponding P/E on Year 1 EPS	(16.2)
Corresponding P/E on Year 2 EPS	(11.9)
Corresponding P/S on Year 1 revenue	47.9
Corresponding P/S on Year 2 revenue	5.0

	Year										Ter-minal
	1	2	3	4	5	6	7	8	9	10	
Revenue	$15	$147	$337	$421	$526	$592	$666	$749	$842	$948	
EBIT	(50)	(67)	(33)	116	145	180	203	228	257	289	
Cash taxes on EBIT	0	0	1	42	52	65	73	82	92	104	
NOPLAT	(50)	(67)	(34)	74	93	115	130	146	164	185	
Depreciation/ amortization	(1)	(2)	(3)	8	11	12	13	15	17	19	
Gross cash flow	(51)	(69)	(37)	82	103	127	143	161	181	204	
Change in working capital	0	5	10	13	16	18	21	23	26	29	
CapEx	0	2	4	5	6	7	8	9	10	11	
Free cash flow	(52)	(76)	(52)	64	80	102	115	129	145	163	1,632
Present value	(48)	(60)	(36)	39	42	46	45	44	43	42	417
EBIT	(50)	(67)	(33)	116	145	180	203	228	257	289	
Net interest income	4	5	4	5	6	6	7	8	9	10	
Pretax income	(46)	(62)	(30)	120	150	187	210	236	266	299	
Taxes	0	0	1	43	54	67	76	85	96	108	
Net income	(46)	(62)	(31)	77	96	120	135	151	170	192	

Sum DCF	$156
Terminal value	$417
Excess cash at beginning	$164
Fully discounted value (market cap)	$738
Approximate share price	**$30.9**

Reprinted with permission from U.S. Bancorp Piper Jaffray Equity Research. Figures are in millions, except per share. CapEx is capital expenditure; WACC, weighted average cost of capital; FCF, free cash flow; P/E, market price per share–to–earnings per share; EPS, earnings per share; P/S, price-to-sales; EBIT, earnings before interest and taxes; NOPLAT, net operating profit less adjusted taxes; and DCF, discounted cash flow.

Appendix 4B
Capital Cash Flow
Analysis

This appendix explains how to use capital cash flow analysis (CCFA) when assessing firm value. CCFA is similar to APV except that under CCFA, the value of the interest tax shield is calculated by discounting with the unlevered cost of equity, as opposed to the cost of debt. The CCFA method is illustrated using the data for the target firm in Exhibit 4.2.

The first three steps of the APV and the CFFA approaches are identical.

The **fourth step** under CCFA is calculating the interest tax shield and its continuing value, discounting these values at the cost of unlevered equity:

	Year 0	Year 1	Year 2	Year 3	Year 4	Year 5
Interest tax shield		4.80	5.02	4.97	4.67	4.23
Continuing value*						59.79
Discount factor (12.42%)		0.890	0.791	0.704	0.626	0.557
Present value		4.27	3.97	3.50	2.92	35.65
Total	50.32					

*Continuing value is calculated with a discount rate of 12.42% (cost of unlevered equity) and a growth rate of 5%.

Note that the present value of the interest tax shield under CCFA ($50.32) is lower than that under APV ($119.67). This result is not surprising as the discount rate used for CCFA (12.42 percent) is higher than the discount rate used under APV (8.00 percent).

The **fifth step** under CCFA is to add the present value (PV) of the free cash flows and the present value of the interest tax shield:

PV of free cash flows	552.40
PV of interest tax shield	50.32
Entity value	602.71
Less debt value	(200.00)
Equity value of firm	402.71

The equity value of the firm given by CCFA ($402.71) is 15 percent lower than the equity value given by the APV approach ($472.07). The use of CCFA for valuation purposes should be considered when it is uncertain whether the target and the acquirer can benefit from the interest tax shield.

Appendix 4C
DCFA When a Firm's Capital Structure Changes

This appendix explains how to solve the problem of circularity for a target firm with the use of discounted cash flow analysis (DCFA).

The **first step** is calculating the free cash flows, which are given for the target firm in Exhibit 4.2.

The **second step** is estimating the entity value at the end of Year 5, defined as the continuing value discounted at the WACC. As before, we assume that (1) after Year 5, the company will grow by 5 percent per year to perpetuity, and (2) from Year 5, the company's capital structure will be stable, which means that the WACC will be constant to perpetuity. In this context, the continuing value (CV) is given by the following expressions:

$$CV_5 = E_5 + D_5 = \frac{\text{Free Cash Flow}_5 \times (1 + g)}{\text{WACC}_5 - g} \qquad \textbf{(4C.1a)}$$

$$CV_5 = E_5 + 154.39 = \frac{58.00 \times (1 + 5\%)}{\text{WACC}_5 - 5\%} \qquad \textbf{(4C.1b)}$$

where E_5 is the equity value at the end of Year 5; D_5, the value of debt at the end of Year 5; and WACC$_5$, the WACC at the end of Year 5, equal to

$$\text{WACC}_5 = r_{e5} \times \frac{E_5}{D_5 + E_5} + r_{d5} \times (1 - tx) \times \frac{D_5}{D_5 + E_5} \qquad \textbf{(4C.2a)}$$

$$\text{WACC}_5 = r_{e5} \times \frac{E_5}{154.39 + E_5} + 8\% \times (1 - 30\%) \times \frac{154.39}{154.39 + E_5} \qquad \textbf{(4C.2b)}$$

where r_{e5} is the cost of equity at the end of Year 5, given by the Capital Asset Pricing Model (CAPM):

$$r_{e5} = r_f + \beta_{e5} \times (r_m - r_f) \qquad \textbf{(4C.3a)}$$

$$r_{e5} = 6.5\% + \beta_{e5} \times 7.5\% \qquad \textbf{(4C.3b)}$$

where β_{e5} is the equity beta at the end of Year 5, equal to

$$\beta_{e5} = \beta_{eu} \times \left[1 + \frac{D_5}{E_5}(1 - tx)\right] \qquad \textbf{(4C.4a)}$$

$$\beta_{e5} = 0.79 \times \left[1 + \frac{154.39}{E_5}(1 - 30\%)\right] \qquad \textbf{(4C.4b)}$$

By substituting Equations 4C.4b in 4C.3b, 4C.3b in 4C.2b, and 4C.2b in 4C.1b, the entity value at the end of Year 5 can be estimated to be $876.32.

The **third step** is calculating the present value of the target firm's entity value. The easiest approach is to start with the entity value at the end of Year 5 and to work backward, year by year. By definition, the entity value at the end of Year 4 is equal to the free cash flow and the entity value of Year 5, discounted at the WACC at the end of Year 4; the entity value at the end of Year 3 is equal to the entity cash flow and the equity value of Year 3, discounted at the WACC at the end of Year 3; and so on. The results for the target firm are as follows:

	Year 0	Year 1	Year 2	Year 3	Year 4	Year 5
Free cash flows		2.00	16.00	30.00	44.00	58.00
Entity value	602.38	669.85	731.45	786.76	835.28	876.32
Debt value	200.00	209.20	207.13	194.57	176.09	154.39
Equity value of firm	402.38	460.65	524.32	592.19	659.19	721.93
WACC	11.53%	11.59%	11.66%	11.76%	11.86%	11.95%

Therefore, the equity value is $402.38.

Appendix 4D
The Black-Scholes
Model

Although a number of approaches exist for valuing an option, the framework that has gained the greatest acceptance is the Black-Scholes Model. According to the Black-Scholes Model, the value of a European call option (C) is given by

$$C = SN(d_1) - Ee^{-rt}N(d_2)$$

and the value of a European put option (P) is given by

$$P = Ee^{-rt}N(-d_2) - SN(-d_1)$$

where
$$d_1 = \frac{\ln(S/E) + (r + 0.5 \times \sigma^2) \times t}{\sqrt{\sigma^2 \times t}}$$

$$d_2 = d_1 - \sqrt{\sigma^2 \times t}$$

and S is the value of the underlying asset; E, the exercise price; σ, the volatility; t, the time to maturity; r, the risk-free interest rate; and $N(d)$, the probability that a random variable that follows a standardized normal distribution will be lower than or equal to d.

To illustrate how the Black-Scholes Model can be used for valuing a company's equity, consider a company that has assets with a book value of $10 million, and the standard deviation of the asset value is 20 percent. The book value of the company's debt is $7 million, and the debt has a maturity of five years. The five-year treasury bond yield is 10 percent.

It is possible to model the company's equity as a call option, where

- The value of the underlying asset (S) is the book value of the assets, that is, $10 million.

- The value of the exercise price (E) is the book value of the debt, that is, $7 million.

- The volatility (σ) is 20 percent.

- The time to expiration (t) is five years.

- The risk-free rate (r) is 10 percent.

In this context,

$$d_1 = \frac{\ln(10/7) + (0.10 + 0.5 \times 0.20^2) \times 5}{\sqrt{0.20^2 \times 5}}$$

$$= 2.1392 \text{ and } N(d_1) = 0.9838$$

$$d_2 = 2.1392 - \sqrt{0.20^2 \times 5} = 1.6920$$
$$\text{and } N(d_2) = 0.9547$$

Therefore, the company's equity is worth

$$C = 10 \times 0.9838 - 7e^{-10\% \times 5} \times 0.9547 = \$5.78 \text{ million}$$

If the entity value is \$10 million and the equity value is \$5.78 million, the market value of debt is worth \$4.22 million (\$10 − \$5.78).

5 Accounting Dilemmas in Valuation Analysis

MARKET VIEW
Seattle FilmWorks, Inc.—Overvalued?

Seattle FilmWorks, Inc., is a leading direct-to-consumer marketer and provider of high-quality amateur photo-finishing services and products. The company offers an array of services and products primarily on a mail-order basis.

From 1990 to 1997, FilmWorks posted an annual average earnings growth rate of 25 percent. The company's return on equity averaged 32 percent over the period 1992–1997, earning it a spot on Forbes' 1997 list of the "200 Best Small Companies." And not surprisingly, the company's stock price increased from just more than $3 per share in 1992 to more than $22 per share in 1997. A Forbes article, however, attributed the company's spectacular success to a combination of smart marketing and questionable accounting.*

A review of the company's 1997 annual report revealed that FilmWorks capitalized the cost of its direct mailings to prospective customers, amortizing this cost over three years rather than immediately expensing it. Although FilmWorks' treatment of its marketing costs did not explicitly violate generally accepted accounting principles, most analysts agreed that the treatment was highly aggressive. Concern over the company's accounting centered on its implicit assumption that customers would repeat year after year. Because

*Scott Woolley, "An Unflattering Close-up," *Forbes,* 13 January 1997, 58–59.

of the uncertainty surrounding customer behavior, most analysts prefer to see a company expense such costs.

FilmWorks' 1997 annual report revealed that more than $13.8 million in marketing costs remained capitalized on the company's balance sheet, representing more than 27 percent of total assets. If the company had expensed its $17.3 million in 1997 marketing outlays, earnings would have been only $0.48 per share instead of the $0.57 actually reported. On the basis of the company's trailing price-to-earnings multiple of 47 times earnings, FilmWork's share price appeared overvalued by more than $4 per share, or almost 20 percent of its share price.

• • •

The analytical techniques for assessing past and future company performance discussed in Chapter 2 are only part of the valuation process. Any financial review and pro forma analysis would be incomplete without also considering the comparability and reliability of the accounting data. Thus, this chapter addresses the various accounting measurement and reporting dilemmas that may affect valuation analyses. Specifically, this chapter addresses the following key questions:

- Given the differences in generally accepted accounting principles (GAAP) that may exist between companies, and even within a company over time, is it necessary for an analyst to restate a target company's financial statements before undertaking a financial review and pro forma analysis?

- What income statement transformations may be necessary for an analyst to correctly estimate a target company's permanent earnings, and hence free cash flows?

- What balance sheet transformations may be necessary for an analyst to correctly estimate the equity value of a target company?

- What cash flow statement transformations may be necessary for an analyst to correctly estimate a target company's cash flow from operations, and hence free cash flows?

Assessing Economic Reality

To illustrate the kind of accounting dilemma that may arise when a financial review is undertaken, consider the data in Exhibit 5.1. This exhibit shows the income statement and selected financial ratios for two economically identical companies. The two companies, First-in, First-out

Exhibit 5.1 Inventory Costing Methods and Valuation Analysis

	FIFO Company	LIFO Company
Sales	75,000	75,000
Less: Cost of goods sold	(34,500)	(42,300)
Gross margin	40,500	32,700
Less: Other operating expenses	(15,000)	(15,000)
Net income after taxes	25,500	17,700
Earnings per share	2.55	1.77
Current ratio	1.67:1	1.57:1
Working capital	10,800	3,000
Inventory turnover	2:1	3:1
Debt-to-equity ratio	1:5.17	1:4.91
Return on assets	10.8%	8.0%
Return on equity	14%	12.1%
Return on sales	34%	24%

(FIFO) Company and Last-in, First-out (LIFO) Company, differ *only* with regard to the accounting method used for measuring their cost of goods sold and ending inventory. A review of this data tells the story: As inventory costs are rising, FIFO Company appears to be financially better off than LIFO Company. FIFO's earnings (and hence, earnings before interest, taxes, depreciation, and amortization [EBITDA]) are higher; the liquidity indicators of working capital and current ratio are higher; the borrowing capacity, as indicated by the debt-to-equity ratio, is greater; and the profitability indicators of return on sales, return on equity, and return on assets are all superior. Only the inventory turnover ratio appears better for the LIFO Company. Can the analyst assume that these accounting results depict economic reality?

Holding the question of income taxes aside, the answer is an emphatic "No!" The two companies are economically equivalent, despite what the financial data might otherwise indicate. In essence, the different assumptions about inventory cost allocation inherent in LIFO and FIFO mask the real economic performance of the two companies. If the analyst also considers the effect of income taxes and assumes that each company uses the same inventory costing approach for both tax purposes and financial statement reporting, the answer is quite surprising. The LIFO Company is economically more valuable because it preserves greater cash flow as a consequence of its lower taxable earnings. Thus, contrary to the financial indicators, the LIFO Company may be a superior acquisition target. What the valuation analyst must consider is whether to undertake an accounting transformation for one or both companies to make the financial data, and hence the comparative financial analysis, more directly comparable.

At the heart of this, and most, dilemmas in accounting data is the following question: Is the quality of the available accounting information sufficient for financial review and pro forma preparation without some form of data transformation? The following sections discuss key accounting dilemmas relating to the income statement, balance sheet, and statement of cash flows that are likely to be a source of bias in financial data. Practical approaches for dealing with these dilemmas are also considered.

Income Statement Transformations: Forecasting Permanent Earnings and Free Cash Flows

Recurring and Nonrecurring Events

It is widely accepted in the financial community that the purchase price to be paid for an asset should be the present value of the asset's *future* cash flows. Allowing earnings to be a proxy for cash flows, this basic tenet can be restated as: The value of a target company today is the discounted value of the firm's *future* permanent earnings. Therefore, the price that a buyer should be willing to pay for a target company is a function of its expected *recurring* or permanent earnings. Nonrecurring earnings, by their nature, are transitory and should not be considered as part of the future value of the firm.

Thus, preparing pro forma financial statements involves forecasting the future **permanent earnings** of a target company. Permanent earnings — that is, recurring operating earnings excluding such one-time items as discontinued operations, extraordinary and unusual items, and one-time write-offs and charges — are the principal source of free cash flows. One key to successfully forecasting permanent earnings is deciding which income statement accounts to project and which to ignore.

Fortunately, the income statement disclosure practices in most countries make identification of the nonrecurring components of earnings relatively straightforward. These single-period events are typically highlighted on the income statement, often labeled "unusual," "abnormal," or "extraordinary." In some countries, however, where there is no requirement for separately identifying recurring and nonrecurring items, the valuation analyst will need to carefully review the components of

Exhibit 5.2   Nonrecurring Single-Period Events: Shiseido
              Company Ltd. Consolidated Statements of Income
              (for years ended 31 March 1995 and 1994)

	1995	1994
Net sales	¥540,361	¥549,178
Cost of sales	159,164	173,441
Gross profit	381,197	375,737
Selling, general, and administrative expenses	344,707	345,712
Income	26,490	30,025
Other income (expenses)		
Interest and divided income	3,490	5,027
Interest expense	(739)	(1,034)
Gain on sales of marketable securities	3,139	5,120
Loss on earthquake disaster (see below)	(1,692)	—
Loss on close down of stores	(1,320)	—
Others, net	36	(114)
	2,914	8,999
Income before taxes	29,404	39,024
Income taxes	(21,013)	(25,287)
	8,391	13,737
Minority interests in net income of consolidated subsidiaries	2,184	183
Amortization of equity in net assets of consolidated subsidiaries over investment cost	35	47
Equity in earnings of affiliates	652	687
Adjustments on foreign current statement translation	120	14
Net income	¥11,382	¥14,668

The companies suffered a loss resulting from the Hanshin-Awaji earthquake of 17 January 1995 and subsequent fire accidents, which are shown in the accompanying consolidated statements of income for the year ended 31 March 1995. The loss includes provisions for the estimated future loss in connection with the disaster and consists of the following:

Disposal of fixed assets	¥693
Disposal of damaged goods	518
Supports and aids to suffering people in the area	317
Others	164
	¥1,692

Values are in millions of yen.

the income statement to identify any single-period events that should be ignored for pro forma statement purposes. For example, consider the income statement disclosures for Shiseido Company Ltd., a leading Japanese cosmetic retailer. Exhibit 5.2 presents the company's 1995 income statement. On 17 January 1995, the Hanshin district of Osaka, Japan, suffered a massive earthquake that damaged or closed many of the company's retail outlets. The one-time loss associated with this event amounted to nearly ¥1.7 billion (see shaded area of Exhibit 5.2). Unfortunately, this disclosure appears in a section of the income statement that is normally reserved for recurring events, consequently causing some confusion over whether this item should be included in forecasts of the company's permanent earnings. Forecasting this unusual loss into future periods would introduce a downward bias in the valuation of such a company.

The Shiseido illustration presents a fairly clear-cut case, but not all cases are so unambiguous. For example, when a company undertakes a large asset write-off to remove nonproductive assets from the balance sheet, the event is often described as "taking a bath." This cleansing of the balance sheet usually produces an income statement loss that traditionally appears among the recurring items on the income statement. As these write-offs are transitory (or nonrecurring) in nature, they should be ignored for the purposes of forecasting a firm's permanent earnings.

Now let's look at the important area of revenue reporting. Not only do revenue reporting practices often differ among companies in the same industry, but they frequently differ on the basis of local accounting practices of different countries.

Revenue Recognition Policy

Divergent revenue recognition practices may be a considerable source of bias in accounting data. Here are a few cases to consider:

- In Hong Kong, profit on installment sales is generally recognized in proportion to the cash payments received, whereas in the U.K., it is more common to recognize all revenues, except for amounts attributed to financing activities, at the point of sale.

- In Germany, revenue recognition is usually delayed until any right-to-return period has expired. In the United States, recognition usually occurs immediately at the time of sale, as long as it is possible to estimate the amount of any expected sales returns (which are booked at the time of sale).

- In Japan, companies rarely recognize long-term contract revenue on a percentage–of–completed work basis. Instead, Japanese companies usually delay revenue recognition until a contract is completed.

In each of the above illustrations, one of the approaches results in a lower level of current revenues. And not only will revenues be lower, but so too will be EBITDA and estimates of a target's permanent earnings. If the valuation analyst fails to recognize the downward-biasing effect of these revenue recognition policies, any valuation based on these conservative reporting policies is likely to result in a similarly conservative estimate of firm value.

Because forecasted revenues are so important to the process of valuing a firm, a review of a target company's revenue recognition policy is an excellent place to begin an analysis of income statement data. When evaluating the revenue recognition policy of a potential acquisition, it is important for the analyst to compare the policy in use with accepted industry practice. The use of an industry-accepted method is reassuring but does not guarantee that a company's revenue stream will be risk free or even bias free. Aside from the lack of predictability of revenues, valuation analysts are frequently concerned about companies that are overly aggressive in their revenue recognition. Overaggressive revenue recognition is often referred to as **front-end loading** and occurs when a company records sales prematurely, perhaps before a firm offer to buy has been received or, if goods are being produced under contract, before the company has attained sufficient completion levels.[1] Front-end loading is largely a concern in countries such as Canada, the U.K., and the United States. In these countries, it is not uncommon to observe companies using aggressive accounting practices in an effort to *maximize* reported accounting earnings. Front-end loading, however, is rarely a concern in countries such as Germany and Japan. In these countries, the net income reported for accounting purposes is often the same net income reported for tax purposes, and consequently, managers usually use conservative accounting practices to avoid or limit taxation.

Front-end loading causes revenues and EBITDA, as well as estimates of permanent earnings, to be overstated. These overstatements can translate into overly optimistic forecasts of corporate profitability and hence target-firm valuations. Fortunately, a target's current cash flow from operations (CFFO) is largely immune to the effects of aggressive revenue recognition because of the inclusion of such working capital accounts as trade receivables and deferred (or unearned) revenue. Thus, if an analyst compares a company's current net income with its CFFO (the cash-basis equivalent of net income) over multiple periods, it is possible to assess the reliability of the firm's revenue recognition policy to accurately portray its cash flow–generating ability.

Some analysts evaluate the strength of the relationship between a firm's revenue recognition policy and its ability to generate cash flows by calculating a ratio of cash sales to accrual sales. Cash sales, or cash collections on sales, is calculated by adjusting net sales from the income statement for any change in trade receivables and customer prepayments. When the value of this ratio is consistently low (i.e., less than 0.7), it is often indicative of aggressive revenue recognition, suggesting that current levels of reported revenues may be an *inappropriate* basis for forecasting future revenue levels. This information indicates the extent to which a company's revenue recognition method can be relied upon to produce reliable forecasts of future revenues and cash flows when pro forma statements are being developed.

When an analyst evaluates a target's revenue-generating function, he or she is usually trying to identify factors that may cause a deceleration in or deterioration of a company's revenue flows. In addition to identifying the various economywide and firm-specific factors that may adversely affect revenues, the analyst must also evaluate two other risk factors: (1) the risk that the revenues have been recorded too early and that a final sale may not be consummated (i.e., front-end loading risk), and (2) the risk that once consummated, the sale may not yield the anticipated level of cash inflows (i.e., cash collection risk). A firm's exposure to these risks can be effectively minimized through the company's accounting policy choices. A firm that adopts a conservative revenue recognition policy effectively minimizes front-end loading risk. A firm that implements a well-conceived credit-granting policy and maintains a sufficient reserve for covering any future uncollectible amounts effectively minimizes cash collection risk.[2]

Recall that for each type of revenue risk, the accounting model calls for the creation of a reserve account to reflect the degree of riskiness associated with the cash flows generated by the revenue function. These reserve accounts — the allowance for sales returns and the allowance for uncollectible accounts, respectively — are contra-asset accounts on the balance sheet and have parallel accounts on the income statement — sales returns, a contra-revenue account, and the bad debt expense account, respectively. The analyst should review these risk-related accounts with two questions in mind: (1) Does the reserve account indicate that a firm's cash flow from revenues is exposed to a high degree of risk? and (2) does the size of the reserve account appear reasonable given the analyst's assessment of the firm's exposure? The second question requires the analyst to assess the reasonableness of management's estimate of a firm's

Exhibit 5.3   Revenue Recognition Policy Analysis—
              Fairfield Communities, Inc.

	1996	1995
Selected financial data (in millions)		
Time-share revenues (net)	$114,592	$85,460
Loans receivable (net)	152,069	139,674
Loan loss provision	5,390	6,505
Loan loss provisions/time-share revenues (net)	4.7%	7.6%
Industry average	7–9%	

Footnote Excerpt: Allowance for Loan Losses

The company's loans receivable are regionally diversified. Generally, vacation ownership interests and lots are sold under installment contracts requiring a 15 percent downpayment and monthly installments, including interest, for periods of up to seven years.
The company provides for losses on loans receivable by a charge against earnings at the
time of sale at a rate based on historical cancellation experience and management's
estimate of future losses.

riskiness. Some managers have intentionally underestimated these reserve accounts as a means of improving their firm's reported profitability, hence artificially increasing firm value.

To illustrate, consider the revenue recognition policies of Fairfield
Communities, Inc., a U.S.-based developer of time-share resorts. Fairfield sells the annual right to vacation for one week at any of the company's resorts for the duration of a buyer's lifetime. The purchase price
is typically financed with a downpayment of 15 percent and a seven-year,
nonrecourse note for the balance.

An analysis of Fairfield's annual report disclosures (see Exhibit 5.3
for excerpts) reveals that the company's 1996 loan loss provision
amounted to only 4.7 percent of time-share revenues, as contrasted with
the industry average of 7 to 9 percent, and was down from 1995's provision of 7.6 percent. Although Fairfield maintains that its default experience had been well below the industry average, an analyst might be concerned about what might happen if the U.S. economy declines. Given
the nonrecourse nature of its receivables, Fairfield could face a substantial write-off of receivables if, and when, such an economic slowdown occurs. If Fairfield were required to increase its provision for loan losses,
both earnings and total assets would decline, as would estimates of its
future CFFO and hence firm value. In essence, Fairfield's management
appears very aggressive in its assessment of the company's exposure to
possible loan default. A concerned valuation analyst might want to in-

crease the size of the company's loan loss provision, perhaps to the low end of the industry average, *before* undertaking any forecast of permanent earnings.[3]

As the Fairfield Communities case illustrates, when an analyst determines that a company has adopted an aggressive revenue recognition policy, it is possible for him or her to transform questionable data by adjusting the appropriate risk-reserve accounts (i.e., sales returns, bad debts expense, or both). However, when a company has been overly conservative in its revenue recognition policies, it is often difficult for the analyst to know by how much to adjust revenues and receivables.[4]

The Fairfield Communities example also illustrates the difficulty an analyst often faces when analyzing a target company's revenues; it is clearly one of the most important areas of valuation review. Consequently, the analyst should, at a minimum, consider the following items:

- Develop an understanding of a company's principal revenue-generating activity. Prepare a list of the potential macro-level factors (e.g., currency movements, expected inflation rate, interest rate movements) and micro-level factors (e.g., barriers to entry, management track record and stability, new competitor products, labor unrest) that might materially affect the company's revenue flows.

- Review the company's discussion of revenues in the management discussion and analysis and the summary of significant accounting policies to identify how and when it recognizes revenues. If the method in use is not the industry standard, explore any reasons why the company is using an alternative method.

- Compare the cash collections from sales with net sales reported on the income statement, in conjunction with the average receivable collection period. Although there is a naturally occurring lag between revenue recognition and cash collection, the lag period, as measured by the average receivable collection period, should not exceed the normal cash collection cycle of an industry. An excessive or growing lag period usually indicates an aggressive revenue recognition policy, a substandard credit-granting policy, poor credit management, or a combination of these factors.

Valuation analysis begins with a thorough historical financial review. The analysis of a company's revenue recognition policy can be seen to be central to this activity. A review of a company's revenue recognition policy provides evidence of the reliability of that data as a description of past performance and as an indicator of future performance. As most pro forma analyses begin with a projection of revenues, validating the reasonableness of a company's reported revenue streams is crucial to the construction of an effective pro forma statement.

In the next section, we consider the primary cost drivers of a company's operating income: cost of goods sold and depreciation and amortization.

Inventory Costing Policy

For most companies, the two largest deductions from revenue in the calculation of net income before taxes are cost of goods sold and the amortization and depreciation expense. Hence, in addition to the revenue-review tasks just described, the valuation analyst should review the accounting policies associated with these major expense items before undertaking any financial review.

With respect to cost of goods sold, the principal accounting methods used worldwide include FIFO (first-in, first-out), the specific identification method, and the weighted-average method. LIFO (last-in, first-out) is permitted only in such countries as Argentina, Brazil, Germany, Italy, Japan, Mexico, Spain, and the United States.[5] In a few countries, such as Japan, HIFO (highest-price-in, first-price-out) and its close variant, latest purchase price, also may be used.

This diversity in accepted GAAP for inventories makes it essential for the analyst to carefully evaluate a company's chosen inventory method. The LIFO/FIFO illustration in Exhibit 5.1 demonstrates that the inventory costing decision can have a material effect not only on cost of goods sold, and hence a firm's profitability (and any valuations based on earnings), but also on ending inventory on the balance sheet and hence a firm's liquidity and asset management ratios.

Concerned that the balance sheet value of ending inventory under LIFO, HIFO, and latest purchase price might become materially understated relative to its fair value, some countries have mandated the disclosure of certain information to help analysts correctly value a firm's ending inventory. Exhibit 5.4, for example, presents the inventory footnote disclosures from the 1993 General Motors Corporation annual report. These disclosures reveal that GM uses LIFO to value most of its inventory and that if FIFO had been used instead, the inventory values reported on the balance sheet would have been $2,519.0 million and $2,668.1 million higher as of 31 December 1993 and 1992, respectively.

Exhibit 5.4   General Motors Corporation Selected Financial Disclosures

Significant Accounting Policies: Inventories

Inventories are stated, generally, at cost that is not in excess of market. The cost of substantially all U.S. inventories other than the inventories of Saturn Corporation (Saturn) and GM Hughes Electronics Corporation (GMHE) is determined by the last-in, first-out (LIFO) method. If the first-in, first-out (FIFO) method of inventory valuation had been used for inventories valued at LIFO cost, such inventories would have been $2,519.0 million higher at 31 December 1993 and $2,668.1 million higher at 31 December 1992. As a result of decreases in U.S. inventories, certain inventory quantities carried at lower LIFO costs prevailing in prior years, as compared with the costs of current purchases, were liquidated in 1993 and 1992. These inventory adjustments improved pretax operating results by approximately $134.4 million in 1993 and $294.7 million in 1992. The cost of inventories outside the United States and of Saturn and GMHE is determined generally by FIFO or average-cost methods.

Selected financial data (in millions)

	1993	1992
Net income before taxes	$2,575.3	$(3,333.1)
Cost of goods sold	106,421.9	105,248.4
Inventories (net)	8,615.1	9,343.6
Total assets	188,200.9	190,196.0
Shareholders' equity	5,597.5	6,225.6

These disclosed values are often referred to as the **inventory reserve** and can be used not only for revaluing the ending inventory on the balance sheet but also for estimating GM's EBITDA *as if* GM had been using the FIFO method.

To illustrate this data transformation, observe that the inventory reserve is a measure of the *difference* between the current (or replacement) cost of ending inventory and its LIFO-calculated cost basis. By adding the inventory reserve to the balance sheet value of LIFO-costed ending inventory, the analyst is able to restate the inventory account to its current value. Thus, if GM had been using FIFO instead of LIFO, the company's inventory at year end 1993 would have been approximately $11,134.1 (8,615.1 + 2,519.0), instead of the $8,615.1 million actually reported.

Note also that if GM had been using FIFO in all prior years, retained earnings would have been greater by $1,637.35 million ($2,519 × [1 − 0.35]), and the company's tax payments would have increased by $881.65 million ($2,519 × 0.35), assuming an effective tax rate of 35 percent. As the GM data illustrate, the effect of this transformation can be quite material: GM's inventories and shareholders' equity are up by 29 percent![6]

It is also possible to disaggregate GM's LIFO/FIFO earnings differential on a year-by-year basis. The change in the value of the inventory reserve from one year to the next approximates the *difference* between EBITDA under LIFO and that under FIFO. In the case of GM, the inventory reserve at year end 1993 was $2,519.0 million and $2,668.1 million at year end 1992, or a decline of $149.1 million. Thus, GM's 1993 EBITDA under FIFO would have been $149.1 million *less* than that actually reported using LIFO.

Whether the valuation analyst should restate a target's earnings for the use of LIFO or FIFO is debatable. Clearly, if the analyst is comparing one target with another, this restatement is desirable to provide an unbiased comparison of results. If the analyst's task does *not* involve a comparison of acquisition alternatives, however, restatement from LIFO to FIFO may be not only unnecessary but also undesirable. As FIFO tends to produce the highest level of EBITDA, restatement to FIFO may cause an acquirer to pay top dollar for a potential acquisition; on the other hand, restatement from FIFO to LIFO may provide a more realistic valuation.

The question of whether to restate a company's earnings also arises when a firm has changed its method of accounting for inventory and cost of goods sold. To facilitate the comparison of a company's financial results over time, companies are discouraged from making changes in accounting policy. Most accounting changes, other than those mandated by local accounting standard setters, tend to result in a higher level of reported earnings. For example, a change in accounting method from LIFO to FIFO will, under most circumstances, result in a higher level of reported profits. Anecdotal evidence suggests that managers often undertake these policy changes to help disguise a company's otherwise poor operating performance.

Exhibit 5.4 illustrates one additional type of event that occasionally affects the financial results of companies using the LIFO method, namely, that earnings (and hence, firm valuation) may be artificially increased by a reduction in inventory levels. A liquidation of inventory levels may occur because of improved inventory management, because of the adoption of a just-in-time inventory system, or simply in response to a downturn in business. When this occurs, LIFO cost of goods sold consists of two components: (1) the cost of inventory acquired or manufactured during the current period, and (2) the cost of inventory acquired or manufactured during prior periods. Because of creeping inflation, prior-period costs may be much lower than current manufacturing costs, causing EBITDA to be artificially increased. This type of artificial increase is a good example of what some analysts refer to as **phantom profit,** in that the additional profits associated with the inventory liquidation do *not* increase a company's CFFO or free cash flow. In fact, an inventory liquidation will ultimately *reduce* these cash metrics because such phantom profits are subject to income taxes.

Exhibit 5.4 reveals that GM's EBITDA was artificially increased by $134.4 million, or about 5.2 percent, in 1993 and by $294.7 million in 1992, because of LIFO inventory liquidations. As a consequence, the company's income taxes were also increased by approximately $47.1 million and $103.2 million, respectively, assuming an effective tax rate of 35 percent. In the eyes of most experienced analysts, LIFO-inventory liquidation profits are of questionable quality. On the other hand, the additional tax paid on the liquidation profit may be less detrimental to the company than the high cost of carrying excess quantities of inventory.

Following the cost of goods sold, the next largest deduction against operating revenues are the charges associated with the use of a company's long-term assets, namely, the amortization and depreciation expense. Because of the magnitude of these deductions, and therefore their effect on a company's forecasted earnings, we now consider these expenses.

Amortization and Depreciation Policy

One of the most important accounting conventions is the matching concept which requires that all expenses incurred in generating revenues be reported on the income statement in the same period in which the related revenues are reported. Under this convention, companies are required to estimate the amount by which their long-term productive assets — their property, plant, and equipment and such intangible assets as franchises, patents, and goodwill — are used up each period. For capital-intensive companies and companies in industries characterized by significant investments in intangible assets, the amortization and depreciation expenses reported in the income statement can be very large. Although large in value, these estimated expenses are merely allocations of *previous* cash outlays. Consequently, they are added back to earnings when a firm's CFFO and free cash flow are calculated. As a result of adding these amounts back, these cash flow–based metrics remain largely unaffected by a firm's amortization and depreciation policy decisions. Amortization and depreciation policy decisions *do,* however, affect valuations based on price-to-earnings (P/E) or price-to-earnings before interest and taxes (P/EBIT) multiples.

Depreciation Policy. Despite relative worldwide consistency in the set of accepted approaches to estimating depreciation, the valuation analyst must be cognizant of the following practices when undertaking a comparative financial review:

- Many countries — such as Australia, France, Italy, Korea, The Netherlands, Singapore, Sweden, and the U.K. — permit, and sometimes require, the periodic revaluation of noncurrent assets, with depreciation expense calculated not only on an asset's historical cost but also on any revalued amounts. In these countries, the depreciation expense will be overstated compared with depreciation in those countries that do not permit the revaluation of noncurrent assets. Thus, valuation using an unadjusted earnings multiple model (i.e., P/E or P/EBIT) may lead to a systematic understatement of firm value attributable to the higher depreciation charges resulting from noncurrent asset revaluation.

- In countries such as the U.K. and the United States, in which there may be considerable policy differences in the calculation of tax and book income, the prevalent depreciation approach for published financial data is the straight-line method. However, in countries such as Germany, Italy, and Japan, in which there is considerable overlap in the determination of tax and book income, the prevalent depreciation treatment is double-declining balance. In these countries, only those deductions taken against book income may be deducted against taxable income. As a consequence, book income tends to be systematically depressed as managers use accounting policy decisions to lower the amount of income subject to taxation. Thus, unadjusted earnings–based valuation of companies from these countries will be systematically downwardly biased.

- Despite the presence of essentially identical assets, the economic life used in the calculation of depreciation may vary considerably between companies, even within the same industry. For example, Lufthansa, the German airline, depreciates its fleet of aircraft over an average estimated life of ten years, whereas British Air-

ways, its U.K.-based competitor, depreciates its fleet over an estimated life of approximately seventeen years. Thus, the reported
earnings of Lufthansa, and other German companies, will tend to
be consistently lower than those of comparable U.K. firms. This
systematic difference is likely to downwardly bias any unadjusted
earnings–based (but not cash flow–based) valuations.

- In France, Germany, Italy, Belgium, and Korea, a company may
  use excess depreciation (e.g., depreciation charges in addition to
  the regular depreciation allocation) to reduce its exposure to income taxes. These excess charges are usually found in those countries in which book income is used as the basis for calculating corporate income taxes. Excess depreciation will yield a systematic
  downward biasing of reported earnings and, hence, a downward
  biasing of any valuation based on unadjusted earnings.

As the above examples illustrate, there may be considerable depreciation differentials between companies holding essentially equivalent
assets. Information contained in the shareholders' equity accounts often
enables the analyst to restate a company's earnings for excess depreciation. And where differentials exist in estimated useful lives, restatement
adjustments are similarly possible. For example, in the case of Lufthansa
and British Airways, to place the two airlines on a common depreciation
basis, Lufthansa's depreciation charges could be reduced by an average
of 41 percent $(1 - [10/17])$ to reflect Lufthansa's shorter estimated lives
and faster write-off schedule. However, restatement for differences in
systematic depreciation method is usually quite speculative because information relating to the average remaining life of a company's depreciable assets is rarely disclosed.[7] The only certain way of accounting for
depreciation policy differentials is by using a cash flow–based valuation
model. In so doing, not only does the calculation of free cash flow compensate for variance in depreciation method but also for excess depreciation and any variance in estimated lives.

Amortization Policy.   With respect to the amortization of intangible assets, there is almost universal agreement that all intangible assets
should be capitalized to the balance sheet and amortized against earnings over the intangible's expected economic life using the straight-line
method. But, alas, the work of an analyst is rarely so simple. Consider,
for example, the following deviations from this standard:

- Not every country limits the selection of an intangible's amortization policy to the straight-line approach. Australian companies, for example, have come under scrutiny in recent years for use of the inverse-sum-of-the-years'-digits method. Under this method, the periodic amortization charge is an increasing function, with the smallest deductions taken in the early years of an intangible's useful life and the largest in the latter years. In essence, this method rear-end loads the amortization of the intangible, causing current earnings to be relatively overstated.

- Despite the overwhelming use of the straight-line method, there is considerably less agreement regarding the estimated economic life of essentially identical intangible assets, both between and within countries. For example, most companies in Canada adopt a forty-year write-off period for goodwill, whereas in Japan and Korea, a five-year write-off is the norm.

- Not all countries require that amortization be taken on capitalized intangible assets. Consider, for example, the case of Guinness Plc, one of the world's leading beverage companies headquartered in the U.K. Approximately 20 percent of the company's total assets (or £1.4 billion) are represented by the intangible asset "brands," which includes such well-known brand names as Johnnie Walker scotch, Gordon's gin, and Guinness stout. According to the footnotes to the company's financial statements, Guinness takes no amortization against these assets until the directors foresee an end to an asset's useful life. Compared with the reported earnings of a similar company in most other countries, Guinness' earnings would be materially overstated because of its failure to amortize the cost of its acquired brands against the revenues generated by those assets. On the basis of Guinness' 1995 net income before taxes of £876 million and an estimated intangible life of twenty years, the company's pretax earnings would decline annually by approximately £70 million (£1.4 billion ÷ 20 years) if the company amortized its brands account.

- Not all countries require that intangibles be capitalized to the balance sheet. Consider, for example, goodwill. In Italy, Japan, and The Netherlands, goodwill may be written off immediately against shareholders' equity.[8] As a consequence, there is no reduction in the future earnings of a company attributable to the amortization

of goodwill, when amortization is required. Thus, companies using this write-off approach will report higher future earnings than
companies not afforded this opportunity. To illustrate, consider
again Guinness Plc. According to the company's footnotes, by year
end 1995, approximately £1,300 million of acquired goodwill, representing 16 percent of total assets, had been written off to shareholders' equity. If this amount had been capitalized to the balance
sheet and then amortized over twenty years (the maximum period permitted by International Accounting Standards Committee standards), Guinness' 1995 net income before taxes would
have declined by £65 million (£1,300 ÷ 20), or about 7.4 percent.
Although the write-off–to–equity approach is not generally accepted in the United States, companies in the United States often
obtain a similar outcome because a little-known accounting rule
permits companies to minimize the amount of goodwill capitalized to the balance sheet after an acquisition. The U.S. accounting rule allows an acquirer company to establish a fair market
value for "in-process research and development" at an acquired
company and to immediately write off that amount. The higher
the value assigned to the in-process research and development,
the lower the value assigned to goodwill on the consolidated
balance sheet. This rule can be particularly important for high-
technology acquisitions, which are often characterized by significant investments in research and development.

Despite the apparent commonality in accounting practices between
countries, the number and effect of exceptions related to depreciation
and amortization are quite significant. As depreciation and amortization
charges are merely allocations of prior-period cash outlays, the analyst
has two options when attempting to value a target company: (1) Try to
restate for the policy differences, particularly if using an unadjusted
earnings–based valuation model, or (2) use a cash flow–based valuation
model if restatement is impossible and the amounts associated with the
policy differentials appear significant.

The restatement dilemmas discussed thus far have largely concerned
the income statement and the analyst's desire to accurately forecast a
company's permanent earnings. We now consider potential balance sheet
restatements. These restatements are usually driven by the analyst's desire to recalibrate a company's total assets, debt, or net worth. Such re-
calibration may be desirable for estimating in an unbiased manner the
equity value of a target company.

Balance Sheet Transformations: Forecasting the Equity Value of a Company

In this section, we examine a number of balance sheet accounting dilemmas that include asset capitalization, asset revaluation, and off–balance sheet debt. Data transformations for overcoming these dilemmas may be desirable to ensure an unbiased financial review and, in the case of off–balance sheet debt, to avoid an overestimation of the equity value of a target company.

Asset Capitalization Policy

Asset capitalization policy refers to those accounting decisions to record — or not to record — an asset on a company's balance sheet. In general, the differences that may arise between company asset capitalization policies can be segmented into two groups:

- Differences in accounting treatment at the time of asset acquisition

- Differences in accounting treatment subsequent to asset acquisition

The first category involves such policy decisions as whether to capitalize research and development outlays, marketing costs (see the Seattle FilmWorks vignette at the beginning of this chapter), and interest costs on borrowings associated with the self-construction of an asset. The second category involves such policy decisions as whether to amortize the capitalized cost of such intangibles as brand names and goodwill.

Capitalization of an expenditure is important from an earnings and cash flow perspective. An expenditure that is *not* capitalized will be currently expensed, causing a reduction in earnings and cash outflow to occur in the same accounting period. An expenditure that *is* capitalized delays the matching process, causing the income effect to be recognized in a period subsequent to the actual cash outflow (i.e., causing current earnings to be overstated).

Exhibit 5.5 presents the generally accepted asset capitalization policies for a selection of countries. This exhibit indicates that the range of acceptable accounting treatments for research and development expenditures, for example, is quite broad: All research and development is capitalized in Brazil; some may be capitalized in Japan; and almost none may be capitalized in the United States. Reported accounting results will

Exhibit 5.5   Asset Capitalization Policies

Country	Research and Development Costs	Interest on Borrowings
United States	Expensed currently (except for software development companies).	Capitalization required for self-constructed assets.
U.K.	Research costs expensed, but some development costs capitalized.	Capitalization permitted but not widely practiced.
Germany	Expensed currently.	Capitalization permitted but not required.
Italy	May be expensed or, if capitalized, written off over five years; practice is dictated by tax laws.	Interest on debt obtained specifically for the acquisition or construction of an asset must be capitalized (as required by tax law).
Japan	Research and development for existing products expensed currently but capitalized for new products (with five-year write-off).	Capitalization not permitted (except for real estate development companies).
Korea	Usually capitalized if the costs (1) are related to specific products or technology, (2) are identifiable, and (3) are reasonably expected to be recovered; otherwise they are expensed.	Capitalization required.
Sweden	Capitalization is permitted (with five-year write-off).	Capitalization permitted on self-constructed assets.
Brazil	Capitalized; amortized over expected period of benefit.	Capitalization required for self-constructed assets.

also vary globally as a result of differences in the acceptable period of amortization for those research and development expenditures that are capitalized. For example, the permissible period of amortization varies from a fixed five-year period in Japan and Sweden to a variable period of expected benefit in Brazil. Finally, Exhibit 5.5 reveals similar divergence in the accounting for interest costs. Note that the capitalization of interest on borrowings related to the self-construction of an asset is required in Brazil, Korea, and the United States; is not permitted in Japan; and is optional in Germany, Sweden, and the U.K.

These divergences in capitalization and amortization policy raise a number of analytical issues. First, with the exception of companies domiciled in countries such as Germany, Italy, and Japan, in which corporate financial reporting policies are largely driven by tax considerations, the analyst should always investigate for the presence of **rear-end loading.** Regrettably, in an effort to improve current profitability, some companies postpone the recognition of certain expenses, thus violating the matching principle, by inappropriately capitalizing these expenses to the balance sheet. A company engaged in rear-end loading understates current-period expenses, causing current net income and total assets to be overstated. Eventually, the inappropriately deferred expenses *do* pass through to the income statement in the form of amortization, and when that occurs, future-period expenses are overstated, causing net income to be understated.

To illustrate the effects of rear-end loading, consider the case of America Online, Inc. (AOL), a leading provider of electronic interactive services. Under U.S. GAAP, the costs of obtaining new AOL customers may be either immediately expensed or deferred and amortized over the expected average life of an AOL account. AOL initially elected the latter approach and amortized its deferred subscriber acquisition costs over twenty-four months. By 1995, AOL's capitalized marketing costs of more than $77 million exceeded the company's earned income to date by more than $110 million (AOL had an accumulated deficit of $33 million). In late 1996, after considerable public criticism of its asset capitalization policy, AOL took a pretax write-off of $385 million. According to one *Wall Street Journal* writer, the large write-off "underscores just how massive the company's marketing efforts have been — and how illusory its profits really were" (see Sandberg 1996). Investors were apparently pleased to see AOL adopt the more transparent accounting treatment, as the company's share price was bid up considerably in the weeks after the write-off. The new treatment apparently enabled analysts to predict the company's future permanent earnings with greater certainty.[9]

A second analytical concern relates to the divergence from accepted practice regarding such high-profile expenditures as interest costs. U.S. GAAP, as well as that of Brazil and many other countries, require that all costs incurred in the acquisition of an asset and the preparation for its intended use be capitalized into the asset's balance sheet valuation. A natural extension of this general philosophy is to require the capitalization of interest on funds borrowed during the period of an asset's preparation or construction. Under this practice, the amount of interest to be capitalized is based on the interest charges actually incurred for a specific project. If the actual interest charges are unknown, a firm is permitted to use its weighted average cost of debt and the average borrowings associated with the project to estimate the amount of interest to be capitalized. Although the capitalized interest charges are ultimately written off in the form of future depreciation charges, some analysts worry that current earnings will be overstated (as will valuations based on those earnings) because borrowing costs are being capitalized rather than expensed. Although current earnings appear to be improved, cash flows are actually reduced by the debt-service cash payments.

Many professional analysts view the capitalization of interest to be a GAAP-approved form of rear-end loading, observing that because the cash outflow for interest charges occurs currently, it is inappropriate to defer the expense deduction until depreciation of the capitalized expenditures occurs at a later date. These professionals usually scan the footnotes to the company's financial statements to assess the level of currently capitalized interest and then charge those amounts off against retained earnings, net of the related deferred income tax effect, under the assumption that the interest charges were almost certainly expensed for tax purposes.

Exhibit 5.6 presents interest capitalization data for an international real estate development company. The shaded data tell the story: In the absence of interest capitalization, the company would have reported a 1998 net loss before taxes of $33,154 million ($12,260 − $45,414) instead of a net profit of $12,260 million. The restated net loss is much closer to the company's CFFO, which was also negative because of the large cash outflow for borrowing costs.

Asset Revaluation Policy

In the previous section we considered the accounting policy dilemma of whether to *capitalize* a cash expenditure. Now we address the related question of whether to *revalue* an asset to reflect changes in its underlying value that are unrelated to the periodic amortization or depreciation of the asset.

It is well known that an asset's underlying value may increase in response to general or specific inflationary factors. An asset may also decrease in value as a company and/or its products fall out of favor with consumers. When the revenue-producing value of an asset declines — called an "impairment" by accountants — it is generally accepted that the value of the asset should be written down if the diminishment in value is considered to be permanent. An asset write-down is normally executed by a charge against earnings and an equivalent charge against the im-

Exhibit 5.6   Real Estate International, Inc.—Capitalization of Interest

	1997	1998
Consolidated statement of earnings (in millions)		
Total revenues	$36,144	$39,076
Cost and expenses	6,650	11,184
Development service expense	18,290	7,424
Interest expense	39,138	45,414
Interest capitalized	(39,138)	(45,414)
Selling, general, and administrative expenses	6,432	8,208
Total	31,372	26,816
Income before taxes	4,772	12,260
Income taxes	2,196	5,640
Net income	2,576	6,620
Consolidated balance sheet (in millions)		
Assets		
Cash and investments	$59,754	$28,626
Accounts and notes receivable	43,318	61,704
Inventories of land	1,000,230	1,038,394
Rental real estate	26,876	26,488
Property and equipment	6,254	5,624
Other assets	7,622	8,842
Total	1,144,054	1,169,678
Liabilities and shareholders' equity		
Accounts payable and accrued liabilities	47,634	41,816
Notes payable	820,910	840,094
Common stock	200	200
Additional paid-in capital	60,950	60,950
Retained earnings	214,360	226,618
Total	1,144,054	1,169,678

paired asset. If, however, an asset has been previously revalued upward using a revaluation reserve account — a component of shareholders' equity — the write-down should first be charged against the revaluation reserve account. In the event that the write-down exceeds the balance in the revaluation reserve, any excess should be charged against current earnings.

Of concern to most valuation analysts is the vagueness inherent in existing international accounting standards that provides company executives with considerable leeway in the decision of *when* to take such impairment write-downs and in *what amount.*

To avoid paying for essentially worthless or otherwise overvalued assets carried on a target company's balance sheet, an acquirer should always undertake a rigorous due diligence review of all financial statement accounts before finalizing an acquisition price. This review is normally undertaken as part of the historical financial review that precedes the preparation of a target valuation. As the valuation analyst reviews a company's historical data in anticipation of developing pro forma statements, he or she should look for assets and other accounts that should be written down (or up) in value. The analyst's dilemma is usually not that some revaluation will be necessary but rather knowing the amount of the revaluation. Outside consultants are often helpful in providing valuation assistance for specific commodity-related assets such as real estate, antiques, and nonquoted investments.

In some countries, such as the U.K., it is generally accepted practice to periodically revalue those assets whose values are affected by the inflationary effects of general and specific price-level movements. Thus, in these countries much of the analyst's task will already be done. Nonetheless, the analyst will want to verify any upward valuation adjustments to ensure that they have not been overly optimistic. If a company's assets have been revalued in accordance with local GAAP and the analyst wants to compare the financial performance of the revalued firm with that of a company without revaluation, the adjusted financial data will need to be restated. As the revaluation reserve is usually reported as a component of shareholders' equity, the easiest way to effect such a restatement is by writing the previous upward revaluation off against the revalued assets.[10]

Off–Balance Sheet Debt

Off–balance sheet debt —financial obligations that are not reported on the face of the balance sheet — plagues the financial reporting practice of every country in the world. In some countries, the incidence of off–balance sheet debt is more prevalent than in others; however, no country escapes this accounting problem, and its presence places a considerable responsibility on the valuation analyst to identify *all* forms of existing company debt during the due diligence review.[11] The three most common forms of off–balance sheet debt are

- Unconsolidated debt of a subsidiary or joint venture
- Contingent liabilities
- Executory contracts

Unconsolidated Debt. Generally accepted accounting practice with respect to the consolidation of controlled subsidiaries varies greatly among countries. In the United States, the financial results of all majority-controlled subsidiaries (except those in bankruptcy or in the process of being sold) must be consolidated with the financial results of the parent company. In other countries, however, controlled subsidiaries may remain unconsolidated. This presents the challenging situation that debt obligations legally attributable to a parent company may remain unconsolidated. Even in the United States, however, the debt of a joint venture that is guaranteed by the venture partners may remain off the balance sheet to the partners because joint ventures are accounted for by the equity method (see Exhibit 6.1). As a consequence, the debt position of the parent will appear less highly leveraged than in fact it really is. To overcome this disclosure deficiency, it is a simple matter for the analyst to increase both the assets and the liabilities of the parent company to reflect the quantity of subsidiary debt carried on the books of the unconsolidated affiliate or joint venture that may accrue to the parent by virtue of legal guarantees. This restatement will permit an analyst to obtain a clearer picture of a parent's potential outstanding debt.

To illustrate the extent to which unconsolidated debt may affect a parent's solvency, consider the case of General Motors and its wholly owned financing subsidiary General Motors Acceptance Corporation (GMAC). Before 1988, GM accounted for GMAC on an unconsolidated basis using the equity method. Beginning in that year, GM consolidated the operations of GMAC. The effect of this accounting change is illustrated by comparing the total debt-to-equity ratio for GM in 1992, both with and without the operations of GMAC:

Total debt-to-equity without consolidation	18.5%
Total debt-to-equity with consolidation	29.7%
Change	61.0%

These figures illustrate the dramatic effect that can result when a parent fails to include debt of an unconsolidated subsidiary or joint venture: GM's debt-to-equity ratio increased by 61 percent when GMAC's obligations were added to those of the parent company.

Contingent Liabilities. Contingent liabilities represent a category of potential liabilities. Whether a contingent liability is reported in a company's financial statements depends largely on management's assessment of the probability of the liability's expected occurrence. Under statement of financial accounting standards (SFAS) No. 5 in the United States and international accounting standard (IAS) No. 10, if a contingent loss is probable and can be reasonably estimated, a liability should be formally accrued on the balance sheet, along with a loss on the income statement. If, on the other hand, a loss is only reasonably possible, or if it is probable but the amount of the loss cannot be reasonably estimated, only footnote disclosure is required.

Unfortunately, the threshold of probable loss for the purposes of applying SFAS No. 5 or IAS No. 10 is not explicit in the authoritative literature. It is generally considered to be well above a 50 percent probability — somewhere between a probability of 70 to 90 percent. But the conditions that indicate a probable liability versus a reasonably possible liability vary among managers and often among auditors. More often than not, probable liabilities end up being reported only in the footnotes or, unfortunately, not at all.

Consider, for example, the case of Bristol-Myers Squibb Company, Dow Corning, and Merck, three international pharmaceutical companies involved in the manufacture of silicone implants. In the late 1980s, medical tests revealed that the implants were capable of leaking and that silicone could be linked to various health problems experienced by implant patients. Because of uncertainty regarding the extent of liability associated with the defective implants, none of the companies accrued losses (or liabilities) for the class action lawsuits filed against them until early 1994, at which time the firms agreed to contribute various sums to a trust fund on behalf of the implant patients.

This case illustrates the all-too-frequent reluctance on the part of managers to recognize a loss and the related liability associated with contingent future events. The desire to avoid unpleasant news is quite natural, and consequently analysts may need to take an aggressive stance regarding the restatement of published financial statements with respect to these contingent claims.[12]

Executory Contracts.   A final category of off–balance sheet debt involves a group of contractual agreements called executory contracts. These contractual commitments are accounted for off the balance sheet because the event triggering the commitment has not yet occurred. As a consequence, executory contracts are principally disclosed through the footnotes, much like a contingent liability. Examples include operating leases, purchase and supply agreements, take-or-pay contracts, and working capital maintenance agreements.

To illustrate the accounting dilemma created by these contracts, consider the following contractual arrangements:

- A company borrows $1 million from a bank, agreeing to repay the borrowed amount, plus interest of $150,000, over twelve months.

- A company signs a noncancelable, nontransferable lease on retail space, agreeing to pay $1.15 million in rent over the next twelve months.

In both cases the company has incurred an economic liability of approximately $1.15 million over the one-year period, ignoring the small differential associated with the time value of money. However, only in the first contract is the company obligated to record an accounting liability for future payments. The second relationship depicts a typical operating lease, which in most countries requires no recognition on the balance sheet of the future lease payments. Instead, the lease payments are recognized only on the income statement, as a lease expense when paid.

It is often difficult for cash flow–minded analysts to understand why the accounting profession differentiates operating leases and similar executory contracts from other accounting liabilities. Perhaps the best explanation of this can be seen by examining the similarities and differences in the two preceding contractual arrangements. Although both contracts involve approximately equivalent cash outflows, they differ as to the amount of consideration received at contract signing. With the bank loan, consideration of $1 million was immediately received, and thus a liability for the repayment of that amount must be recorded. With the operating lease, however, only a *promise* of future consideration — the opportunity to use the retail space — was received.

For valuation purposes, this distinction is irrelevant. What matters is that the company has a noncancelable obligation to make future cash payments. Given this viewpoint, it is a simple matter for an analyst to restate a company's statements for these unreported obligations if adequate information exists. As Exhibit 5.7 reveals, some countries — such as Brazil, Italy, and Japan — fail to capitalize any type of lease, and for those countries that do — such as Germany, Korea, and Sweden — the level of financial disclosure can be quite limited. For those companies that provide adequate footnote disclosure, the restatement of financial statements to depict noncapitalized leases and other off–balance sheet debt items on the balance sheet are relatively straightforward.

Exhibit 5.7   Accounting for Leases

Country	Operating Leases	Capital Leases
Brazil	All leases, regardless of economic substance, are treated as operating leases. If capital leases are treated as operating leases, footnote disclosure of the asset and liability is required.	Not applicable.
Germany	Leases are carried off the balance sheet but must be disclosed in footnotes if material.	Accounting treatment follows complex tax rules.
Great Britain	Treatment and criteria are similar to those in the United States.	Criteria are similar to those in the United States; however, capitalized leases are carried at face value.
Italy	All leases, regardless of economic substance, are treated as operating leases. No footnote disclosures are required.	Not applicable.
Japan	Substantially all leases are treated as operating, but no disclosures are required.	Not applicable.
Korea	Treatment and criteria are similar to those in the United States.	Treatment and criteria are similar to those in the United States. Present value of lease obligations is reported if significantly different from face value.
Sweden	Leases are carried off the balance sheet unless the lease contract requires acquisition of the leased assets at some point during the lease period.	If a lease agreement provides for a deferred acquisition, at terms specified in the lease contract, balance sheet disclosure is recommended. Leases are valued at face value of obligations.
United States	Leases are carried off the balance sheet, with footnote disclosure of future minimum noncancelable lease payments.	Capitalized assets and liabilities are carried at present value of minimum future lease payments.

To illustrate this restatement, consider the financial data of World Enterprises, Inc. (WE), a multinational company headquartered in the United States. Exhibit 5.8 shows that WE leases substantial quantities of retail space via operating leases. Assuming that WE's incremental cost

Exhibit 5.8   World Enterprises, Inc.—Operating Leases

Consolidated balance sheet (30 July 1997)
(U.S. dollars, in thousands)

Assets

Total current assets	$529,544
Net property, plant, and equipment	264,118
Excess of cost over net assets of subsidiaries acquired less applicable amortization	60,597
Other assets and deferred charges, at cost less applicable amortization	10,626
Total assets	$864,885

Liabilities and stockholders' equity

Total current liabilities	$271,293
Deferred federal and state income taxes	14,167
Long-term debt, excluding current installments	11,133
Stockholders' equity	
Common stock of $0.10 par value. Authorized, 100 million; issued, 37,461,475.	3,746
Capital in excess of par value	108,971
Retained earnings	455,575
Total stockholders' equity	$568,292
Total liabilities and stockholders' equity	$864,885

Footnote Disclosures: Leases

The company conducts the major portion of its retail operations from leased store premises under leases that will expire within the next twenty-five years. Such leases generally contain renewal options. In addition to minimum rental payments, certain leases provide for payment of taxes, maintenance, and percentage rentals based on sales in excess of stipulated amounts.

Total rental expense was as follows:	
Minimum rentals	$55,980
Percentage rentals	10,735
	$66,715

At 30 July 1997, minimum rental commitments under noncancelable leases were as follows:

Year	
1998	$55,892
1999	54,884
2000	53,434
2001	52,107
2002	50,606
2003–2007	210,166
2008–2012	129,807
2013–2017	4,572
After 2017	4,918
	$616,386

of borrowing at 30 July 1997 is 10 percent, an estimate of the present value of the minimum future lease payments after 1997 is approximately $350.8 million. Using this figure, the analyst can then increase WE's long-term assets by $350.8 million and its liabilities by an equivalent amount.[13]

Cash Flow Statement Transformations: Forecasting CFFO and Free Cash Flow

A key component of any financial review must involve a consideration of the amount, composition, sources, and sustainability of cash flow. Because of the importance of cash flow data to sophisticated users of financial statements, most countries now require the presentation of a statement of cash flows (SCF). Not only is cash flow data readily available in most countries (except Belgium, France, Germany, India, Italy, The Netherlands, and Switzerland, where presentation of such information is optional), but the information also appears in a relatively consistent format, segmented into three broad categories (see Appendix 2B for additional information):

- Cash flows from operations (CFFO)
- Cash flows from investing (CFFI)
- Cash flows from financing (CFFF)

Because the cash flows of a company are an explicitly measurable quantity, the decisions regarding the selection of alternative accounting methods and the estimation of the expected useful lives of fixed and intangible assets do *not* affect cash flow metrics. Of concern, however, are the classification decisions by management that do affect the *individual* SCF components — CFFO, CFFI, and CFFF — and thus may affect firm valuation.

To illustrate this concern, consider Exhibit 5.9, which presents the 1993 SCF for Blockbuster Entertainment Corporation. Blockbuster is the largest video store chain in the world, with operations in more than fifteen countries. According to the company's annual report, Blockbuster's principal sources of revenues are videotape rentals in company-owned stores and product sales to franchisee-owned stores. The company's footnotes reveal that Blockbuster amortizes its significant investment in videotapes over periods ranging from nine to thirty-six months. A valuation analyst might be concerned with the Blockbuster

Exhibit 5.9 Blockbuster Entertainment Corporation—
Consolidated Statement of Cash Flows

	1993	1992
Cash flows from operating activities (CFFO)		
Net income	$243,646	$148,269
Adjustment to reconcile net income CFFO		
Depreciation and amortization	396,122	306,829
Amortization of film costs	87,281	—
Additions to film costs and program rights	(110,422)	—
Interest on subordinated convertible debt	6,362	8,945
Gain from equity investment	(2,979)	—
Changes in operating assets and liabilities, net of effects from purchase transactions		
Increase in accounts and notes receivable	(29,444)	(9,347)
(Increase) decrease in merchandise inventories	(83,333)	(1,379)
(Increase) decrease in other current assets	(974)	(5,254)
Increase (decrease) in accounts payable and accrued liabilities	(62,529)	(37,159)
Increase in income taxes payable and related items	83,655	20,391
Other	(5,101)	16,732
	522,284	448,027
Cash flows from investing activities (CFFI)		
Purchases of videocassette rental inventory	(451,116)	(296,139)
Disposals of videocassette rental inventory	40,595	37,618
Purchases of property and equipment	(164,541)	(98,393)
Net cash used in business combinations and investments	(673,241)	(252,888)
Other	(2,216)	(22,893)
	(1,250,519)	(632,695)
Cash flows from financing activities (CFFF)		
Proceeds from the issuance of common stock, net	595,698	80,769
Proceeds from long-term debt	2,373,786	328,583
Repayments of long-term debt	(2,152,239)	(222,523)
Cash dividends paid	(18,275)	(7,154)
Other	(18,839)	(6,071)
	780,131	173,604
Increase (decrease) in cash and cash equivalents	51,896	(8,306)
Cash and cash equivalents at beginning of year	43,358	51,664
Cash and cash equivalents at end of year	95,254	43,358

Values are in thousands of U.S. dollars.

practice of reporting its cash purchases of videotapes as an investing activity rather than as part of the company's operating activities. (See the shaded area in Exhibit 5.9.) If Blockbuster's net videotape purchases were reclassified as part of operating activities, the company's 1993 CFFO would decline by nearly 80 percent from more than $522 million to more than $111 million (522,284 − 451,116 + 40,595), similarly reducing the company's free cash flows. Since videotapes are known to have relatively short economic lives, treatment of videotape purchases as an operating cash flow is more consistent with this asset's expected revenue-generating life.

Because the CFFO is so critical to the calculation of free cash flow, it is important for the analyst to validate a company's definition and measurement of CFFO. Failure to do so for Blockbuster, for example, would result in a significant overvaluation error.

Summary

In this chapter we considered a number of important accounting measurement and reporting dilemmas that a valuation analyst is likely to encounter. Although it is unlikely that an analyst will confront all of the dilemmas in any one valuation project, some data transformation is almost always required, ranging from rearranging and combining income statement or balance sheet items, to modifying the accounting measurement methods themselves. In some instances, there will be sufficient information for the analyst to transform the financial data from its original presentation to some preferred form of presentation, whereas in other cases, when little information is available, the analyst will merely be able to note the presence of a dilemma and to subjectively incorporate its likely effect on financial ratios and other measures of risk and return. In any case, the analyst will need to identify and resolve such dilemmas *before* the financial review and development of the pro forma statement.

Academic researchers have addressed the question of whether accounting data transformation is cost effective, but their findings have not been definitive. For example, White, Sondhi, and Fried (1998) advocate the restatement of cost of goods sold, ending inventory, net income, and various ratios of LIFO firms to allow increased comparability with FIFO firms. However, Dawson, Neupert, and Stickney (1980) and Trombley and Guenther (1995) suggest that the improvements in comparability are sufficiently marginal that such adjustments are simply not worth the effort involved. Other researchers have investigated the question of whether restatement of foreign GAAP financial statements to U.S. GAAP provides higher quality and more comparable information for users of financial statements. Again, the findings do not provide an unambiguous answer. Although Barth and Clinch (1996), Herrmann, Inoue, and Thomas (1996), and Rees (1995) find that foreign GAAP reconciliation to U.S. GAAP provides value-relevant information, Meek (1983); Amir, Harris, and Venuti (1993); and Chan and Seow (1996) found no evidence to suggest that transformation is cost beneficial. One important issue regarding cross-country accounting reconciliation appears to be that even though, say, a U.S. and Japanese company might issue financial statements prepared using the same GAAP, the financial results are still not strictly comparable because of differences in the cultural, economic, and institutional settings of the two countries. An analyst should also consider that although it may be possible to restate *some* accounting method differences, it is almost impossible to adequately restate for management estimate differences found in estimated salvage values, expected product returns, and warranty estimates, which are culturally and institutionally dependent.

Because so much ambiguity exists around the issue of whether to transform, what specific advice can we offer the valuation analyst? Recall that differences in accounting policy are likely to have a far greater effect on unadjusted earnings–based valuations (e.g., P/E and P/EBIT multiples) than on cash flow– or adjusted earnings–based valuations (i.e., EBITDA multiples). This is because the adjustments called for in cash flow–based or EBITDA-based models often overcome most differentials in accounting policy. Hence, when concerns about data restatement are high, analysts should consider using a cash flow– or adjusted earnings–based valuation approach. However, because even these valuation models are to some extent accounting based, their use may not overcome all data concerns (e.g., revenue recognition policies, the estimation of such revenue offsets as sales returns and bad debts, and inventory policy). In such cases, the analyst should undertake as many transformations as can be easily and readily executed in conjunction with a cash flow– or adjusted earnings–based valuation method.

Exhibit 5.10 shows a comprehensive financial statement restatement and illustrates how four common accounting dilemmas can be resolved. Notice that following restatement for the four dilemmas, some of the key financial ratios of interest to valuation analysts are materially affected (e.g., return on assets, current ratio, debt-to-equity, and days' inventory on hand), whereas others are relatively unaffected (i.e., quick ratio) or only marginally affected (e.g., times interest earned). Finally, observe that the company's net profit increased from 942 to 1,026 million guilders as a consequence of the restatement.

Exhibit 5.10   Financial Statement Restatement: An Illustration

Global Enterprises NV (GE) is a multinational corporation with operations in sixty countries around the world. The company maintains its headquarters in The Netherlands and prepares its financial statements according to Dutch accounting standards. GE's abbreviated consolidated balance sheet and profit-and-loss statement for the year ended 31 December 1999 is presented below. A review of the footnotes to the financial statements reveals the following additional information:

Brands

The company has a significant investment in acquired brands, the cost of which amounts to 1,020 million guilders. Amortization of acquired brands is not provided except where the end of the useful economic life of an acquired brand can be foreseen. The directors have reviewed the amounts at which brands are stated and are of the opinion that there has been no impairment in the brands' recognized values and that the end of their useful economic lives cannot be foreseen.

Goodwill

Goodwill arising on the acquisition of new businesses is calculated by reference to the fair value of net assets acquired. Goodwill, the cost of which amounts to 1,300 million guilders, is written off if, in the opinion of the directors, its value has become impaired or if the related business is sold or otherwise disposed of. The directors have reviewed the goodwill account and are of the opinion that there has been no impairment.

Stocks

Inventories are principally valued using the last-in, first-out method. If the first-in, first-out method had been used, the inventories would have been 1,400 million guilders higher at 31 December 1999 and 1,000 million guilders higher at 31 December 1998.

Leases

The company has entered into several long-term, noncancelable lease agreements that, in the opinion of the directors, do not meet the requirements of a finance lease. As such, all leases are treated as operating leases. Pursuant to the Accounting and Reporting Guidelines issued by the Council for Annual Reporting, the future minimum lease payments under such agreements are as follows:

Year	Amount (in millions of guilders)
2000	400
2001	380
2002	350
2003	320
2004	300
Thereafter	3,500
Total	5,250

Exhibit 5.10   Financial Statement Restatement: An Illustration (*continued*)

Although GE's accounting policies are acceptable in The Netherlands and are largely permissible under International Accounting Standards Committee standards, potential transformations include the following:

- Amortization of brands over ten years
- Amortization of goodwill over five years
- First-in, first-out method for inventory
- Capitalization of future lease commitments

Because insufficient information is available for determination of when the brands and goodwill were first acquired, restatement is assumed as of 1 January 1999. Furthermore, it is assumed that the new brands and goodwill policies have been implemented for tax purposes to minimize taxable income and that the new inventory policy would not be implemented for tax purposes, as it would result in a higher taxable net income. Finally, a review of the company's footnotes suggests that the long-term weighted average cost of borrowing is approximately 10 percent.

The accounting entries for achieving the four transformations are as follows (with Dr. meaning *debit* and Cr. meaning *credit*):

(1) Brands

Dr. Profit-and-loss account	66	
Dr. Provision for deferred income taxes	36*	
Cr. Accumulated amortization: Brands		102[†]

* Reflects a statutory tax rate of 35 percent.
[†] (1,020 ÷ 10 years = 102)

(2) Goodwill

Dr. Profit-and-loss account	169	
Dr. Provision for deferred income taxes	91	
Cr. Accumulated amortization: Goodwill		260[‡]

[‡] (1,300 ÷ 5 years = 260)

(3) Inventories

Dr. Stocks	1,400	
Cr. Provision for deferred income taxes		490
Cr. Profit and loss account		910

With respect to inventories, only 260 (400 × 0.65) of the total change in the profit-and-loss account relates to 1999; the remainder, 650 (1,000 × 0.65), relates to prior years.

(4) Leases

Dr. Leased asset	3,320[§]	
Cr. Lease liability; due in one year		364
Cr. Lease liability; due after one year		2,956

[§] Present value of future minimum lease payments at 10 percent.

(continued)

Exhibit 5.10   Financial Statement Restatement: An Illustration (*continued*)

After restatement, a comparison of select financial ratios indicates the following:

	Original	Restated
Return on sales	19.0%	20.7%
Return on assets	7.8%	6.2%
Return on equity	16.5%	15.4%
Current ratio	2.19×	2.67×
Quick ratio	0.89×	0.89×
Long-term debt-to-equity	59.5%	101.0%
Times interest earned	5.14×	5.51×
Day's inventory on hand	440 days	629 days
Noncurrent asset turnover	0.88	0.56

Global Enterprises NV: Profit-and-Loss Statement (for year ended 31 December 1999, in millions, guilders)

	Original	Adjustments	Restated
Turnover from continuing operations	4,950	(1) (102)	4,950
Trading costs	(3,150)	(2) (169)	(3,021)
Profit before interest and taxation	1,800	(3) 400	1,929
Net interest charges	(350)		(350)
Profit before taxation	1,450		1,579
Taxation (35% statutory rate)	(508)		(553)
Net profit	942		1,026

Global Enterprises NV: Balance Sheet (as of 31 December 1999, in millions, guilders)

	Original	Adjustments	Restated
Fixed assets			
Acquired brands	1,020	(1) (102)	918
Tangible assets (net)	4,630		4,630
	5,650		5,548
Leased assets	—	(4) 3,320	3,320
Current assets			
Stocks	3,800	(3) 1,400	5,200
Debtors	1,716		1,716
Cash at bank	872		872
	6,388		

Exhibit 5.10 Financial Statement Restatement: An Illustration (*continued*)

	Original	Adjustments		Restated
Creditors (due in one year)				
Short-term borrowings	(2,760)			(2,760)
Other creditors	(160)			(160)
Lease liability	—	(4)	(364)	(364)
Net current assets	3,468			
Total assets less current liabilities	9,118			13,372
Creditors (due after one year)		(1)	36	
Long-term borrowing	(3,000)	(2)	91	(3,000)
Provisions	(400)	(3)	(490)	(763)
Lease liability	—	(4)	(2,956)	(2,956)
Total net assets	5,718			6,653
Equity		(1)	(66)	
Share capital, plus share premium	4,000	(2)	(169)	4,000
Profit-and-loss account	3,018	(3)	910	3,693
Goodwill reserve	(1,300)	(2)	260	(1,040)
Total equity	5,718			6,653

Notes

1. See, for instance, MacDonald (2000). Nelson, Elliott, and Tarpley (2000) report that earnings management most frequently occurs (in order of frequency) in reserves, revenue recognition, business combinations, intangibles, fixed assets, investments, leases, and compensation, among others.

2. In some countries, such as China and Switzerland, companies are not required to estimate future uncollectible amounts and instead write off receivables only after an account has been proven to be uncollectible — an event that may take years to confirm. One consequence of this direct write-off approach to accounting for bad debts is that earnings may be substantially overstated. Smith (1995) estimates that if the worthless receivables carried on the books of some Chinese multinational companies were written off, it would lower current-year earnings by up to 70 percent. As a consequence, the valuation analyst should verify that uncollectible accounts are being properly estimated and matched against current earnings, if for no other reason than to avoid paying for worthless receivables.

3. The accounting entry for recording an estimate of a company's bad debt expense is as follows (with Dr. meaning *debit* and Cr. meaning *credit*):

Dr. Bad debt provision (expense) $XX
    Cr. Allowance for uncollectible accounts $XX

This entry reduces both net income before taxes and the net realizable balance of accounts receivable. To restate Fairfield's financial statements for an increase in the loan loss provision, a similar entry would be called for.

4. For example, the financial statements of the Hoechst Group, a leading German chemical company, reveal the following:

> The Group inventories contain services performed but not yet billed within the scope of long-term construction contracts amounting to DM 523 million. They relate to projects that are not billed to the customer until the plant is successfully commissioned. Under German commercial law, profits from these orders are not recognized as income until the year in which the work is billed (completed contract method).
>
> The IAS [international accounting system] recommends the percentage of completion method in such cases, meaning that revenue is recognized according to the stage of contract performance completed. Had we applied the IAS in this case, the Group profit before taxes on income would have been DM 49 million higher.

Thus, Hoechst provides sufficient information to restate the company's pretax profits, assuming the use of percentage-of-completion method instead of the more conservative completed-contract method. The adjustment of DM 49 million represents more than 2 percent of the company's profits, and restatement can be executed by the following entry:

Dr. Cost of goods sold	523	
Dr. Accounts receivable (unbilled)	572	
Cr. Inventories		523
Cr. Revenues		572

5. A uniquely American tax regulation requires that if LIFO is used for tax purposes, it must also be used when financial results are reported to shareholders. Given the very favorable tax consequences associated with the use of LIFO, it is not surprising that the vast majority of publicly held companies in the United States use LIFO for both tax and accounting purposes.

6. Assuming that an analyst wants to evaluate a target company *as if* FIFO had been used for both tax and accounting purposes, the transformation would be accomplished by the following adjusting entry (using GM's 1993 figures and assuming an effective tax rate of 35 percent):

Dr. Inventory	$2,519.00	
Cr. Income taxes payable		$881.65
Cr. Retained earnings		$1,637.35

7. One approach some analysts use to estimate the average expected remaining life of a company's depreciable assets is to calculate the ratio of accumulated depreciation to the gross carrying value of depreciable assets. By comparing this ratio over time, an analyst can arrive at an estimate of the average expected useful life of a bundle of depreciable assets.

8. Although the write-off–to–equity method for goodwill is not acceptable in the United States, the practice is similar to the restatement procedures that most lending institutions follow. Because goodwill generally lacks a resale market, lending institutions usually reduce a borrower's borrowing base by the amount of goodwill carried on the borrower's balance sheet. This restatement is executed by writing off any goodwill and similar intangibles with questionable resale value against the borrower's net worth, as follows:

Dr. Retained earnings	$XX	
Cr. Goodwill (net)		$XX

This restatement produces a revised measure of shareholders' equity called "tangible net worth."

9. In May 2000, AOL agreed to pay a $3.5 million penalty to settle an allegation from the Securities and Exchange Commission (SEC) that the Internet company improperly accounted for its advertising and marketing costs in the mid-1990s. The SEC alleged that AOL should never have used the deferral approach because the volatile nature of the Internet market precluded reliable forecasts of revenues.

10. The necessary adjusting entry to achieve the restatement is as follows:

Dr. Revaluation reserve	£XX	
Cr. Revalued asset		£XX

11. Recall from Chapter 3 the definition of the equity value of a firm:

$$\text{Equity Value} = \text{Total Value} - \begin{array}{l} \text{Market Value of Debt,} \\ \text{Minority Interest,} \\ \text{Preferred Stock, and} \\ \text{Contingency Claims} \end{array}$$

Failure to identify all forms of existing debt may lead to an overestimation of forecasted equity value.

12. The procedure necessary for capitalizing off–balance sheet debt is straightforward. First, calculate the present value of the expected future cash outflows necessary to satisfy the obligation. Second, determine whether the obligation is associated with the acquisition of an asset or the occurrence of a loss. Finally, capitalize the liability to the balance sheet, with a corresponding entry to an asset or a loss account (as in the case of Dow Corning and Merck) as follows:

Dr. Expected loss on implant lawsuits	$XX	
Cr. Reserve for lawsuit awards		$XX

13. More specifically, the accounting entry would appear as follows:

Dr. Leased assets	$350.8 million	
Cr. Short-term lease obligations		$50.8 million
Cr. Long-term lease obligations		$300.0 million

The analyst should note that restating the balance sheet with this entry also requires a consideration of the effect of the restatement on the income statement. With capitalization, the lease expense needs to be replaced by depreciation expense on the newly capitalized asset and interest expense on the lease liability. Hence, capitalization requires that the analyst make certain assumptions about such items as depreciation method, salvage value, and expected life of the newly capitalized asset.

6 Financial Reporting and Tax Considerations for Mergers and Acquisitions

MARKET VIEW
The Allied Waste Industries' Acquisition

In September 1996, Allied Waste Industries, Inc., offered to pay $1.48 billion for the solid waste disposal operations of Laidlaw Inc.* Some industry analysts described the offer as something akin to a "minnow swallowing a whale" in that Laidlaw's waste operations were about five times larger than those of Allied. Analysts also questioned the propriety of the offering price; of the $1.48 billion price tag, $900 million, or 61 percent, would represent "goodwill."

Under the acquisition agreement, Allied agreed to pay Laidlaw $1.2 billion in cash, $117 million in discounted notes, and 14.6 million new Allied common shares valued at approximately $113 million, along with warrants for another 20.4 million shares valued at $50 million. Despite the large number of shares involved in the transaction, Allied would be required to account for the acquisition using "purchase accounting."

In early January 1997, Allied sold Laidlaw's Canadian waste operations to USA Waste Services Inc. for $520 million. As part of this sale, Allied wrote off $300 million in goodwill acquired as part of the original Laidlaw acquisition. When questioned by industry analysts about the January sale, Allied's chief

---

*J. Bailey, "Allied Waste to Buy Line from Laidlaw, *Wall Street Journal,* 19 September 1996, A3.

accounting officer Peter Hathaway explained: "Under U.S. tax regulations, goodwill acquired in conjunction with an asset acquisition is tax deductible, but only if the goodwill relates to U.S. assets. Thus, we sold Laidlaw's Canadian operation in part to generate cash to help pay for the acquisition and in part to remove the $300 million in goodwill from our balance sheet that would not be tax deductible."

• • •

Although mergers and acquisitions have historically been a within-country phenomenon, the 1990s witnessed an explosive growth in cross-border merger and acquisition activity. Wessel (2000) reported for instance, that cross-border mergers and acquisitions grew fivefold from 1990 to 1999, with an increase of 50 percent in 1999 alone. As firms tried to globalize, they found it less costly and far less difficult to buy access to foreign marketplaces than to try to build that access. With this trend came the need to understand generally accepted merger and acquisition accounting and taxation issues on a global basis.

One consequence of a merger or acquisition is usually the requirement of preparing consolidated financial statements; that is, preparing a single set of financial statements reflecting the combined operations of an acquirer and any majority-owned subsidiary companies. The requirement of preparing consolidated financial statements for financial reporting purposes and tax purposes is rarely the same, however, in different countries. Hence, this chapter focuses on understanding how, and when, the financial data from two (or more) companies are aggregated in the preparation of consolidated financial statements after a merger or acquisition.

Specifically, this chapter addresses the following key questions:

- Under what circumstances are consolidated financial statements prepared for financial reporting purposes?

- How does the financial structure of a merger or acquisition affect the accounting for such transactions?

- Does the use of alternative consolidation accounting practice affect firm valuation?

- Under what circumstances are consolidated financial statements prepared for tax purposes?

- What is "goodwill," how is it accounted for, and what are its tax implications?

An understanding of these issues will help analysts and managers decide how an acquisition transaction should be executed — with cash or with stock.

Financial Reporting: To Combine, or Not to Combine?

In most countries around the world, when one company obtains a majority shareholding in another, the "parent company" is required under local generally accepted accounting principles (GAAP) to prepare **consolidated financial statements.**[1] These combined financial statements were originally introduced to avoid the potential problem of information overload that might result if investors received individual financial statements for a multitude of companies that might comprise a conglomerate or holding company. Combining the operating results of many diverse businesses, however, resulted in a different type of analytical problem, namely, obscuring the results of the various combined businesses and precluding investors from determining exactly which businesses were successful and which were not. This disclosure problem is mitigated to some extent by the disclosure of sales and income data along key business-segment lines (i.e., segment reporting). Unfortunately, equity markets still struggle to value diversified companies, as evidenced by the fact that the aggregate market value assigned to a conglomerate is frequently less than the value assigned to the individual business components comprising the conglomerate (i.e., a "conglomerate discount"). This valuation problem is almost certainly exacerbated by the preparation of consolidated financial statements.

In some countries, such as India and Indonesia, consolidation of majority-owned subsidiaries is not mandatory; and in Brazil, Italy, and Japan, consolidation is required only when a parent company is publicly held.[2] When a subsidiary is not consolidated, it is accounted for on the parent's financial statements using either the **cost method** or the **equity method,** with results that are not entirely satisfactory from an analytical perspective. As Exhibit 6.1 reveals, when the cost method is used to account for a majority-owned subsidiary, both the parent's income statement and balance sheet are likely to be incomplete with respect to the subsidiary's operations; and if the equity method is used, the parent's balance sheet (but not income statement) is likely to be informationally

Exhibit 6.1   Unconsolidated Reporting:
Cost Method versus Equity Method

Cost Method

In late 1994, Jyoti Structures Ltd. of Calcutta, India, acquired a 100 percent ownership interest in Prakash Fabricators, Inc., for 4.7 million rupees, which was the fair market value of Prakash's net assets. Jyoti also assumed responsibility for 3 million rupees of Prakash debt. In the following year, Prakash earned profits of 1.9 million rupees, all but 0.5 million of which were retained by Prakash to finance a planned capital asset expansion. Following generally accepted accounting practice in India, Jyoti accounted for its wholly owned Prakash subsidiary using the cost method and consequently recorded the above information in its accounts as follows (where Dr. indicates *debit* and Cr., *credit*):

```
1994:   Dr. Investment in Prakash Fabricators, Inc.    4.7 million
            Cr. Cash                                                  4.7 million
            (To record the initial investment in Prakash Fabricators, Inc.)

1995:   Dr. Cash                                         0.5 million
            Cr. Dividend income                                       0.5 million
            (To record the receipt of dividend income from Prakash
                Fabricators, Inc.)
```

Thus, at year end 1995, Jyoti's balance sheet reflected an investment of 4.7 million rupees in its Prakash subsidiary, and Jyoti's income statement reflected dividend income of 0.5 million rupees.

Analysis: Despite the fact that Jyoti became responsible for Prakash's 3 million rupees in debt, this information was not disclosed on Jyoti's balance sheet, thereby understating the company's total debt position and overstating its equity value. And because only 0.5 million of Prakash's total net income of 1.9 million rupees was incorporated into the Jyoti accounts, the earnings of the new entity Jyoti-Prakash were understated by 1.4 million rupees, causing its permanent earnings and free cash flows to be understated.

Equity Method

If Jyoti had instead used the equity method to account for its investment in Prakash, the following entries would have been recorded in Jyoti's accounts:

```
1994:   Dr. Investment in Prakash Fabricators, Inc.    4.7 million
            Cr. Cash                                                  4.7 million
            (To record the initial investment in Prakash Fabricators, Inc.)

1995:   Dr. Investment in Prakash Fabricators, Inc.    1.9 million
            Cr. Equity in the earnings of unconsoli-
                dated subsidiary                                      1.9 million
            (To record Jyoti's ownership interest in the earnings of Prakash
                Fabricators, Inc.)

        Dr. Cash                                        0.5 million
            Cr. Investment in Prakash Fabricators, Inc.               0.5 million
            (To record the receipt of a "liquidating dividend" from Prakash
                Fabricators, Inc.)
```

Exhibit 6.1 Unconsolidated Reporting:
Cost Method versus Equity Method (*continued*)

Analysis: At year end 1995, Jyoti's balance sheet would reflect a net investment of 6.1 million rupees (4.7 + 1.9 − 0.5) in Prakash, and its income statement would fully reflect the subsidiary's contribution to the combined entity's total profit (i.e., the "equity in the earnings of unconsolidated subsidiary" of 1.9 million is added to Jyoti's earnings on its income statement); but Prakash's debt of 3 million rupees remains off the balance sheet, causing the equity value to be overstated.

Conclusion

Because the equity method is equivalent to a "one-line consolidation," observe that a single line item ("equity in the earnings of unconsolidated subsidiary") summarizes Prakash's entire income statement on Jyoti's income statement; and on the balance sheet, a single line item ("investment in Prakash Fabricators") summarizes Jyoti's net investment in its subsidiary. From an investor's vantage point, the equity method is clearly more informative than the cost method, although this method also has some limitations. Note that although the parent's income statement incorporates the overall operating results of the subsidiary, the balance sheet does not. Unfortunately, as was the case with the cost method, the balance sheet under the equity method fails to reflect the debt position of the subsidiary. For this reason, many analysts criticize the equity method as a vehicle that permits off–balance sheet debt.

---

incomplete. Neither the cost method nor the equity method adequately portrays a majority-owned subsidiary's debt position on the parent's balance sheet, and only the equity method fully recognizes the operating results of the subsidiary. In short, despite the concern that consolidated financial statements may make it more difficult for an analyst to value a highly diversified entity, consolidated financial statements *do* provide a more complete picture of an economic entity than unconsolidated financial statements. Exactly how consolidated financial statements are prepared is the focus of the next section.

Consolidated Reporting: Pooling versus Purchase Accounting

When a company decides to gain control over another, it may do so in several different ways: share purchase, share exchange, or asset purchase. In the first two approaches, the acquirer becomes the majority shareholder of the newly acquired subsidiary, and consequently, the subsidiary becomes a member or affiliate of the parent's family of companies.

Under an asset purchase, the acquirer acquires only the operating assets (and possibly liabilities) of a company but not its legal, organizational structure.[3] Having sold its operating assets, the unaffiliated company is free, subject to possible covenant-not-to-compete agreements, to do with its resources whatever it desires (e.g., go into another business, liquidate, etc.).

If an acquisition is executed by a share purchase or an asset purchase, the **purchase method** — or what is sometimes called "acquisition accounting" — must be used to account for the transaction. On the other hand, if the acquisition is executed by a share exchange, it *may* be permissible to use the **pooling-of-interests method** — or what is sometimes called "merger accounting." In those countries in which the pooling method is not allowed, all mergers and acquisitions are accounted for with the use of the purchase method. As Exhibit 6.2 reveals, use of the pooling method is not permitted in Australia, France, Mexico, Spain, or the United States (after 2001), among other countries. More importantly, in those countries in which pooling is permitted, the requirements that must be satisfied for use of the method are usually quite onerous; consequently, the pooling method is disallowed in many merger and acquisition transactions.

Purchase Method. To help visualize the difference between the purchase and pooling methods, consider a simple acquisition between two independent companies.[4] Assume that Global Enterprises Ltd. (GE Ltd.) of the U.K. purchased 100 percent of the voting shares of British Subsidiary Ltd. (BS Ltd.), another U.K. company, for £275,000. Immediately before the acquisition, the balance sheets of the two companies appeared as follows:

	GE Ltd.	BS Ltd.
Assets	£700,000	£300,000
Liabilities	£150,000	£100,000
Shareholders' equity	550,000	200,000
Total equities	£700,000	£300,000

Assume further that the investment bankers GE hired to help assess the appropriate acquisition price for BS conclude that the fair market value of BS's identifiable net assets was £250,000, or £50,000 more than the company's net book value of £200,000. Thus, GE's offering price of

Exhibit 6.2   Consolidated Reporting Practices

	Consolidation Accounting		Goodwill Accounting	
Country	Purchase	Pooling	Capitalize/ Amortize	Direct Write-Off
Australia	✓	—	✓ (20 years)	—
Brazil	✓	✓	✓	—
Canada	✓	✓	✓ (40 years)	—
Denmark	✓	✓	✓	✓
France	✓	—	✓	✓
Germany	✓	✓	✓	✓
Hong Kong	✓	✓	✓	✓
Italy	✓	✓	✓	✓
Japan	✓	✓	✓ (5 years)	—
Korea	✓	✓	✓ (5 years)	—
Mexico	✓	—	✓ (20 years)	—
The Netherlands	✓	✓	✓ (10 years)	✓
Spain	✓	—	✓ (10 years)	—
U.K.	✓	✓	✓	—
United States	✓	—	✓	—
IASC standard	✓	✓	✓ (20 years)	✓
European Union standard	✓	✓	✓	✓

A check mark shows that the method is permitted; a dash, the method is not permitted; and (# of years), maximum goodwill amortization period; where unspecified, amortization period is "useful economic life." IASC is international accounting standards committee.

£275,000 includes goodwill in the amount of £25,000; **goodwill** is the excess of the purchase price paid (£275,000) over the fair market value of the acquired net assets (£250,000). GE may have been willing to pay a premium in excess of the appraised value of BS's net worth for several reasons: the presence of a loyal customer base for BS's products, a competent management group, an efficient distribution system, or anticipated cost savings and other synergies between the operations of GE and BS.

Immediately after the payment of £275,000 to BS's shareholders, GE will record its investment in BS as follows:

        Dr. Investment in BS Ltd.   £275,000
              Cr. Cash   £275,000

GE's unconsolidated balance sheet will then appear as

	GE Ltd.
Assets	£425,000*
Investment in BS Ltd.	275,000
Total assets	£700,000
Liabilities	£150,000
Shareholders' equity	550,000
Total equities	£700,000

*£700,000 less £275,000 paid to the BS shareholders.

As the acquisition transaction took place between GE and the former shareholders of BS, the balance sheet of BS will remain unchanged *unless* GE decides to use **push-down accounting** for its new wholly owned subsidiary.

Under push-down accounting, the balance sheet values of the newly acquired subsidiary are restated to reflect the purchase price paid by the acquirer to acquire the subsidiary. In essence, the parent company imposes (or pushes down) a new cost basis on the new operating subsidiary. Hence, if GE's investment bankers assess the fair market value of BS's total assets to be £350,000 and conclude that BS's liabilities are fairly valued at their book value of £100,000 (i.e., indicating a fair market value of the entire company of £250,000), BS's balance sheet would be revised as follows under push-down accounting:

	BS Ltd. (Original)	BS Ltd. (Restated)
Assets	£300,000	£350,000
Goodwill	0	25,000
Total assets	£300,000	£375,000
Liabilities	£100,000	£100,000
Shareholders' equity	200,000	275,000
Total equities	£300,000	£375,000

As a consequence of the implementation of push-down accounting, BS's management will now be expected to earn an acceptable rate of return on the fair market value of BS's net assets (i.e., £275,000) — a more difficult task than simply earning an acceptable rate of return on the historical cost of those same assets (i.e., £200,000). Most parent companies *do* impose push-down accounting on their subsidiaries for performance evaluation purposes and as a means of ensuring that the subsidiary managers operate on the basis of the same financial data as the parent company management.

At the end of the fiscal year, GE will be required under U.K. accounting standards to prepare and issue consolidated financial statements. To prepare its consolidated balance sheet, GE will need to transfer the recently purchased subsidiary net assets to its consolidated balance sheet, and this can be accomplished with the following consolidation entry:

Dr. Assets (from BS)	£350,000	
Dr. Goodwill	25,000	
Cr. Liabilities (from BS)		£100,000
Cr. Investment in BS Ltd.		275,000

Note how the account "investment in BS Ltd." is removed from GE's unconsolidated balance sheet and replaced on the consolidated balance sheet by the specific assets and liabilities, valued at their fair market value, acquired in the BS acquisition. Under purchase accounting, the subsidiary's net asset value is "stepped-up" to its fair market value at the time of consolidation, regardless of whether push-down accounting is imposed on the subsidiary.[5]

After the above consolidation entry, GE's consolidated balance sheet will appear as follows:[6]

	GE Ltd. Before Investment in BS	GE Ltd. After Investment in BS	GE Ltd. Consolidated
Assets	£700,000	£425,000	£425,000
Assets (from BS)	—	—	350,000
Investment in BS Ltd.	—	275,000	—
Goodwill	—	—	25,000
Total assets	£700,000	£700,000	£800,000
Liabilities	£150,000	£150,000	£150,000
Liabilities (from BS)	—	—	100,000
Shareholders' equity	550,000	550,000	550,000
Total equities	£700,000	£700,000	£800,000

Before ending our consideration of the purchase method, a brief word about the consolidated income statement is necessary. Under the purchase method, the earnings of an acquired subsidiary are consolidated with those of the parent on a *prospective* basis only; that is, if an acquisition occurs at midyear, only those subsidiary earnings from the second half of the year (i.e., *after* the acquisition has been consummated) may be consolidated with the earnings of the parent. In essence, the subsidiary's earnings from the first half of the year belong to the prior shareholders of the subsidiary and are not consolidated with those of the new owner.

Pooling of Interests.   The pooling method, or merger accounting, may be used in some countries, but only where a set of stringent regulations have been satisfied. If a share exchange is executed and pooling is permitted, the consolidated financial statements will appear substantially different from those arising under the purchase method. To illustrate, let us return to our example in which GE Ltd. acquires BS Ltd.; however, instead of giving the BS shareholders £275,000 in cash, assume that GE gives the BS shareholders GE shares valued at £275,000. Exactly how many GE shares will be exchanged for the BS shares will be determined by the relative market price of GE stock versus BS stock on an agreed-upon date before the merger date.[7] Note that this transaction is essentially equivalent to the share purchase transaction described above except that the consideration given to the BS shareholders is GE stock and not cash.

Under the pooling method, the value assigned to GE's investment in BS is neither the market value of the GE stock distributed to the BS shareholders (i.e., £275,000) nor the market value of the BS stock received in the exchange; instead, the value assigned to GE's investment in BS is the *book value of the acquired net assets,* or £200,000. Consequently, GE's investment in BS will be recorded in the GE accounts as follows:

| Dr. Investment in BS Ltd. | £200,000 | |
| Cr. Capital stock | | £200,000 |

It is worth repeating: The value assigned to the GE capital stock given to the former BS shareholders is the book value of the acquired net assets *not* the GE shares' fair market value of £275,000. As a consequence, it can be seen that in this instance, the pooling method has significantly *undervalued* both the investment in BS and the GE shares distributed to BS's former shareholders; for this reason, many countries do not permit the use of the pooling method.

For preparation of the consolidated financial statements at year end under the pooling method, the following consolidation entry will be executed to bring BS's assets and liabilities into the consolidated accounts:

Dr. Assets (from BS)	£300,000	
Cr. Liabilities (from BS)		£100,000
Cr. Investment in BS Ltd.		200,000

The consolidated balance sheet under the pooling method will appear as follows:

	GE Ltd. Before Investment in BS	GE Ltd. After Investment in BS	GE Ltd. Consolidated
Assets	£700,000	£700,000	£700,000
Assets (from BS)	—	—	300,000
Investment in BS Ltd.	—	200,000	—
Total assets	£700,000	£900,000	£1,000,000
Liabilities	£150,000	£150,000	£150,000
Liabilities (from BS)	—	—	100,000
Shareholders' equity	550,000	750,000*	750,000*
Total equities	£700,000	£900,000	£1,000,000

*Includes £200,000 assigned to the GE shares issued to the former BS shareholders.

As in the case of purchase accounting, the account "investment in BS Ltd." is replaced with the specific assets and liabilities acquired from BS, except that in this instance the BS assets and liabilities are valued at their existing book values. As a consequence, no goodwill is recognized in the consolidated accounts despite the fact that GE's managers agreed to exchange GE shares valued at £275,000 for BS's net assets having a fair market value of £250,000 (i.e., indicating the presence of £25,000 in goodwill). The absence of goodwill, which in most countries must be amortized against net earnings, is one reason why most acquirers prefer the pooling method — there is no drag on future consolidated earnings resulting from the amortization of goodwill. Another reason why the pooling method is preferred is that the carrying values of the acquired subsidiary assets are not stepped up to their higher fair market value (in this case, £275,000). The stepped-up basis of assets under the purchase method means that the level of *future* depreciation charges will be higher than that under the pooling method; as a consequence, consolidated earnings — and such performance measures as return on assets — will almost certainly be less under the purchase method than under the pooling method. Recent research confirms that companies that use the pooling-of-interest method *do* enjoy a valuation premium relative to companies that use the purchase accounting method.

A final issue concerns the consolidated income statement. Unlike the purchase method, in which only the subsidiary's earnings from the date of acquisition are consolidated, under pooling *all* prior earnings, as well as future earnings, are consolidated. Thus, if an acquisition is executed at midyear, and the pooling method is permitted, the subsidiary's earnings for the *entire year* would be consolidated with those of the parent. This "pooling of prior earnings" can have a very positive effect on the income statement of a parent that is having a poor operating year and hence is another reason why some managers prefer the pooling approach.

Pooling versus Purchase Accounting: The Effect on Firm Valuation

As a practical matter, all managers prefer more earnings to less; thus it comes as no surprise that pooling accounting is largely preferred to purchase accounting. Under pooling, there is neither goodwill to amortize nor a stepping up in the cost basis of depreciable assets (and hence, higher depreciation charges). Hence, does the use of pooling accounting affect firm valuation? Apparently it does.[8] According to Fink (1999) most companies are still valued on the basis of traditional price-to-earnings multiples. Since the hits to earnings from goodwill amortization or higher depreciation on the stepped-up basis of property, plant, and equipment inflate the price-to-earnings multiples of companies using pooling versus those using purchase accounting, the share prices of pooling-based companies may appear overvalued. Alternatively stated, an acquirer may be induced to pay a higher-than-justified multiple for a pooling-based target company.

Whether the premium associated with pooling-based companies is justified is ultimately a tax-dependent issue, to which we now turn. First, however, a final comment is merited: The accounting valuation dilemma created under pooling is yet one additional argument in favor of the use of the discounted cash flow approach to firm valuation: Valuations based on free cash flows explicitly account for the effects of higher amortization and depreciation charges associated with purchase-based transactions.

Tax Considerations of Mergers and Acquisitions

Consolidation practices for income tax purposes vary considerably around the world. In the United States, for example, when consolidated tax reporting is permitted — and considerable restrictions exist — companies often file consolidated tax returns in order to take advantage of operating loss carryforwards or tax credits from unprofitable subsidiaries to shelter the earnings of other profitable subsidiaries. In many countries (e.g., Canada), however, consolidated tax returns are simply not permitted. In these countries each corporation must file its own tax return and pay its own income taxes. Worldwide, *international* consolidated tax returns are *never* permitted *as long as* the foreign subsidiary has a legitimate business purpose. In essence, all foreign subsidiary income is taxed in the country in which it is earned, unless the subsidiary has no legitimate business purpose, in which case the income may be taxed in multiple countries.[9]

A result similar to foreign income consolidation is often reached, however, if the parent company is incorporated in a country with a rule similar to the U.S. "controlled foreign corporation" (CFC) rule. Under the CFC rule, some or all of the net income of a foreign subsidiary that qualifies as a controlled foreign corporation will be taxed to the U.S. parent corporation as a "deemed dividend," taxable in the year earned rather than in the year repatriated. These rules arise because some companies, in an attempt to escape or defer taxation, have established subsidiaries in low- or no-tax countries called "tax havens" (e.g., Bermuda, the Cayman Islands, Malta, and the Seychelles). Were it not for these rules, the parent corporation would succeed in transferring all or part of its profits from a high-tax environment to a tax haven by selling goods to these CFC subsidiaries at the lowest possible transfer price and then causing the subsidiary to resell at the highest possible price to the final customers. Under CFC rules, often called "transparency regimes" in countries other than the United States, the tax authorities of the parent company's country of residence evaluate the business role of each subsidiary, and if a subsidiary is judged to be a mere conduit of goods or services (i.e., having no independent legitimate business purpose), such laws force the profits of the foreign subsidiary to be taxed in the home-country tax return of the parent, *as if* a dividend of the profits had been paid to the parent corporation.

Under the U.S. Internal Revenue Code, a consolidated tax return may be filed only when the companies involved are U.S. companies and when the parent company owns at least 80 percent of the subsidiary. Furthermore, because the U.S. Internal Revenue Service does not recognize the equity method, U.S. companies rarely pay taxes on any income except self-generated income. The one exception involves dividends received from an affiliate or subsidiary. To avoid double taxation of these dividend earnings, however, the U.S. Internal Revenue Code allows an exclusion of up to 100 percent of the dividends received by a U.S. parent company from a U.S. subsidiary. This exclusion does not apply to dividends received by a U.S. parent from a foreign subsidiary.

Just as existing accounting rules may influence the structure of a merger and acquisition, so too should the income tax consequences of a transaction be considered to ensure an optimal tax outcome. In the United States, for example, if a merger or acquisition is executed between an acquirer and a target company's shareholders — that is, the acquirer company either buys shares directly from the target's shareholders or exchanges shares directly with the shareholders — the transaction is considered to be *tax free* to both the acquirer and the target company (but is potentially a taxable transaction to the target's former shareholders). As a consequence, even though the acquisition may be accounted for as a purchase for financial reporting purposes, the new subsidiary will continue to calculate its taxes as it did before the acquisition; that is, no step up in the value of the acquired assets is permitted, and consequently no additional tax depreciation is obtained. In essence, this type of transaction produces no particular tax advantages for the consolidated entity, unless of course the acquired company has operating loss carryforwards or unused tax credits. If, on the other hand, the acquirer company buys the net or gross assets *directly* from the target company and places the assets in a newly created subsidiary, the new subsidiary (and indirectly the parent) may claim additional tax depreciation on the stepped-up asset values implied by the transaction. Under this set of circumstances, the transaction is a taxable event for the target company.

As the above discussion suggests, tax regulations related to mergers and acquisitions can be quite complex and are almost certain to be country specific. Space does not permit a review of these regulations on a country-by-country basis. Suffice it to say that a thorough review of these regulations is essential before the execution of a domestic or international merger or acquisition.

Minority Interest

Thus far we have considered only the situation in which an acquirer company obtains a 100 percent ownership interest in a subsidiary. But what accounting issues arise when an equity position of between 51 and 100 percent is acquired? To comprehend the accounting issues under these circumstances, one must first understand the **full consolidation** approach.

Most countries use the full consolidation approach, which is premised on the notion of "control." Under this method, even though a parent does not own 100 percent of a subsidiary, *all* of the subsidiary's assets and liabilities are consolidated with those of the parent under the supposition that the parent *controls* 100 percent through its voting majority. To illustrate the full consolidation approach, let us return to our original example of BS and GE. Now, however, let us assume that GE obtained only a 90 percent shareholding in BS by means of a share exchange, and that merger accounting must be used because all of the requirements for use of the pooling-of-interests method have been satisfied. GE's 90 percent investment in BS will be recorded in its GE accounts as follows:

Dr. Investment in BS Ltd.	£180,000*	
Cr. Capital stock		£180,000
*90% × £200,000 = £180,000		

In anticipation of the preparation of consolidated financial statements, the following consolidation entry will be executed in GE's accounts:

Dr. Assets (from BS)	£300,000	
Cr. Liabilities (from BS)		£100,000
Cr. Investment in BS Ltd.		180,000
Cr. Minority interest		20,000*
*10% × £200,000 = £20,000		

Notice that GE records 100 percent of BS's assets and liabilities on its consolidated balance sheet despite the fact that legally, GE owns only

90 percent. As a consequence, it is necessary to create a new balance sheet account — the minority interest account — to represent the portion (10 percent) of BS's consolidated net assets not actually owned by GE. After the above consolidation entry, GE's consolidated balance sheet will appear as follows:

	GE Ltd. Unconsolidated	GE Ltd. Consolidated
Assets	£700,000	£700,000
Assets (from BS)	—	300,000
Investment in BS Ltd.	180,000	—
Total assets	£880,000	£1,000,000
Liabilities	£150,000	£150,000
Liabilities (from BS)	—	100,000
Minority interest	—	20,000
Shareholders' equity	730,000	730,000
Total equities	£880,000	£1,000,000

Observe that the "minority interest" account appears as a credit balance on GE's consolidated balance sheet although it is neither a debt obligation nor a component of shareholders' equity. It is merely a balancing account required under the full consolidation approach.[10] Of some debate is how the "minority interest" account should be treated when such financial ratios as the debt-to-equity ratio are being calculated. In most financial institutions, the "minority interest" account either is considered to be a component of debt or is excluded altogether when such ratios are calculated.

Accounting for Goodwill

Another consideration in our review of consolidated reporting practices involves the accounting for goodwill under the purchase method. As already noted, goodwill arises when one entity purchases another and pays more than the fair market value of the acquired company. In our original illustration, GE acquired a 100 percent shareholding in BS by purchasing shares from the BS shareholders for £275,000 in cash. An analysis by GE's investment advisers indicated that the fair market value of BS was only £250,000. (BS's book value was £200,000 at the time of the transaction.) As a consequence, GE concluded that the acquisition transaction involved goodwill of £25,000, which was recorded on the consolidated balance sheet with the following entry:

Dr. Assets (from BS)	£350,000	
Dr. Goodwill	25,000	
Cr. Liabilities (from BS)		£100,000
Cr. Investment in BS		275,000

Once goodwill has been recorded on the consolidated financial statements, there are two prevailing approaches to account for it:[11]

- Amortize the goodwill against consolidated earnings over the expected useful life of the goodwill.

- Write the goodwill off immediately against shareholders' equity.

The first method is the most widely used globally. The only difference in the accounting for goodwill among the countries using this approach is the length of time typically assumed to be the useful economic life of goodwill. In Canada, amortization of goodwill over forty years is quite common, whereas in Japan, amortization over five years is the norm. The write-off–to–equity method, on the other hand, is the dominant practice in The Netherlands and, although not prevalent, is also permitted in Denmark, Germany, and Italy, among other countries. (See Exhibit 6.2 for a listing of countries in which the direct write-off treatment of goodwill is permitted.) The direct write-off method is commonly executed with the following entry booked to the consolidated accounts:

Dr. Retained earnings (or other equity reserve account)	£25,000	
Cr. Goodwill		£25,000

This method *removes* the goodwill from the consolidated balance sheet and consequently eliminates the drag on a company's future consolidated earnings due to goodwill amortization, which is the principal reason for the method's popularity.[12]

A third, less prevalent, method requires that goodwill be capitalized on the balance sheet after an acquisition but does not require any periodic amortization of the capitalized goodwill. Instead, the goodwill is subject to an annual impairment test by management. If, and when, the goodwill is determined to be impaired, it is then written down against earnings. This approach was recently adopted in the United States, effective 2001.

Tax Considerations of Goodwill.   An important issue in formulating the appropriate financial structure for an acquisition is the tax deductibility of goodwill. As noted above, goodwill arises only under purchase accounting, which must be used for all share and asset purchases, as well as for those share exchanges that are not accorded treatment under the pooling-of-interests method. To help understand the existing tax regulations with regard to goodwill, it is necessary to differentiate between goodwill arising on a share acquisition, using either cash or shares as the consideration to acquire the shares of the target, and goodwill arising on an asset acquisition.

Exhibit 6.3 summarizes the tax deductibility of both types of goodwill for a selection of countries. Note that goodwill associated with a

Exhibit 6.3   International Goodwill Tax Regulations

Country	Share Purchase Goodwill	Asset Purchase Goodwill
Australia	—	—
Canada	—	75% deductible; double-declining balance (28.5 years)
France	—	—
Germany	—	100% deductible; straight-line amortization (15 years)
Italy	—	100% deductible; straight-line amortization (5 years)
Japan	—	100% deductible; straight-line amortization (5 years)
The Netherlands	—	—
Spain	—	—
U.K.	—	—
United States	—*	100% deductible; straight-line amortization (15 years)

A dash shows that goodwill is not tax deductible.

*The U.S. Internal Revenue Code section 338-H10 permits a company, under certain conditions, to elect to treat a stock acquisition as an asset acquisition to gain goodwill deductibility under section 197 of the Revenue Reconciliation Act of 1993.

share purchase is not tax deductible in *any* country, whereas goodwill associated with an asset purchase is tax deductible in Canada, Germany, Italy, Japan, and the United States, among other countries. In some countries, the deductibility of asset-purchase goodwill is further constrained by the requirement that the assets must be purchased by one domestic company from another. In this way, the tax deductibility of the goodwill is a tax-neutral event; that is, the domestic selling company pays income taxes *on* the goodwill, and the domestic buying company gains a tax deduction *for* the goodwill, all within the same country.[13]

Summary

To try to summarize the key issues for such a complex topic as the financial reporting and tax considerations of mergers and acquisitions is difficult. It is perhaps most useful to organize a summary around the six key questions that need to be addressed in anticipation of a merger or acquisition:

1. Do local accounting standards require the preparation of consolidated financial statements?

2. How was the transaction structured financially — as a share purchase, an asset purchase, or a share exchange?

3. Do local accounting standards permit both pooling-of-interests and purchase accounting methods?

4. If purchase accounting is required, is goodwill present in the transaction?

5. What accounting treatments for goodwill are permitted under local accounting standards?

6. Was a 100 percent ownership interest obtained?

Exhibit 6.4 provides a comprehensive illustration of how consolidated financial statements are prepared in a typical merger or acquisition, along with a detailed consideration of the consolidation process.

Exhibit 6.4   Consolidated Financial Statements: A Detailed Illustration

On 1 July 1998, World Enterprises, Inc. (WE Inc.), a Canadian company, acquired a 100 percent ownership interest in Global Subsidiary Inc. (GS Inc.), another Canadian company, for $300,000 in WE voting shares. (All values are in Canadian dollars, and the two companies are assumed to be independent.) At the time of the transaction, GS had a fair market value of $250,000 and a book value of $200,000.

A review of the structure of the transaction and of the local accounting principles produced the following answers to the six key questions:

1. Canadian accounting standards require the preparation of consolidated financial statements.

2. The transaction was structured as a share exchange.

3. Both pooling-of-interests and purchase accounting methods are permitted under Canadian accounting standards.

4. Goodwill in the amount of $50,000 will need to be accounted for if purchase accounting is used.

5. Goodwill must be capitalized to the balance sheet and then amortized against earnings over forty years.

6. Since a 100 percent ownership interest was obtained, no minority interest account is required.

Purchase Method

If the acquisition is accounted for with the purchase method, WE will record its investment in GS as follows:

Dr. Investment in GS Inc. $300,000
        Cr. WE Capital stock $300,000

The consolidated balance sheet will appear as follows:

	WE Inc. Balance Sheet	GS Inc. Balance Sheet		Consolidated Balance Sheet
		Historical Cost	Fair Value	
Cash	$100,000	$50,000	$50,000	$150,000
Accounts receivable (net)	75,000	30,000	30,000	105,000
Inventory	90,000	40,000	40,000	130,000
Property, plant, and equipment (PP&E) (net)	285,000	155,000	205,000	490,000
Investment in GS	300,000	—	—	—
Goodwill	—	—	—	50,000
Total assets	$850,000	$275,000	$325,000	$925,000
Accounts payable	$50,000	$25,000	$25,000	$75,000
Notes payable	100,000	50,000	50,000	150,000
Capital stock	550,000	125,000 }	250,000	550,000
Retained earnings	150,000	75,000 }		150,000
Total equities	$850,000	$275,000	$325,000	$925,000

Exhibit 6.4   Consolidated Financial Statements: A Detailed Illustration (*cont.*)

The consolidated balance sheet reflects a combination of WE's balance sheet and GS's balance sheet, stated at fair market value, and is achieved by means of the following consolidation entry:

Dr. Cash	$50,000	
Dr. Accounts receivable (net)	30,000	
Dr. Inventory	40,000	
Dr. PP&E (net)	205,000	
Dr. Goodwill	50,000	
Cr. Accounts payable		$25,000
Cr. Notes payable		50,000
Cr. Investment in GS		300,000

Observe how GS's PP&E is stepped up from its book value of $155,000 to its fair market value of $205,000 and also how the excess of the purchase price ($300,000) over GS's fair market value ($250,000) is recorded as goodwill ($50,000). Finally, note how the "investment in GS" is replaced by the specific assets and liabilities, stated at fair market value, acquired from GS.

Pooling of Interests

If the acquisition is accounted for with the pooling method, WE will record its investment in GS as follows, valuing the capital stock distributed to GS's former shareholders at the book value of GS's net assets:

Dr. Investment in GS	$200,000	
Cr. WE Capital stock		$200,000

The consolidated balance sheet will appear as follows:

	WE Inc. Balance Sheet	GS Inc. Balance Sheet Historical Cost	Fair Value	Consolidated Balance Sheet
Cash	$100,000	$50,000	$50,000	$150,000
Accounts receivable (net)	75,000	30,000	30,000	105,000
Inventory	90,000	40,000	40,000	130,000
PP&E (net)	285,000	155,000	205,000	440,000
Investment in GS	200,000	—	—	—
Goodwill	—	—	—	—
Total assets	$750,000	$275,000	$325,000	$825,000
Accounts payable	$50,000	$25,000	$25,000	$75,000
Notes payable	100,000	50,000	50,000	150,000
Capital stock	450,000	125,000 ⎫	250,000	375,000
Retained earnings	150,000	75,000 ⎭		225,000
Total equities	$750,000	$275,000	$325,000	$825,000

(*continued*)

Exhibit 6.4   Consolidated Financial Statements: A Detailed Illustration (*cont.*)

The consolidated balance sheet reflects a combination of WE's balance sheet and GS's balance sheet, both stated at historical cost, and is achieved by means of the following consolidation entry:

Dr. Cash	$50,000	
Dr. Accounts receivable (net)	30,000	
Dr. Inventory	40,000	
Dr. PP&E (net)	155,000	
Cr. Accounts payable		$25,000
Cr. Notes payable		50,000
Cr. Investment in GS		200,000

In addition, since a pooling of interests is executed retroactively, in order to ensure that the consolidated retained earnings is equal to the sum of WE's retained earnings ($150,000) plus GS's retained earnings ($75,000), the following consolidation adjusting entry is also required:*

Dr. Capital stock	$75,000	
Cr. Retained earnings		$75,000

After this adjusting entry, the consolidated shareholders' equity will total $600,000, but the values in the individual equity accounts have now been altered to achieve a particular outcome: Consolidated retained earnings will equal the sum of WE's retained earnings plus GS's retained earnings.

Consolidated Income Statements

Since the acquisition transaction took place at midyear, the consolidated income statement under the purchase method combines the earnings of GS with those of WE on a prospective basis only, whereas under pooling, the earnings of GS for all of 2000 are combined with those of WE, as follows:

	2000 Income Statements				Consolidated Income Statement	
	WE Inc.		GS Inc.			
	Jan–June	July–Dec	Jan–June	July–Dec	Pooling	Purchase
Sales	$8,000	$9,000	$4,000	$4,500	$25,500	$21,500
Cost of sales	(4,000)	(4,500)	(2,000)	(2,250)	(12,750)	(10,750)
Selling, general, and administrative costs	(1,500)	(1,700)	(750)	(850)	(4,800)	(4,050)
Extra depreciation	—	—	—	—	—	(1,667)[†]
Amortization	—	—	—	—	—	(1,250)[‡]
Income taxes	(1,000)	(1,200)	(500)	(600)	(3,300)	(2,800)
Net income	$1,500	$1,600	$ 750	$ 800	$ 4,650	$ 983

[†] Extra depreciation taken on the stepped-up increment to PP&E: $50,000/30 years = $1,667.
[‡] Amortization taken on the goodwill of $50,000: $50,000/40 years = $1,250.

Exhibit 6.4 Consolidated Financial Statements: A Detailed Illustration (*cont.*)

Observe that under purchase accounting, the consolidated net income is less than that under the pooling method for several reasons. First, under the purchase method, only the second half of GS's 2000 earnings are consolidated with those of WE. Second, the consolidated purchase method earnings are reduced by the amortization of goodwill ($1,250) and the extra depreciation ($1,667) on the stepped-up basis of GS's PP&E.

---

*The transfer from the consolidated contributed capital account to retained earnings is normally executed by a debit to "additional paid in capital" unless the balance in that account is insufficient, in which case a portion of the transfer is also obtained from the "capital stock at par value" account by reducing the parent's par value per share.

Notes

1. For our purposes, a majority-owned subsidiary is one in which the parent's voting shareholding *exceeds* 50 percent.

2. The implications of this practice can be far-reaching: If a parent company wants to consolidate a recent acquisition, it can arrange to execute the acquisition at the parent-company level, whereas if the parent wants to avoid consolidation, perhaps because of a subsidiary's high debt level, the acquisition can be executed by an existing or recently created, but unlisted, subsidiary. Thus, a parent company can, in some countries, exercise considerable discretion in the accounting for a merger or acquisition by controlling the organizational level at which an acquisition is executed.

3. One advantage of the asset purchase approach is that an acquirer can limit its purchase to those specific assets that it wants to own or control; however, an asset purchase can also be quite broad in scope, encompassing both the assets *and* liabilities (or net assets) of a company. When the net assets of a company are acquired, the acquirer also assumes responsibility for settlement of the subsidiary's liabilities — a factor that will reduce the total price paid for the purchased net assets.

4. The assumption that the two companies are "independent" is important. If the two companies were not independent — that is, they engaged in various intercompany purchase or sale transactions, or borrowed or lent money to one another — any intercompany transactions would need to be eliminated *before* the consolidated financial statements could be prepared. Elimination entries avoid double counting of any intercompany profits and eliminate nonsensical items such as a receivable from (or payable to) the consolidated entity itself.

5. Occasionally, when the book value of a subsidiary's net assets is overstated relative to its fair market value, it is necessary to "step down" the subsidiary's net asset value, that is, to write the subsidiary's net asset values down to their lower fair market value. In some countries, an alternative to stepping down the sub-

sidiary's net asset value is to value the subsidiary at its overstated book value and to also record **negative goodwill** (a credit balance) for the amount by which the subsidiary's net assets are overvalued. This latter alternative is not permitted under U.S. GAAP but is permitted under International Accounting Standards Committee (IASC) accounting standards and the accounting standards of many countries. For example, in Germany, negative goodwill may be carried on the credit side of the balance sheet and may be amortized (added) to the consolidated net earnings over time (usually five to fifteen years); alternatively, the negative goodwill may be immediately added to the parent's equity reserves. See Appendix 6A for an illustration of negative goodwill in the United States.

6. If, instead of a share purchase, GE purchased 100 percent of BS's net assets (i.e., both BS's assets and liabilities but not its legal corporate structure), the following entry would be recorded in the GE accounts at the time of the net asset purchase:

Dr. Assets (from BS)	£350,000	
Dr. Goodwill	25,000	
Cr. Liabilities (from BS)		£100,000
Cr. Cash		275,000

GE's consolidated balance sheet will appear as follows:

	GE Ltd. (Consolidated)
Assets	£425,000
Assets (from BS)	350,000
Goodwill	25,000
Total assets	£800,000
Liabilities	£150,000
Liabilities (from BS)	100,000
Shareholders' equity	550,000
Total equities	£800,000

Thus, whether an acquisition is executed as a share purchase *or* as a net asset purchase has no effect on the final consolidated financial statements; the consolidated statements will appear the *same* under either approach.

7. Erickson and Wang (1999) report evidence that acquiring firms manage earnings upward in the periods before merger agreement in an attempt to increase share price and lower the cost of acquiring a target.

8. For a comparison of the effect of pooling versus purchase accounting on the firm's equity value, see Hong et al. (1978), Jennings et al. (1996), and Vincent (1997).

9. If a parent company conducts operations in a foreign country, as contrasted with operating an independent subsidiary in the foreign country, any foreign income is subject to taxation in *both* the foreign and home country. In this case, any foreign income will be consolidated with a company's domestic income for purposes of assessing taxes due in the home country. To avoid double taxation, the home country usually gives the taxpaying corporation a tax credit for any foreign taxes paid. Thus, if a U.S. corporation conducts operations in Hong Kong, where the statutory tax rate is 16.5 percent, any foreign earnings would be subject only to a further incremental 18.5 percent in U.S. taxes. (The U.S. statutory tax rate is 35 percent: $35 - 16.5 = 18.5$.) If, on the other hand, the U.S. company conducts operations in Germany, where the statutory tax rate is 45 percent, no further U.S. taxes would be levied on the consolidated German income, but neither would a tax credit (against U.S. taxes) be received for any German tax payments *above* the U.S. statutory rate.

10. A simpler methodology not requiring the creation of a minority interest account is the **proportionate consolidation** method. Under this approach a parent company consolidates only the value of a subsidiary's assets and liabilities that it actually owns. To illustrate, using our example from above, GE's consolidation entry will appear as follows:

Dr. Assets (from BS)	£270,000*	
Cr. Liabilities (from BS)		£90,000*
Cr. Investment in BS		180,000

*90% × £300,000 = £270,000; 90% × £100,000 = £90,000

The partial consolidation approach is intuitively easier to understand and eliminates the need for the "minority interest" account. However, most members of the financial community believe that control is a far more important criteria than ownership, and consequently, the proportionate consolidation method is not widely used throughout the world, except for joint ventures.

11. Lee and Choi (1992) show that goodwill accounting has an effect on the premium that the acquirer pays for the target.

12. A little-known accounting rule in the United States effectively allows an acquiring company to minimize the amount of goodwill ultimately booked after an acquisition — an outcome similar to the write-off–to–equity method. The accounting rule in question permits an acquirer to establish a fair market value for the "in-process research and development assets" at an acquired company and to immediately write off that amount. The higher the value assigned to the in-process research and development, the lower the value that ultimately must be assigned to goodwill on the consolidated statements. This accounting rule can be particularly important for high-technology and pharmaceutical acquisitions, in which the level of research and development expenditures is often quite significant. To illustrate, consider the 1994 acquisition activity of three high-technology companies:

Company	Cost of Acquisitions (millions)	Value of Research and Development Write Offs (millions)	Write Offs as a Percentage of Acquisition Cost
3Com	$220.0	$192.9	88%
Novell	$529.7	$425.9	81%
Exar	$24.1	$16.9	70%

For these three companies, 70 to 88 percent of the initial cost of an acquisition was written off at the time of the transaction.

13. This regulation explains why in 1996, when Allied Waste Industries, Inc., purchased the Canadian and U.S. waste operations of Laidlaw Inc. for $1.4 billion, Allied quickly resold the Canadian assets to yet another firm. The transaction involved $900 million in goodwill, of which $300 million related to the Canadian operations and would *not* have been tax deductible. By retaining only the U.S. assets, Allied preserved the tax deductibility of the $600 million in goodwill associated with the recently purchased U.S. operations. (See the Allied Waste acquisition vignette at the beginning of this chapter.)

Appendix 6A
Negative Goodwill

In September 1996, Keystone Consolidated Industries, Inc., a U.S.-based manufacturer of steel wire and related products, acquired DeSoto Inc., another U.S.-based manufacturer, for $29.3 million in common stock, $3.5 million in preferred stock, and the assumption of certain liabilities. The acquisition was accounted for using the purchase method and involved negative goodwill.

Consistent with U.S. GAAP, the negative goodwill was written off against DeSoto's noncurrent assets until those accounts were fully eliminated, leaving a remaining balance of $27.1 million in negative goodwill. Since U.S. GAAP do not permit the offset of negative goodwill against current assets, the remaining balance of negative goodwill was capitalized to the consolidated balance sheet (see data below). The footnotes to the consolidated statements revealed the following about Keystone's treatment of the negative goodwill: "Negative goodwill, representing the excess of fair value over cost of individual net assets acquired in the DeSoto acquisition, is amortized by the straight-line method over 20 years (remaining life of 19.75 years at December 31, 1996) and is stated net of accumulated amortization of approximately $76,000 at December 31, 1996."

Keystone Consolidated Industries, Inc., and Subsidiaries:
Partial Consolidated Balance Sheet, 31 December 1995 and 1996
(in thousands, except share data)

	1995	1996
Current liabilities		
Notes payable and current maturities of long-term debt	$18,750	$34,760
Accounts payable	26,534	34,419
Accounts payable to affiliates	39	159
Accrued pension cost	7,170	—
Accrued OPEB cost	7,776	8,368
Other accrued liabilities	19,297	28,631
Total current liabilities	79,566	106,337
Noncurrent liabilities		
Long-term debt	11,195	17,020
Accrued pension cost	39,222	—
Accrued OPEB cost	97,868	100,818
Negative goodwill	—	27,057
Other	8,464	16,466
Total noncurrent liabilities	156,749	161,361
Redeemable preferred stock, no par value;		
500,000 shares authorized; 435,456 shares issued	—	3,500
Stockholders' equity (deficit)		
Common stock, $1 par value, 12 million shares		
authorized; 5,637,641 and 9,190,139 shares issued		
at stated value	6,362	9,920
Additional paid in capital	20,013	46,347
Net pension liabilities adjustment	(36,257)	—
Accumulated deficit	(27,599)	(25,085)
Treasury stock: 1,134 shares, at cost	(12)	(12)
Total stockholders' equity (deficit)	(37,493)	31,170
	$198,822	$302,368

7

Some Final Thoughts

MARKET VIEW
General Electric's Proposed Honeywell Acquisition

In October 2000, General Electric Company, the world's largest company in market value, announced its intention to acquire Honeywell International, Inc., a leading manufacturer of avionics for aircraft, for approximately $47 billion. Because of the global reach of the two companies, the acquisition would require the approval of not only Canadian and U.S. antitrust regulators but also the European Union (EU) Competition Commission.

By early May 2001, Canadian and U.S. regulators had approved the transaction with only minor conditions, namely, that certain industry divestitures valued at less than $200 million would be required. However, on 8 May 2001, the Competition Commission notified GE of its concerns regarding the takeover: Approval would necessitate divestitures totaling more than $5 billion, if approval was granted at all!

Competition Commissioner Mario Monti said: "We are responsible in all competition cases for monitoring the effects on the European market, independent of the nationality of the companies involved. Both companies are American, but they operate with their products worldwide."

In Washington, D.C., U.S. governmental officials slammed the EU reluctance to approve the deal. In New York, analysts were far more nonchalant:

"C'est la vie in the world of M&A," commented one Wall Streeter. On 3 July 2001, the EU commission officially voted to block the acquisition.

• • •

In the previous six chapters, we have explored a variety of topics regarding the process of valuing a company. The journey involved a consideration of accounting and reporting dilemmas, financial modeling techniques, taxation and financial reporting consequences of alternative deal structures, and the variety of valuation frameworks commonly used in today's financial markets. In this chapter, we try to bring closure to this journey.

Valuation: A Debriefing

When undertaking a merger or acquisition, it is crucial for an acquirer to undertake a sound valuation of the target company; to do otherwise is a certain invitation for the winner's curse. Once a strategically appropriate acquisition candidate has been identified, the process of conducting the due diligence investigation begins. The first step for the analyst is to collect data — financial as well as nonfinancial. Then he or she must analyze these data in order to fully understand the target's business and to assess its financial well-being. Usually, this financial review is based on accounting data; however, before the analyst can undertake this phase of the due diligence investigation, he or she must first verify the integrity and appropriateness of the accounting data. Indeed, issues such as the target's inventory policy or the depreciation and amortization policy may affect the financial review considerably. Once the veracity of the basic data has been determined, the analyst can then turn his or her attention to the target's future and begin preparing the pro forma financial statements that will reflect the analyst's most likely expectations about the target's future. The final step is for the analyst to actually value the target. In Chapters 3 and 4, we considered two categories of valuation frameworks: direct valuation methods and relative valuation methods.

Direct Valuation Methods.   Direct valuation methods provide an explicit assessment of target firm value. The principal direct valuation methods include discounted cash flow analysis (DCFA), adjusted present value (APV), the equity method, and economic value (EV) analysis. The logic behind the first three methods is similar: The value of a target is

Exhibit 7.1   Summary of Direct Valuation Methods

Method	Cash Flows	Discount Rate
DCFA	Free cash flows	WACC
APV	Free cash flows	Cost of unlevered equity
	Interest tax shields	Cost of debt
Equity method	Equity cash flows	Cost of equity

DCFA is discounted cash flow analysis; WACC, weighted average cost of capital; and APV, adjusted present value.

given by the sum of its future (appropriate) cash flows, discounted at an (appropriate) discount rate. Exhibit 7.1 summarizes the appropriate cash flows and discount rate of each method.

When firm value is being forecasted, a target's future is usually divided into two forecast periods. For the first period, the analyst tries to model the target's specific annual operating cash flows using pro forma financial statements. For the second period, the analyst must make an assumption regarding the target's growth to perpetuity in order to capture the effect of the target's remaining future cash flows (i.e., beyond the pro forma period) in a single metric: The target's continuing value.

DCFA and APV estimate a target's equity value by calculating the difference between the market value of the entity and the market value of its debt. Under DCFA, the market value of the entity is the sum of its free cash flows discounted at the weighted average cost of capital (WACC). When a target's capital structure changes, however, DCFA often leads to a problem of circularity. In this case, APV is likely to produce more reliable valuation results. APV distinguishes between two elements of firm value: The value of the target's operations (i.e., the sum of the free cash flows, discounted at the cost of unlevered equity) and the effect of the target's capital structure on firm value (i.e., the sum of the interest tax shields, discounted at the cost of debt). The market value of the entity is simply the sum of these two elements. One advantage of APV is that it allows the analyst to more carefully tailor the valuation analysis and thereby explicitly identify the different sources of value inherent in a target firm.

The equity method, on the other hand, estimates a target's equity value directly, by discounting the equity cash flows at the cost of equity. As this method focuses on the shareholders' perspective, venture capitalists and investors frequently use it.

The logic behind EV analysis is different, however, as this method does not rely on cash flows but instead on economic income. As it is closer to the data provided in the financial statements, EV analysis is used both as a valuation method and as a tool for improving managerial performance.

Relative Valuation Methods.   Relative valuation methods estimate a target's value relative to a benchmark usually provided by a group of industry-comparable companies. Two categories of relative valuation metrics are widely used: (1) multiples that relate a target's value to its earnings, and (2) multiples that relate a target's value to its revenues. The first category includes the price-to-earnings (P/E) ratio; the price-to-earnings before interest and taxes (P/EBIT) ratio, which neutralizes the effect of capital structure; and the price–to–earnings before interest, taxes, depreciation, and amortization (P/EBITDA) ratio, which neutralizes the effect of the depreciation and amortization policy, as well as that of capital structure. Because some targets lack a history (or future) of positive earnings, it is impossible for a P/E, P/EBIT, or P/EBITDA multiple to be computed for these companies. Consequently, a second category of relative valuation metrics has emerged, which includes such multiples as the price-to-sales ratio.

Some Caveats to Consider

When valuing a target, the analyst must remember a number of caveats. First, whichever valuation method is used, a target's value is highly sensitive to the assumptions the analyst uses to model the target's future. As revealed by the Nokia valuation in Chapter 3, the assumption regarding Nokia's growth to perpetuity was found to be crucial: With a growth rate of 5 percent, Nokia's value was twelve times greater than with a growth rate of 0 percent. Consequently, the analyst should *always* consider running sensitivity analyses and simulations to assess the effect of each key assumption on the valuation results. Second, each valuation framework has its strengths and weaknesses. Consequently, when possible, it is always best for an analyst to use several valuation methods. If the different approaches yield results that are relatively comparable, the analyst can have some degree of confidence that the financial modeling and valuation results are reasonable. On the other hand, if the different approaches yield results that are significantly different, the analyst should have little confidence and should consider investigating the sources of the difference. These caveats cause us to be mindful of one of this book's key themes: *Valuation is an art to be learned, not a science to be practiced.*

Closure

The valuation of a target firm for merger or acquisition can be a lengthy process. Once an acquirer has determined a range of values for the target's equity, the acquirer must then negotiate a final price with the target's management and/or shareholders. If the target rejects the acquirer's offer, a hostile conflict may begin. Even if a friendly agreement can be reached between an acquirer and a target, the merger or acquisition is rarely free of impediments. For example, a competing bidder might enter the scene with a higher valuation. Also, the proposed transaction might not receive necessary governmental and antitrust regulatory approvals, as illustrated by the GE-Honeywell vignette at the beginning of this chapter. And even if the merger or acquisition is completed, potential pitfalls still remain, such as the integration of the acquirer and the target. In short, so many factors can cause a merger and acquisition transaction to fail that it is surprising that any merger and acquisition transactions succeed at all.

Thus, for those managers who try to cross these waters, we end this journey by reiterating the five principal reasons for the destruction of merger and acquisition value:

1. Overestimation of target firm growth and/or market potential

2. Overestimation of expected cost and/or revenue synergies

3. Overbidding

4. Failure to undertake a thorough due diligence

5. Failure to successfully integrate an acquiree after the merger or acquisition

The successful valuation analyst will always keep these five points in mind and work to avoid them.

Bibliography

Agrawal, A., J. F. Jaffe, and G. N. Mandelker. "The Post-Merger Performance of Acquiring Firms: A Re-Examination of an Anomaly." *Journal of Finance* 47, no. 4 (1992): 1605–1621.

Amir, E., T. S. Harris, and E. K. Venuti. "A Comparison of the Value-Relevance of U.S. versus Non-U.S. GAAP Accounting Measures Using Form 20-F Reconciliations." *Journal of Accounting Research* 31 (1993): 230–264.

Bailey, J. "Allied Waste to Buy Line from Laidlaw." *Wall Street Journal,* 19 September 1996, A3.

Barth, M. E., and G. Clinch. "International Accounting Differences and Their Relation to Share Prices: Evidence from U.K., Australian, and Canadian Firms." *Contemporary Accounting Research* 13, no. 1 (1996): 135–170.

Berger, P. G., and E. Ofek. "Diversification's Effect on Firm Value." *Journal of Financial Economics* 37, no. 1 (1995): 39–65.

Berkman, H., M. E. Bradbury, and J. Ferguson. "The Magic of Earnings in Terminal Value Calculations." *Journal of Financial Statement Analysis* 3, no. 4 (1998): 27–32.

Bruner, R. F., and K. M. Eades. "Best Practices in Estimating the Cost of Capital." *Financial Practice and Education* 8, no. 1 (1998): 13–28.

Burns, G. "What Price the Snapple Debacle?" *Business Week*, 14 April 1997, 42.

Burton, T. M. "Lilly Will Swallow $2.4 Billion Charge." *Wall Street Journal,* 24 June 1997, A4.

Chan, K. C., and G. S. Seow. "The Association between Stock Returns and Foreign GAAP Earnings versus Earnings Adjusted to U.S. GAAP." *Journal of Accounting and Economics* 21, no. 1 (1996): 139–158.

Choi, F. D. S., H. Hino, S. K. Minn, S. O. Nam, J. Ujiie, and A. I. Stonehill. "Analyzing Foreign Financial Statements: The Use and Misuses of International Ratio Analysis." *Journal of International Business Studies* 14, no. 1 (1985): 113–131.

Copeland, T. E., and P. T. Keenan. "How Much Is Flexibility Worth?" *McKinsey Quarterly,* no. 2 (1998a): 38–49.

———. "Making Real Options Real." *McKinsey Quarterly,* no. 3 (1998b): 123–136.

Dawson, J. P., P. M. Neupert, and C. P. Stickney. "Restating Financial Statements for Alternative GAAP: Is It Worth the Effort?" *Financial Analysts Journal* 36, no. 6 (1980): 38–46.

Dewers, E. A., and B. Lev. "A Rude Awakening: Internet Shakeout in 2000." Working paper, University of Rochester and New York University, November 2000.

Ehrdhardt, M. and P. Daves, "The Adjusted Present Value: The Combined Impact and Growth and the Tax Shield of Debt or the Cost of Capital and Systematic Risk," working paper, University of Tennessee, June 1999.

Erickson, M., and S. Wang. "Earnings Management by Acquiring Firms in Stock for Stock Mergers." *Journal of Accounting and Economics* 27, no. 2 (1999): 149–176.

Ferris, K., K. L. Tennant, and S. I. Jerris. *How to Understand Financial Statements: A Nontechnical Guide for Financial Analysts, Managers, and Executives.* Englewood Cliffs, N.J.: Prentice-Hall, 1992.

Fink, R. "Going with the Flow." *CFO Magazine*, October 1999, 113–116.

Freudenheim, M. "Lilly Cuts Distribution Unit's Book Value by $2.4 Billion." *New York Times*, 24 June 1997, D7.

Graham, J. R., and C. R. Harvey. "The Theory and Practice of Corporate Finance: Evidence from the Field." *Journal of Financial Economics* 60, no. 2–3 (2001): 187–243.

Gregory, A. "An Examination of the Long-Run Performance of U.K. Acquiring Firms." *Journal of Business Finance and Accounting* 24, no. 7–8 (1997): 971–1002.

Hand, J. "The Role of Economic Fundamentals, Web Traffic, and Supply and Demand in the Pricing of U.S. Internet Stocks." Working paper, University of North Carolina, April 2000.

Hand, J., and L. Lynch. "Two Roles for Summary Accounting Data in Explaining Takeover Premia." Working paper, University of North Carolina and University of Virginia, August 1999.

Haskins, M., K. Ferris, and T. Selling. *International Financial Reporting and Analysis: A Contextual Emphasis.* Burr Ridge, Ill.: McGraw-Hill, 2000.

Healy, P. M., K. G. Palepu, and R. S. Ruback. "Which Takeovers Are Profitable? Strategic or Financial." *Sloan Management Review* 38, no. 4 (1997): 45–57.

Herrmann, D., T. Inoue, and W. B. Thomas. "Are There Benefits to Restating Japanese Financial Statements according to U.S. GAAP?" *Journal of Financial Statement Analysis* 2, no. 1 (1996): 61–73.

Hong, H., R. S. Kaplan, and G. Mandelker. "Pooling vs. Purchase: The Effects of Accounting for Mergers on Stock Prices." *Accounting Review* 53, no. 1 (1978): 31–47.

Ip, G., S. Pulliam, S. Thurn, R. Simon, and K. Scannell. "The Internet Bubble Broke Records, Rules and Bank Accounts." *Wall Street Journal,* 14 July 2000, A8.

Jennings, R., J. Robinson, R. B. Thompson, and L. Duvall. "The Relation between Accounting Goodwill Numbers and Equity Values." *Journal of Business Finance and Accounting* 23, no. 4 (1996): 513–534.

Jensen, M. C., and R. S. Ruback. "The Market for Corporate Control: The Scientific Evidence." *Journal of Financial Economics* 11, no. 1–4 (1983): 5–50.

Kaplan, S. N., and R. S. Ruback. "The Valuation of Cash Flows Forecasts: An Empirical Analysis." *Journal of Finance* 50, no. 4, (1995): 1059–1093.

Kaplan, S. N., and M. S. Weisbach. "The Success of Acquisitions: Evidence from Divestitures." *Journal of Finance* 47, no. 1 (1992): 107–139.

Kim, M., and J. R. Ritter. "Valuing IPOs." *Journal of Financial Economics* 53, no. 3 (1999): 409–437.

Lee, C., and F. D. S. Choi. "Effect of Alternative Goodwill on Merger Premia: Further Empirical Evidence." *Journal of International Management and Accounting* 4, no. 3 (1992): 220–236.

Lev, B. *Financial Statement Analysis: A New Approach.* Englewood Cliffs, N.J.: Prentice-Hall, 1974.

Lipin, S., and B. Bahree. "Failure of Deal for BOC Hurts Air Products." *Wall Street Journal,* 11 May 2000, A3.

Liu, J., D. Nissim, and J. Thomas. "Equity Valuation Using Multiples." *Journal of Accounting Research,* forthcoming.

Loughran, T., and A. M. Vijh. "Do Long-term Shareholders Benefit from Corporate Acquisitions?" *Journal of Finance* 52, no. 5 (1997): 1765–1790.

Luehrman, T. A. "Using APV: A Better Tool for Valuing Operations." *Harvard Business Review* 75, no. 3 (1997a): 145–154.

———. "What's It Worth? A General Manager's Guide to Valuation." *Harvard Business Review* 75, no. 3 (1997b): 132–142.

———. "Investment Opportunities as Real Options: Getting Started with the Numbers." *Harvard Business Review* 76, no. 4 (1998): 51–60.

MacDonald, E. "Are Those Revenues for Real?" *Forbes,* 29 May 2000, 108–110.

Marshall, A. *Principles of Economics.* New York: Macmillan, 1890.

Meek, G. "U.S. Securities Market Response to Alternate Earnings Disclosures of Non-U.S. Multinational Corporations." *Accounting Review* 58, no. 2 (1983): 115–130.

Modigliani, F., and M. H. Miller. "Dividend Policy, Growth, and the Valuation of Shares." *Journal of Business* 34, no. 4 (1961): 411–433.

Moore, G. "Measuring Up: Keep Your Eyes on the Right Metrics." *Forbes,* 3 April 2000, 105–106.

Myers, S. C. "Interactions of Corporate Financing and Investment Decisions: Implications for Capital Budgeting." *Journal of Finance* 29, no. 1 (1974): 1–25.

Nelson, M. W., J. A. Elliott, and R. L. Tarpley. "Where Do Companies Attempt Earnings Management, and When Do Auditors Prevent It?" Working paper, Cornell University and George Washington University, November 2000.

Pécherot, B. "La performance sur longue période des acquéreurs français." *Banque & Marchés* 46 (Mai–Juin 2000): 31–39.

Rajgopal, S., S. Kotha, and M. Venkatchalam. "The Relevance of Web Traffic for Internet Stock Prices." Working paper, University of Washington and Stanford University, November 2000.

Rau, P. R., and T. Vermaelen. "Glamour, Value, and the Post-acquisition Performance of Acquiring Firms." *Journal of Financial Economics* 49, no. 2 (1998): 223–253.

Ravenscraft, D. J., and F. M. Scherer. "Life after Takeover." *Journal of Industrial Economics* 36, no. 2 (1987): 145–157.

Rees, L. L. "The Information Contained in Reconciliations to Earnings Based on U.S. Accounting Principles by Non-U.S. Companies." *Accounting and Business Research* 25, no. 100 (1995): 301–310.

Sandberg, J. "America Online Plans $385 Million Charge." *Wall Street Journal,* 30 October 1996, A3.

Schroeder, M. "SEC Widens MicroStrategy Investigation." *Wall Street Journal,* 24 May 2000, C1.

Sirower, M. *The Synergy Trap: How Companies Lose the Acquisition Game.* New York: The Free Press, 1997.

Smith, C. S. "Chinese Companies Writing off Old Debt." *Wall Street Journal,* 28 December 1995, A4.

Stewart, G. *The Quest for Value.* New York: Harper Business, 1991.

Stickney, C. P., and P. R. Brown. *Financial Report and Statement Analysis: A Strategic Perspective.* 4th ed. Harcourt College Publishers, 1999.

Trombley, M. A., and D. A. Guenther. "Should Earnings and Book Values Be Adjusted for LIFO?" *Journal of Financial Statement Analysis* 1, no. 1 (1995): 26–32.

Trueman, B., M. H. F. Wong, and X. J. Zhang. "Back to Basics: Forecasting the Revenues of Internet Firms." *Review of Accounting Studies,* forthcoming.

Varaiya, N., and K. R. Ferris. "Overpaying in Corporate Takeovers: The Winner's Curse." *Financial Analysts Journal* 43, no. 3 (1987): 64–70.

Vincent, L. "Equity Valuation Implications of Purchase versus Pooling Accounting." *Journal of Financial Statement Analysis* 2, no. 4 (1997): 5–19.

Wessel, D. "Cross-Border Mergers Soared Last Year." *Wall Street Journal,* 19 July 2000, A18.

White, G. I., A. C. Sondhi, and D. Fried. *The Analysis and Use of Financial Statements.* 2d ed. New York: John Wiley & Sons, 1998.

Wooley, S. "An Unflattering Close-up." *Forbes,* 13 January 1997, 58–59.

Index

Boldface page numbers refer to exhibits.

The *Financial Times* delivers a world of business news.

Use the Risk-Free Trial Voucher below!

To stay ahead in today's business world you need to be well-informed on a daily basis. And not just on the national level. You need a news source that closely monitors the entire world of business, and then delivers it in a concise, quick-read format.

With the *Financial Times* you get the major stories from every region of the world. Reports found nowhere else. You get business, management, politics, economics, technology and more.

Now you can try the *Financial Times* for 4 weeks, absolutely risk free. And better yet, if you wish to continue receiving the *Financial Times* you'll get great savings off the regular subscription rate. Just use the voucher below.

8 reasons why you should read the Financial Times for 4 weeks RISK-FREE!

To help you stay current with significant
developments in the world economy ...
and to assist you to make informed business
decisions — the Financial Times brings you:

① Fast, meaningful overviews of international affairs ... plus daily briefings on major world news.

② Perceptive coverage of economic, business, financial and political developments with special focus on emerging markets.

③ More international business news than any other publication.

④ Sophisticated financial analysis and commentary on world market activity plus stock quotes from over 30 countries.

⑤ Reports on international companies and a section on global investing.

⑥ Specialized pages on management, marketing, advertising and technological innovations from all parts of the world.

⑦ Highly valued single-topic special reports (over 200 annually) on countries, industries, investment opportunities, technology and more.

⑧ The Saturday Weekend FT section — a globetrotter's guide to leisure-time activities around the world: the arts, fine dining, travel, sports and more.

For Special Offer See Over

FT FINANCIAL TIMES
World business newspaper